RITES
OF THE
GODS

'All religions are ancient monuments
to superstition, ignorance, ferocity;
and modern religions are only
ancient follies rejuvenated.'

Baron d'Holbach, 1723–89

By the same author

Stone Circles of the British Isles
Prehistoric Stone Circles
Prehistoric Avebury
Rings of Stone

RITES OF THE GODS

Aubrey Burl

J. M. Dent & Sons Ltd
London Melbourne Toronto

First published 1981
© Aubrey Burl 1981

Printed in Great Britain by
Butler & Tanner Ltd Frome and London
for J. M. Dent & Sons Ltd
Aldine House Welbeck Street London

This book is set in 11 on 13pt Ehrhardt

British Library Cataloguing in Publication Data

Burl, Aubrey
    Rites of the gods.
    1. Religion, Prehistoric – Great Britain
    2. Rites and ceremonies – Great Britain
    I. Title
    301.2′1   GN805

ISBN 0–460–04313–7

Contents

List of Maps and Diagrams

List of Colour Plates

Most of these were photographed by Mick Sharp.
Nos. vii, viii, xi and xii were taken by the author.

Photographic Acknowledgments

The author and publishers are grateful to the following for their permission to reproduce the black and white photographs in this book: No. 8, Bristol University Spelaeological Society; 2, 6, 10, 11, 55, 95 are reproduced by courtesy of the Trustees of the British Museum; 7, 56, 70, Devizes Museum; 1, Dr Harold Edgerton; 5, 14, Dr P. V. Glob; 53, 54, 57, Dr Richard Harrison; 89, 90, 100, 101, Hull Museum; 75, Liverpool Museum; 98, Manor House Museum, Ilkley; 71, Ministry of Finance, Belfast; 40, 41, 60, National Monuments Record; 96, 102, National Museum of Ireland, Dublin; 103, National Parks and Monuments Branch, Dublin; 31, 33, Professor M. J. O'Kelly; 3, 38, 39 are Crown Copyright from the Property Services Agency, London; 26, 43, 46, 48, 79, 87 are Crown Copyright, reproduced by permission of the Scottish Development Department; 47, 83, Alastair Service; 4, 12, 13, 20, 21, 22, 24, 27, 28, 29, 30, 32, 35, 36, 44, 45, 49, 50, 51, 59, 62, 63, 64, 68, 72, 73, 74, 76, 77, 78, 82, 85, 88, 91, 92, 97, 104, Mick Sharp; 9, 66, Sheffield Museum; 17, Society of Antiquaries of London; 34, Crown Copyright, Welsh Office, Cardiff; 69, West Air Photography, Weston-super-Mare. Nos 15, 18, 19, 23, 25, 27, 37, 42, 52, 61, 67, 81, 86, 99, were taken by the author.

Jacket photograph courtesy Musée Borély, Marseilles.

To Dr Cyril Bibby
Principal of the former Hull College of Education
who encouraged my researches and who believed in the subject
of Evolution and Prehistory

Preface

Penetrating so many secrets we cease to believe in the unknowable.
But there it sits nevertheless, calmly licking its chops.

H. L. Mencken

No book has ever been written solely about the rituals of prehistoric people in these islands but just after the Second World War the title-song of a popular film surprisingly summarized the themes of supernatural spirits, mysticism, offerings and ceremonies of fertility that are common features of religion from the earliest times down to the end of the Iron Age. In 'Three Coins in the Fountain' the song-writer, Sammy Cahn, described how 'three hopeful lovers' each threw a coin into Rome's Trevi fountain hoping that the gifts would bring them love and happiness. The magic number, three, the water, the appeal to the gods and the intimate activities of men and women to ensure the safety of their lives, all these appear in the words of that unpretentious song. It is unlikely that Mr Cahn had any thought of Celtic votive rites when he composed his lyrics but, knowingly or not, we are all conditioned by beliefs that have survived palely from antiquity.

The Trevi fountain in Rome is only one of hundreds of springs, fountains and wishing-wells, many of them in the British Isles, whose origins reach back into our prehistoric past. Some, like the Well of St Bridget in Co. Clare, surrounded by statues of saints and scenes of the crucifixion, were once the shrines of Brigid, an Iron Age goddess of herds and sowing and of the pagan festival of Spring. These places, where children now drop their innocent pennies, were the centres of fertility rites that could never be shown on our television screens, and the 'three hopeful lovers' are the vapid descendants of Bronze Age men and women who were hurled alive down deep shafts to placate the gods and bring good harvests to the community.

Other modern customs have just as long an ancestry as the wishing-well. In Ireland there are weathered standing stones about which no legends survive. They have nothing buried near them to give a clue to their purpose and yet they are still painted white each year for reasons that have long been forgotten. One is called 'The White Wife', perhaps a memory of a time when it was associated with ritual marriages to a goddess like so many others of these old stones.

Not far from Dundalk in Co. Louth there are the denuded slabs of a prehistoric tomb, three head-high pillars that support a massive granite capstone weighing over thirty tons. On its top, a good thirteen feet above the ground, there are lots of little pebbles. Although the monument must be over four thousand years old people still believe it has supernatural powers of fertility and that if they can cast a stone that does not roll off the uneven and sloping block they will be married within the year.

Inside this tomb, known as the 'Giant's Load' at Proleek, there would have been burials and often it has been the prehistoric dead that have revealed most strikingly the beliefs of the living. By the side of a corpse covered by a mound of chalk on the Yorkshire Wolds archaeologists discovered the cremated bones of a child packed up in a wad of clay. Some miles away the skeleton of an old woman lay under another round barrow. The teeth she had lost in life had been kept and when she was buried they were tucked neatly underneath her chin. Signs of a less peaceful end came from another Yorkshire barrow where the right arm of a heavily built man lacked its hand and most of its forearm, 'probably the result of some conflict, and the cause of the death', according to the excavator. The severed limb had been put on the man's shoulder with the fingertips touching his face. Another body had been hacked up into small pieces before the flesh had decayed, just as other corpses were sometimes tied up in an attempt to stop their ghosts returning to haunt the living.

It seems strange, then, that when so many facts are known about prehistoric burial customs, amulets, standing stones and druids that neither archaeologist nor other writer has attempted a description of them to explain some of the traditions that endure, thin and ghostlike, to this day. There are probably two reasons for this silence. First, once the few well-known and overworked sites such as Stonehenge have been examined, the rest of the information is widely and meagrely spread in excavation reports published in local archaeological journals, and the details are difficult to assemble unless one knows where to look and has access to a good university library. Second, religious activities are not easily reconstructed from the broken pots, the patch of charcoal and the spikelets of burnt human bone from the average Bronze Age burial. It is one matter to analyse the clays of the pot and the age and sex of the cremation but it is quite different to deduce accurately what rites were performed by the mourners. To scholars perhaps the only acceptable work on such a speculative topic would consist of lists of pots and artefacts, collections of plans and measurements, and illustrations of megalithic art because, beyond this, there is little more than surmise, a host of alternative interpretations any one of which may be correct. One misdirected step in these mists leads one towards apparitions, White Goddesses, psychic archaeology and the Never-Never Land of the ley-liners.

Nevertheless, within the sensible limits of what is known, there is ample material for a general book about the people and the relics they left behind them, the charms and fetishes, the funeral mounds, the henges and stone circles, and the rowdy festivals of sowing and harvest that are alluded to so animatedly in the poetry of the Celts. It is this book that I have tried to write for the many readers who are interested in this neglected aspect of our past.

Because there already exist some excellent works about Iron Age religion and the druids, noted in the *Booklist and Notes*, this glorious period has been more briefly described than the less well-known ages before it. Nor is this book a general prehistory of the British Isles or an architectural survey of the magnificent structures that are such delights to visit. Some splendid stone circles such as Stonehenge and Avebury are referred to in passing but this is not a book about monuments. It is about people and their rituals and beliefs.

It has often been the excavations of more obscure sites that have provided the most vivid insights into the strange customs of their builders. Few books mention Broomend of Crichie with its deep grave and its avenue of stones because now almost nothing remains of it. The hill at Dalgety where lonely skulls were found is equally ignored because today there is nothing to be seen there. Few people other than prehistorians have heard of Liff's Low where a Bronze Age chieftain lay with some lumps of red ochre for body-painting, a pair of ferocious boar's tusks by his side. It is places such as these, and Goodland, Duggleby Howe, Tara and Stenness, that receive most attention in the chapters that follow and it is hoped that the reader will find them just as fascinating as I have done.

To avoid confusion over chronology caused by radio-carbon analysis of organic material yielding 'dates' that have sometimes been several centuries too young, all the dates in this book have been converted to what is believed to be their real age and they are followed by BC. On the few occasions when a Carbon-14 determination is quoted its standard deviation is given and 'bc' printed in lower case letters after it. There is, for example, a radio-carbon date from the henge at Arminghall, Norfolk, of 2490 ± 150 bc. In real years this would be about 3250 BC.

I could not end without a word of thanks to the many colleagues who have stimulated this book by their discussions, arguments and downright disagreements. There were also my archaeology students who were courageous enough to suggest that sometimes my opinions were ill-considered. They have since been expunged. The students, of course, remain.

To my fellow excavator and friend, Mick Sharp, many of whose fine photographs enhance the text, particular thanks must be given. Being an archaeologist he has been able to add a proper understanding of the monuments to an artistic appreciation of their tones and structure. He has also an unyielding patience that permits him to wait so long for the light to be at its best that sometimes his windchilled companions have wondered if the sun was still moving along its appointed course. How well justified these tedious vigils were can be seen by anyone who looks at his lovely and illuminating photographs.

David Brown, Librarian of my College, has been unfailingly helpful, and I must especially thank Richard Crabtree for his courteous response to requests for books located anywhere from Ireland to Idaho. June Buckland typed the final draft quickly, precisely and, above all, cheerfully. Margaret, my wife, endured its inception, coped with its despondencies, charmingly concealed her relief when it was done, and no writer who has suffered the turmoil of authorship will doubt me when I say that what merits there are in these pages are largely due to her constant care and encouragement.

Date BC	Period	Particular sites	General events Monuments/*Pottery*	Climate and vegetation
5000	Mesolithic			Becoming warmer
				Pine and hazel forests
				Wild ox, elk, deer, pig, beaver and bear
				Warm and moist
4500				Alder, hazel and oak forests
	Early		Earthen long barrows	Early clearances
4000		Fussell's Lodge long barrow	Long megalithic tombs	
			Passage-graves	Oak, elm, lime, alder forests
	Middle (Neolithic Age)	Fochabers cairn	Cursuses	Elm declining
3500		Newgrange tomb Goodland enclosure Arminghall henge	Early henges and stone circles *Rinyo-Clacton ware*	Red and roe deer, wild pig and ox, domestic cattle
3000	Late	Stonehenge I	Decline of long building	Regeneration of the forests
		Stenness circle-henge	Early round barrows	
		Tara, Mound of the Hostages	First Beaker people	
2500		Slieve Gullion passage-grave	*beakers* Recumbent stone circles	Warm and dry
	Early	Stonehenge II	Beginning of linear cemeteries	Mixed oak forests
2000		Stonehenge IIIA	*urns and food-vessels*	Domesticated sheep
	Middle (Bronze Age)	Berrybrae recumbent stone circle	Enclosed cremation cemeteries	
1500		Wilsford Shaft	*Deverel-Rimbury urns*	
			Decline of henge and stone circle building	
	Late	Itford Hill	Decline in round barrow building	Becoming cooler and wetter
1000		South Cadbury hillfort	Increase in hoards and weapons	Wet and cold
	Early (Iron Age)	Cullen Bog?	Defended homesteads	Spread of birch, ash, beech and hornbeam
500		Tara earthworks?		
	Middle		Yorkshire chariot-burials	
0	Late		First Roman invasion	

A time-chart of British prehistory

1

Avenues to Antiquity, Blind Alleys and Dead Ends

Religion is 'a daughter of Hope and Fear, explaining to Ignorance the nature of the Unknowable'.

Ambrose Bierce (1842–1914), *The Devil's Dictionary*

At the beginning of November 1866 the Reverend William Greenwell, librarian to the Dean and Chapter of Durham Cathedral, began the excavation of a round barrow on the Yorkshire Wolds. The low mound lay two miles north of Weaverthorpe, a little village resting snugly in the valley of the Gypsey Race, sheltered from the winds that blew across the open Wolds above it. Even today the Wolds with their wide, treeless fields are empty places, not very different in atmosphere from the time when prehistoric people farmed there and buried their dead under mounds of earth and chalk. Greenwell, however, was to uncover burials that were quite different from those in a modern cemetery and which revealed the strange and alien thinking of Bronze Age people in Britain.

To the archaeologist prehistoric religion is a shadow that conveys hardly anything of the reality behind it. A photograph of Stonehenge would be recognized by almost every person in this country. Its stones and the lintels on top of them have been made familiar by a thousand advertisements and book-jackets but even those great stones are shadowlike because they tell us very little about the ceremonies that took place inside the ring, the fears and desires of the people who raised the pillars, and the reasons why they laboured so long and tiringly to build Europe's most famous prehistoric monument. There has been no shortage of guesses, fantasies, even downright lies, but the reality remains elusive and may always escape us.

1 *Stonehenge by strobe lighting. The photograph was taken during World War II by Dr Harold Edgerton*

Yet each piece of research by archaeologist, anthropologist, astronomer, brings us a little nearer. Whereas barely a hundred years ago Charles Dickens, in his *Child's History of England*, could describe the prehistoric Britons as 'poor savages, going almost naked, or only dressed in the rough skins of beasts, and staining their bodies, as other savages do, with coloured earths and the juices of plants', we now know those people to have been skilled woodworkers and potters, metalsmiths, expert in the growing of crops and the rearing of livestock, capable of banding together to erect not only huge mounds or barrows of earth for their dead but also monuments as monstrous as Stonehenge or that colossus of antiquity, Avebury, with its canal-deep ditch and its inner circles of forty-ton sarsens. These were the structures of organized societies whose members were as intelligent and adaptable as ourselves but whose beliefs and values were quite different, and for this reason in particular it is difficult to understand their religious customs. Another problem is that so few clues have been left for us to examine.

Although Dickens, in the same work, was probably wrong when he wrote 'It is certain that the Druidical ceremonies included the sacrifice of human victims, the torture of some suspected criminals and, on particular occasions, even the burning alive in immense wicker cages, of a number of men and animals together' his implication that people behaved differently in those days was probably correct. The rites of the ancient British, some of which still linger today, are not to be judged by today's ethics. Any attempt to do so must result in a distorted view of the past. The barrow Greenwell was digging showed this for it was not the straightforward burial that, by today's standards, it should have been.[1]

The barrow, knee-high and circular, was not large, perhaps twenty paces across, and it was composed of earth and chalk. Today it would be excavated a quarter at a time, very slowly and methodically, but Greenwell's method was less demanding. He simply told his labourers to drive a trench from the south directly through the mound, recording in his notebook the bones and pots and flint tools as they appeared. He was a curious man, interested in mediaeval manuscripts and fishing—it was he who gave the description of 'carp's tongue' to a type of later Bronze Age sword—and he did not begin excavating regularly until he was middle-aged. Nevertheless, he contrived to dig into some three hundred barrows, gouging into them in a way that has caused some archaeologists to wish that the hours he spent on his knees had been in prayer rather than in trowelling.

Under the barrow he might have expected to find a single body. Instead his workers came upon a concreted block of human cremated bone and chalk and flint, all fused together by intense heat. Although Greenwell did not understand it, these were bones from a New Stone Age long mound over the eastern end of which a later round barrow had been built. Then the diggers came to the first Bronze Age burial, the skeleton of 'a strongly made man', about thirty years of age, lying crouched on his left side, his left hand to his face. Near him were a bone pin and a marble-sized pebble of quartz. Not far away were the bones of a little child. At the far side of the mound was another skeleton, also crouched as though in sleep, of a 'strongly made old man'. His left hand, too, rested by his face. Two small slabs of chalk had been set upright under his head and some pig bones had been placed near him.

The men and the child appeared to be ordinary burials but at the centre of the barrow was a scooped-out hollow with reddened earth, charcoal and some burnt bone in it, and on top of all this were three skulls, all facing towards the south, one upright with part of the spine still attached to it, the others upside down. All were of young boys.

Greenwell never finished the excavation. A fellow archaeologist helping him, Robert Mortimer, described what happened.

> As night had nearly approached, the barrow was being rapidly completed and unsatisfactorily explored. The tumulus was trenched over with four-tined forks and shovels in a hurried manner by six or seven men as if by 'takework', a method not at all suitable for making antiquarian researches on a scientific principle.[2]

No archaeologist today would disagree with that.

Esh's Barrow, as it is known, has left us with several questions, some of them not very obvious. One mystery is not merely the presence of the three skulls but why they all faced the same direction, south, especially as they were to be covered in thick earth and chalk. Nor can it have been coincidence that both the men had been laid on their left-hand sides with their left hands to their faces, although this may have been no more than a local funerary custom. What might be overlooked, however, are the pig bones and the quartz pebble, counterparts of which will occur repeatedly in this account of religious practices in prehistoric Britain. Skulls, animal bones, the orientation of bodies, burning, water, quartz—all these are fundamental to an understanding of these rites. Before concluding that this was the time of a Golden Age in these islands, as ley-liners would have us believe, or a period when science flourished under the guidance of astronomer-priests skilled in arithmetic, geometry and celestial observations, as some reputable scholars have claimed, it is necessary to accumulate all the evidence that barrows, pits and ritual circles have yielded.

Esh's Barrow was not alone. There are many others on the Wolds, a region which is a microcosm of the ancient mysteries of our heritage. Less than two hours' walk from the barrow towards the coast is the Sharp Howe group of five tumuli, one of them covering the body of an old man with the hind quarters of a pig by his knees. Three-quarters of a mile to the east is an isolated barrow on Folkton Wold, no bigger than Esh's but constructed of dark layers of earth, flint and stones interspersed with thin beds of chalk. Before it had been heaped up its builders had dug out two irregular circular ditches, one inside the other, to enclose a central burial area within which they had placed several bodies in graves. At the south-east, just inside the edge of the inner ring, were three skeletons of adults in separate pits close together. Another lay at the north. At the north-west 'was the body of an infant, laid on the left side with the head to South'. At the centre of the ring, and presumably the focus of the ceremonies that had taken place there, a cairn of flints and stones concealed the disturbed bones of a man and woman. Their skulls were missing. Around them were strewn the smashed remains of a drinking vessel or beaker made about 2300 BC. A few fragments of flint lay near them.[3]

Figure 1 *Some British sites mentioned in Chapter 1:*
1 Skara Brae, HY 230187; 2 Esh's Barrow, SE 959689; 3 Folkton Barrow,
TA 059777; 4 Windmill Hill, SU 087714; 5 Bush Barrow, SU 116413; 6 Rillaton
Barrow, SX 260719

With the exception of the missing skulls which were thought to have been taken by nineteenth-century treasure-seekers there might seem to be nothing very strange about these burials although it was noticeable that all the corpses had been laid so that they faced the western horizon and the setting sun. There was, however, another feature of this barrow which was altogether more sinister. Quite removed from the others, not in the central ring but touching the inner edge of the outer ditch, the Bronze Age people who had brought their dead here had first dug an oval pit and in it had placed the body of a five-year-old child, facing the west with her hands in front of her face. Three small 'drums' of solid chalk from the sea cliffs a few miles away were laid behind her. They were beautifully decorated. Each top had carefully grooved circles on it, each side had panels of geometrical patterns, lozenges, triangles and chevrons. And in zones separated from the others by broad bands were 'eyebrow' motifs that resembled the faces carved on some of the earlier stone-built tombs in

2   *The Folkton Drums, Yorkshire. The 'eye and eyebrow' motifs can be clearly seen on the two outer chalk drums. The middle drum is about 3½ in. high*

Brittany. Some scholars have identified such carvings as the features of the Mother Goddess, a fearsome deity who watched over the spirits of the dead, often depicted in Mediterranean lands, sometimes in Brittany, rarely in Ireland. What a carving of her—if this is what the artist had intended—was doing in a Yorkshire round barrow of the Bronze Age is not at all clear, but it raises the possibility that the little child at Folkton, placed well apart from the other burials, was a sacrifice interred as a dedicatory offering to give power to the sacred ring that would enclose the later burials before the final barrow of earth and chalk covered them all.

The enigmas and enticements of prehistoric religion are not confined to the Bronze Age on the Wolds. Three miles north-east of Folkton, and thousands of years before that barrow was built, people of the Middle Stone Age had camped for a few seasons at Star Carr in the flooded Vale of Pickering, leaving behind them mysterious head-pieces made from the skulls of stags. Just a mile east of Folkton a vast New Stone Age long barrow at Flotmanby stretches conspicuously along the brink of an escarpment, burnt human bones still incarcerated within it. A few miles south there is a line of enormous round barrows of the Late Neolithic—Willy Howe, Wold Newton, Duggleby Howe—put up in the valley of the Gypsey Race, a stream that rises and flows only in dry weather. To the south-east in Rudston graveyard is the tallest standing stone in Britain with the church built right alongside it. Several cursuses, mile-long parallel lines of banks and ditches of the New Stone Age, lead towards it at the end of a chalk ridge. Bronze Age round barrows are commonplace. Later people heaped up hundreds of tinier barrows at Danes Graves nine miles away, a pit beneath one of them containing a complete chariot of the Iron Age. Not far away at Driffield, hand-sized chalk figurines have been found of Iron Age warriors complete with scabbard-belt and sword neatly scratched out. Their heads have been broken off.

There is no simple and easily obtained explanation of what happened in prehistoric rituals. Far away from Yorkshire but also in chalk countryside the ditched enclosure on Windmill Hill in Wiltshire was for a long time supposed to be a settlement and cattle camp of the Neolithic period. Then skeletons of infants were discovered in the ditches, facing east. In the weeks following these excavations there were more

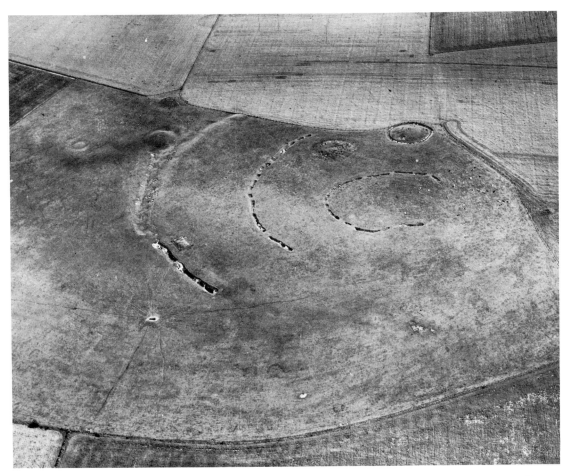

3   *Windmill Hill, Wiltshire. The three rings of ditches during excavation. The small mounds are Bronze Age round barrows built when the neolithic causewayed enclosure had fallen into disuse*

finds, not of whole skeletons but of isolated human skulls, arm bones, femurs, jaws, all meticulously set at the very bottom of the ditches and covered with chalk.[4] One leg bone of a man had the mark of a deep, healed cut in it. Although the children's bones might have been explained away as burials after an epidemic the adult skulls demanded a different interpretation. They could have been relics of burials accidentally disinterred when the ditches were first dug or, perhaps, trophies of battles fought by people who had not enjoyed such a peaceful existence as some archaeologists have believed. Other, uglier possibilities came to mind.

The bones could have been all that survived of human sacrifices at Autumn festivals after the crops were in and the people were turning to their gods in thanksgiving. Even cannibalism was possible. By the 1920s it was known that tens of thousands of years before the time of Windmill Hill, in Yugoslavia, France and Germany, the ancient Neanderthal people, heavyset forerunners of our own ancestors of the Old Stone Age, had killed others of their own kind with clubs and had smashed open the bases of their skulls to extract the brains, less probably for food than in the belief that from such a 'ritual' meal they might gain strength or wisdom from the dead person. At Monte Circeo near Italy a blocked cave led to a chamber where a single skull lay at the centre of a ring of stones, its forehead smashed, its base cracked and chipped from a similar ceremony over 50,000 years ago.

Nearer in time and space to the Windmill Hill skeletons was the famous cave of Great Ofnet in Bavaria where explorers came across two holes that had been scooped out in the limestone floor. There were twenty-seven human skulls packed into the first hole, six in the second, all tightly pressed against each other, all facing west, half hidden under the pile of red ochre that had been poured over them. Jammed in their nests fifteen thousand years ago—twenty children and nine young women with ornaments of deers' teeth and snail shells, four men without trinkets— the skulls had been brought to the cave one at a time after the head had been hacked from its body. At least five of the people had been killed by hatchet-blows. In a cave near Hohlenstein three other skulls had similar murderous fractures on their temples.[5]

Whether we look at the skulls of Neanderthalers with their shattered bases, or the nested Middle Stone Age skulls reddened by ochre, or the buried heads and leg bones at Windmill Hill we are left with questions that are hard to answer. It is easy for the romantic to say that Neanderthal people were cannibals; that the users of the Ofnet cave were headhunters; that the people of Windmill Hill and Folkton Wold practised a cult of head burial. But it is much more difficult for us to be certain that we are right and that we have understood the beliefs of our ancient forefathers.

All over the British Isles are monuments that have lasted from early prehistoric times, some fortunately preserved, others in almost unrecognizable ruin, wrecked by time and men over the centuries. There are circles of upright stones like Stonehenge, and there are less well known but just as impressive rings of banked-up earth or pebbles like Mayburgh in Westmorland where trees grow on a bank as high as a bungalow, where people heaped up one-and-a-half million tons of cobbles around an interior as big as Piccadilly Circus or Times Square.

4   *Machrie Moor II, Arran. The fate of many prehistoric stone circles can be seen in the foreground where a pillar has been pulled over to be turned into two millstones*

Elsewhere there are long mounds with stone-built chambers sometimes filled with human skeletons. There are single stones set on the ridges of hills, or stones standing in rows across wind-stretched moorlands on which today only grey sheep graze. These monuments survive. So do others, invisibly, long buried beneath turf or peat, or entombed under modern roads and towns. They are all silent because the people who raised them are dead and left no writing for us to translate. Whether we stroll around the stones at Avebury, twenty miles north of Stonehenge, touching the rough block that toppled and crushed a mediaeval barber; whether a plane touches down at Heathrow where an Iron Age temple once stood, its wooden porch adorned with ox skulls; whether we visit museums to look at burial urns and Iron Age necklets of gold twisted like a hangman's noose, or see at Colchester or Hull or Edinburgh wooden carvings of men with eyes of agate, their sexual organs detached and lost; in all this we are moving amid the silence of antiquity and it seems, sometimes, that we shall never know why our ancestors made such objects.

There are several apparent ways back into the past but some of them are dead ends, and there are other blind alleys such as the illusory ley-lines that entice their believers farther and farther from the realities of prehistoric existence. Fortunately not all the avenues to antiquity are as foolish as these. There are meanings to be drawn from the wreckage of the old world and it is from these that this book comes with its attempt to say something of the strange, occasionally repugnant customs and beliefs of the inhabitants of prehistoric Britain. Some mysteries can be solved by patient excavation, others by comparing different excavations that may be hundreds of miles and years apart but which provide us with examples of such similar activities that we feel safe in making deductions from them.

Five hundred miles north of Windmill Hill, on the west coast of Orkney Mainland by the shore of the Bay of Skaill is the prehistoric village of Skara Brae, five thousand years old, the stone walls of its houses still six feet high.[6] Buried thousands of years ago by a winter storm the settlement lay forgotten like a northern Pompeii until a nineteenth-century gale set the sands blowing away, leaving some of the walls protruding above the dunes. Seven small houses were discovered. Each had a room with well-constructed furniture of sandstone slabs including a bed on either side of the doorway. Under one bed in a stone-lined cist or coffin were the crouched skeletons of two old women, their bones unbroken and undisturbed. The bodies had been deliberately interred where the wall of the house would pass over their grave sealing it for ever, leaving it uncertain whether these were the relics of natural death, of murder, execution or even sacrifice. Although human bones can carry their own story of age, sex and injury there was nothing at Skara Brae to explain these bodies.

Other excavations give us hints. As far away as Palestine in 6000 BC the inhabitants of villages like Eynan and Jericho buried human bones and skulls inside their homes, sometimes sprinkling them with red ochre. Human burials have been found under the floors of beehive-shaped huts at Khirokitia in Cyprus, a village dating back to the Bronze Age. About the same time but many miles away the Bronze Age villagers of El Oficio in Spain deposited their dead in large jars which were set up inside the houses. At the much earlier neolithic site of Catal Huyuk in Turkey, one of the first large farming settlements, bones and sometimes whole skeletons still clothed and wrapped in rugs were recovered from beneath platforms on which the living slept inside their homes.[7] Even if they had not been aware of the need for hygiene the occupants of these rooms would have found the stench of decomposition unbearable and the corpses of the newly dead must have first been left out in the open on high platforms where vultures could devour their flesh. It was not until the body was reduced to a skeleton, stringy ligaments holding the bones together, that it was transferred to the house, clothed, wrapped and pushed into the darkness of the space beneath the sleeping-floor. Above the beds the wall was painted with a scene of huge, ragged-winged birds hovering over the headless torsoes of human beings, frozen symbols of the reality of death and decay outside.

Although there is no question of a connection between cultures so far apart in time and space it is feasible that these house burials, whether at Catal Huyuk or Skara Brae, developed from a belief that the ghosts of the dead could protect and sustain the walls of the house just as the walls of Jericho were reputedly erected upon the bodies of first-born children.

It can be seen from such comparisons that some of the problems arising from an archaeological excavation may be explained by reference to other excavations and that, insubstantial though they are, people's beliefs can on occasion be recaptured. Sometimes it is valuable to examine the manners, beliefs and taboos of modern primitive groups, looking for parallels among them for the tantalizing pieces of prehistory that the years have left for us. Several instances of such anthropological comparisons occur in this book. Yet another way to an understanding of the past is to read descriptions written by outsides who had known some of the prehistoric societies of western Europe.

Although down to the end of the Iron Age people in prehistoric Britain were illiterate the Romans were not and authors like Tacitus and Julius Caesar have left information for us, such as Caesar's comment that the Druids believed the soul did not die but passed from a corpse to a new body. Knowing this it is easier to understand the ferocity of the naked Iron Age warriors. To them glory in battle was everything and death was of small consequence. There are other instances of archaeological evidence being enlivened from written sources.

In 1952 the body of a fourteen-year-old girl was recovered from a small peat-bog in northern Germany, naked, her fair hair untied, a cloth bound tightly around her eyes.[8] Over her lay branches of birch. A large stone had half sunk in the mud beside her. The left side of her head had been shaved. Despite her amazingly well-preserved condition the girl had lain in the bacteria-free waters of the bog since the time of Christ. The circumstances of the burial, four feet deep in the once brackish, reedy waters, showed without doubt that this was not a natural death, but it was much more difficult to decide if this was the remains of a murder, an execution or a sacrifice. Murder was improbable. The shaven crown and the bandage both implied some form of ceremony. Regrettably, as is so often true, there were limits to what could be learned from the archaeological evidence alone. The few clues did not prove that the girl had been executed for some crime but neither did they rule out the possibility that she might have been ceremonially killed during a festival that her kinsmen had celebrated in some long-gone Spring, Midsummer or Autumn.

As it happened, a Roman historian had described a similar burial. The Windeby girl was killed some two thousand years ago, about the time that the Romans were establishing a border of wooden watchtowers, forts and earthworks between the Rhine and the Danube against the fierce northern tribes, and their historians were recording as best they could some of the savage and unpleasant customs of the German barbarians. Cornelius Tacitus in his *Germania* described the inflexible laws of morality that ruled the nation, accepted willingly by both men and women, with punishment for adultery left wholly with the insulted husband who would shave his wife's head, strip her in front of their families and whip her from the village.[9] So closely does this tally with the nude, hair-cropped body in the Windeby swamp that we may assume the girl, through some act of immorality, had offended her village and had been summarily drowned, pinioned by branches and stones in the shallow waters. It also reminds us that puberty began early and that girls of fourteen might well have been married for two years or more.

There are other instances of the partnership between history and archaeology. Today in Silkeborg Museum in Denmark visitors may look on the face of a man who died about the same time as the Windeby girl and who also was found in a peat-bog, in his case at Tollund in central Jutland, his head preserved so uniquely that even now we can see the stubble of his beard, look at the crow's feet around his eyes. He too had died violently. Two twisted leather thongs were coiled round his throat, passing through an eyelet behind his neck, curling loosely for another

5   *The Windeby burial. The shaven head, the blindfold and the sticks laid across her all show that this girl had been executed*

five feet before ending in a sharp cut. Almost certainly he had been hanged. Then his body had been cut down and flung into the thick waters at the edge of the fen-lake whose tree-covered banks darkened the mud and rushes.[10]

This had not been an execution but a sacrifice. The same historian, Tacitus, mentions a goddess, Nerthus, symbolic of the richness of the earth, the fruitfulness of the crops and the health of cattle, who welcomed the awakening of Spring by a ritual marriage of feasting and intercourse, maybe with a priest, more probably with chosen men who, after their union with her, were killed. Nerthus is often shown in carvings with a gold neck-ring, twisted like a hangman's halter, fitting closely around her throat. In the words of Tacitus:

> In an island of Ocean stands a sacred grove, and in the grove stands a cart draped with a cloth which none but the priest may touch. The priest can feel the presence of the goddess (Nerthus) in this holy of holies, and attends her, in deepest reverence, as her cart is drawn by cattle. Then follow days of rejoicing and merry-making in every place that she honours with her arrival. No one goes to war, no one takes up arms; every object of iron is locked away; then, and only then, are peace and quiet known and prized, until the goddess is again restored to her temple by the priest, when she has had her fill of men. After that, the cart, the cloth, and, believe it if you will, the goddess herself are washed clean in a secluded lake. This service is performed by slaves who are immediately afterwards drowned in the lake. Thus mystery begets terror and a pious reluctance to ask what that sight can be which is allowed only to dying eyes.[11]

Tollund man, his stomach containing a last thin meal of gruel, may also have known the feasting and celebration before he had to pay for that 'sight ... which is allowed only to dying eyes'.

The archaeologist's dilemma is to recognize a religion when he sees it. Museums are filled with so-called ritual objects, meaning often that we cannot find any functional use for them. If it were not for Tacitus we would probably have believed that both the Windeby girl and the Tollund man had been sacrificed but, in fact, we would have been right for only one of them. And just as ancient authors can sometimes solve mysteries for us, so modern place-names can be illuminating about ancient religious sites from which the buildings and structures have long vanished.

The Kentish village of Alkham with its Early English church was originally called *Ealh-ham*, the homestead by the heathen temple, though where or what that temple was we do not know today. Scratchbury Hill, Wiltshire, an Iron Age hillfort, was called *Scucca-burh*, the earthwork of demons, by the Saxons, telling us something of the superstitious dread with which the Saxons regarded these prehistoric places. Hescombe, Somerset, began as *haetse-cumb*, the valley of the witch, and Broxted, Essex, may first have been named *brocces-heofod*, the badger's head, a site of animal sacrifice like Eversheds, Surrey, the place of the wild boar's head. The present-day corrupt pronunciation of what was once *eofor-heofod* shows how time can distort the evidence just as it has transformed many of the legends that are associated with prehistoric sites like stone circles.[12]

Although these rings have little to tell us in themselves, it can hardly be coincidence that whether at Haltadans in the Shetlands or at the Merry Maidens on Land's End or even at Stonehenge, once known as Choir Gaur, the Giants' Dance, there are persistent folk-stories that the rings are groups of people turned into stone for dancing on the sabbath, surely memories of the communal rites that once took place in these circles. An example of the long life of such memories comes from a Cornish story about a burial-mound on Bodmin Moor.[13]

According to legend a druid-priest, the possessor of a magnificent gold cup, lived on the nearby Cheesewring rock and whenever a huntsman came by the druid would offer him a drink from the cup which was inexhaustible. One day a hunter, contemptuous of the cup's reputation, decided to prove he could drain it and drank and drank until he almost choked. Angry at his failure he hurled the wine into the druid's face and galloped off with the cup, only to plunge to his death over the rocks. He and the cup were buried under the round cairn of stones.

For centuries this story was told until, in 1818, the cairn was excavated. Inside, the diggers found the stretched-out skeleton of a man, a bronze dagger—and a gold cup. This was the famous Rillaton cup that is now in the British Museum. It must

6   *The Rillaton Cup, Cornwall. This beautiful vessel, about 3½ in. high, is made of beaten gold and may have been a luxurious imitation of a beaker. It was found in an Early Bronze Age round barrow near the Hurlers stone circles on Bodmin Moor*

have been buried with its owner almost four thousand years ago, long before there were druids in Britain, long before writing, maybe as many as a hundred and fifty generations before the excavation. One wonders how it was possible for a memory, however much distorted, to have endured so long. It seems clear that despite the warpings of time these folk-stories do retain something of their original form. The same is probably true of customs that have lingered on in Europe almost up to the present.

Although there is no proof that they have an ancestry that extends back to some prehistoric period many traditional ceremonies at the time of sowing and harvesting probably have links with the earliest farmers and their superstitions. That the practices are very old is revealed by their being connected with imitative magic, a belief distasteful to the early Christian church. Such magic is based on the primitive belief that if something, normally beyond man's control, is urgently desired then it might be attained by performing actions that closely copied its appearance or sound or character. If rain was needed by an agricultural community then drums might be beaten in imitation of the thunder of rain-bearing clouds. What upset the Church was that ceremonies to ensure a successful harvest were often acted out through the lewd medium of human copulation.

Unable to prevent these age-old customs the Church sometimes added a form of respectability to them. Until recently, in the Ukraine, when the young crops were just becoming green they were blessed by the priest after which young married couples would lie down together at the edges of the fields, rolling over and over, holding each other, in open imitation of sexual intercourse. In the same way, in parts of Germany at harvest-time the men and women who had done the reaping, married or not, also rolled joyfully together among the stubble and chaff.[14]

In pre-Christian times the intercourse would not have been simulated but real, performed as a necessary ritual. Human fertility was believed to encourage the earth itself to be fruitful, guaranteeing a good harvest the next year, and the practice of imitative magic like this probably had a long history before the Church denounced it as depravity.

One cannot imagine such habits with their emphasis on bodily joys actually beginning during Christian times. The attitude of the Church was clearly expressed by Pope Gregory writing to Augustine in AD 601 soon after the latter had arrived in England: 'Lawful intercourse should be for the procreation of children, not for mere pleasure.' The sight of men and women coupling not only for pleasure, though doubtless that also was involved and bawdily acknowledged, but also to evoke richness from the soil, something that was God's business alone, would have been doubly repugnant to a celibate priest who would have done his uttermost to terminate such fertility rites. Where these customs have been noticed it is reasonable to suppose that they are, like the legends, the faded and altered survivals of beliefs that extend backwards over many centuries.

Pregnancy was also an important part of imitative magic and it too was associated with rites designed to perpetuate the fertility of the earth. Up to the last century, in Brittany, the final sheaf to be gathered in from the harvest was made up into a crude human shape and called the 'Mother-Sheaf'. Often a smaller sheaf was put inside it suggesting that the pregnant sheaf would in its turn bring forth more grain. Sometimes the Mother-Sheaf was thrown into a river to make rain, or was made exceptionally heavy, expressing the hope of an even richer crop the following year, or was fed to the cattle to make them thrive.

For anyone hoping to learn about the superstitions, magic and religions of pre-historic people such folk-practices are treacherous for they are easily misinterpreted. Yet when they are put alongside the finds from excavations, the ritual activities of modern primitive societies, the writings of ancient authors, the legends, they all help to build up a picture of what people in this country believed in thousands of years ago.

Archaeology itself deals with solid objects and is limited by them. When the skeleton of a young man was discovered in the hillfort of Maiden Castle in Dorset, an iron ballista-bolt embedded in his backbone, it was reasonable to deduce this was probably the body of an Iron Age warrior killed when the Romans laid siege to the fort around AD 44. Similarly at Spettisbury hillfort a war cemetery was found by navvies working on the Central Dorset Railway who came upon a vast pit in which nearly one hundred bodies had been tumbled, some with savagely hacked wounds. Roman weapons found nearby tell us that this was also an inheritance from the Roman invasion.

Archaeologists can tell from which mountain source a stone axe came, what minerals there are in a bronze bracelet, how old a dug-out canoe is. They can work out the probable cereal-yield from the fields of a Late Bronze Age farm. These are objective matters. But the language, laws, morals, religion of dead societies are different. They belong to the minds of man. Unless they were written down, and even then only if they were recorded accurately, we shall find it hard to recapture them.

Ironically, the very indefiniteness of the evidence that has deterred archaeologists has attracted other writers who have welcomed the opportunities for guesswork. Even one prehistoric burial, especially a lavish one, has been enough to provoke fantasies about a Golden Age altogether unknown to the dead person. Such men were physically and mentally very like ourselves although their beliefs were different. They grew as tall as us, were as intelligent, had rural skills far too developed for a modern townsman to compete against but no more than the skills to be expected from a country dweller lacking modern technology. They were not near-gods.

We might take as an example the burial at Bush Barrow on Salisbury Plain, asking whether this was the grave of a wealthy Stonehenge chieftain and, if so, whether he had also been an astronomer-priest who had been able to predict eclipses of the moon to his awed followers.

Bush Barrow is at the centre of the open and windy plain and today a chalk track, rutted, flinty, puddle-wet in winter, leads to the cluster of twenty-four grassy circular barrows known as the Normanton cemetery. Some of them have ditches and banks around them, the so-called Wessex 'fancy' barrows, and in this cemetery people were buried in the Bronze Age between about 2250 and 1250 BC. When the first mounds were built over four thousand years ago the fresh, grey pillars of Stonehenge hardly a mile to the north were a familiar sight and the line of barrows may have been raised here just because the stone circle was so conspicuous from the ridge.

In the autumn of 1808 Sir Richard Colt Hoare, an antiquarian, decided to explore Bush Barrow with the help of his companion, William Cunnington, and some labourers.[15] Under the mound they discovered the skeleton of a tall, robust man wrapped in the soft fur of an animal skin. By his hand had been placed his bronze dagger, a small ornament of gold and a macehead made of a fossil stone mounted on a wooden handle decorated with bone zigzags. Two more bronze daggers had been left beside him, the wooden hilt of one inlaid with crowds of miniature gold pins so small that Colt Hoare's workmen threw out 'thousands of them with their shovels and scattered them in every direction, before, by the necessary aid of a magnifying glass, we could discover what they were'.

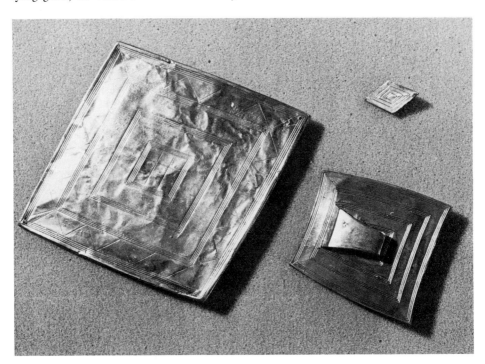

7   *The goldwork from Bush Barrow, Wiltshire. These exquisite hand-made objects were discovered in 1808 by William Cunnington. The larger lozenge is about 7 in. long. Perforations for attaching the articles to a woven tunic can be seen in all their corners*

An axe wrapped in cloth lay by the dead man's shoulder. A leather shield or helmet studded with bronze rivets rested by his head. On his chest was a lozenge of gold incised with delicate geometrical lines in patterns identical to those on the Folkton Drums and matched in beauty by the gold belt-hook at his waist. Over this rich burial the Bronze Age people had piled chalk blocks until the barrow stood like an enormous slant-sided drum, chalk white, brilliant on the skyline from the centre of Stonehenge.

Such a burial is not uncommon and can be dated to the Early Bronze Age in Britain, around 2100 BC, when Stonehenge was undergoing its most outstanding transformation. Whether in Wiltshire or in Scandinavia rich graves like these are well known and the strange ceremonies that accompanied the burials will be described in Chapter Six. The wealth and craftsmanship of his grave-goods surely tell us that the Bush Barrow man was a person of importance in his society.

There is nothing among his possessions that says that this person had studied the movements of the sun or moon. There is no instrument designed for viewing the skies, nothing carved in the shape of sun, moon or star on the axe or daggers or goldwork. In the barrow there is no substance foreign to our world, no moon-rock or Martian dust or mineral from the stars. There is only the body of a middle-aged man buried with his best objects, all of which are easily identified by us as articles that even we might prize.

There is nothing improbable about prehistoric man being interested in the glory of the sun and we shall see that some of his constructions of stones did have alignments built into them towards midsummer sunrise or moonset. Anyone who has seen the burning ball of the midwinter sun sinking between the pillars at Stonehenge, the grill of stones black against the sky, could not doubt that Bronze Age people quite deliberately planned the ring with this phenomenon in mind. Their religious practices were often closely associated with such astronomical events.

From his beginnings Homo sapiens has been concerned with death and with the world in which the living had to exist. For most of the time that man has been on earth his environment has been insecure and he has lacked the means to combat the dangers that surrounded him. It is something of a surprise to realize that for well over two-thirds of the time that men have been in Europe they had to hunt and seek food and shelter during an Ice Age, dependent on the annual migrations of the herds for their livelihood. The fears and strains of this precarious existence were lessened by rituals that were designed to ensure that there would be animals to stalk and water to drink. Fragments of these early rituals from the Old Stone Age have survived for us to interpret.

2

The Birth of the Gods

Who the first inhabitants of Britain were, whether natives or
immigrants, remains obscure; one must remember we are dealing with
barbarians.

Tacitus, *Agricola*, XI

The Old Stone Age in Britain is often dismissed in a few lines as being of no interest,
an age when palaeolithic hunters seldom came close to the bitter edge of their world.
Yet even from so remote a period there are relics of religious practices fourteen thousand or more years old, a time when man first sensed the spirits whose world he
inhabited, spirits that could be generous or vengeful and, more than anything else,
could provide food in a world where food was never certain.

It is a time so long ago that it is almost impossible to imagine. An analogy may
emphasize more clearly its distance from us. If each generation between those early
hunters and ourselves were to be represented by one person with outstretched arms
and all the generations placed side by side, fingertip to fingertip, the line would be
over half a mile long. If one were to walk briskly along it the Romans would be
reached in just over a minute. It would then require another ten minutes of steady
walking, past the warfare of the Iron Age, the stone tombs of the first farmers, the
forests of the Middle Stone Age, past nearly one hundred more arm-stretched people,
before one came finally to the snows and sea-grey skies of the Old Stone Age. It
would take another quarter of an hour to come to the beginning of that age when
Neanderthal men still occupied Europe.

Even towards the end of the Palaeolithic period, fourteen thousand years ago,
there were few people. In winter perhaps no more than two hundred and fifty persons
inhabited the lowlands of England and Wales, little bands trailing the herds, moving
from cave to cave as the animals shifted their winter grazing grounds, camping in
the open air during the warmer summers. From the exposed tundras like Salisbury
Plain there is no trace of these people. It is only in the caves of the Gower peninsula,
of the Mendips and of the Peak District that the slight relics of their religious practices have survived in Britain. In central France and in Spain palaeolithic artists had
for thousands of years been painting animals in the far interiors of caves, or carving
animal shapes out of ivory and bone, sculpting friezes at the entrances to their rock-
shelters. Even before then, in central Europe, mammoth-hunters had fashioned
statuettes of heavy-breasted, big-buttocked women, without faces but with coiled,
plaited hairstyles, hand-sized figurines made from mammoth tusks, clay, bone, limestone, effigies used in some rite within the tents of leather occupied by these hunters.
From Britain there is hardly anything except for the flint tools left in the caves, and
a few burials that provide us with the first glimpse of religious belief in this country.

One matter which for tens of thousands of years had distinguished man from the other members of the animal kingdom was the way in which he disposed of his dead, and in this can be detected the growing awareness that life was more than physical, that existence could be more than a daily searching for food. Man's burial of his dead was not impelled merely by hygiene. Abandoning a corpse at the fringe of the forests for the beasts to devour would have accomplished that. Rather it seems that man began burying his dead as he developed the belief that death was not an end. We are able to detect with how much care the dead were buried, how from very early times they were provided with food, tools, trinkets to take with them into their new spirit world. At first they may have been thought of as remaining, invisible but present, with the living, still sharing their home, performing the same tasks. Later, as myths of the world's creation evolved and as cults of ancestors were shaped into ceremonies of story, dance and mime, so the dead were given other, more unworldly habitations for their unending existence.

Even the so-called 'brutish' Neanderthalers, forerunners of our own ancestors, as long as 60,000 years ago were burying their dead in caves that from the evidence of hundreds of domestic flint tools were still occupied by the living. One burial at La Chapelle-aux-Saints in France was dug out in 1908 and described as that of an ape-like creature, heavy-set, that had walked slumping forward with bent knees, using his feet like a gorilla to pick up food, his brain 'simple and coarse'.[1] From this misrepresentation came the popular image of Neanderthal man. Indeed, the first discovery of one of his burials in 1856 was not even recognized as the skeleton of an intelligent being but was thought to be the remains of a freak. The nineteenth-century anthropologist, Pruner Bey, described him as 'a powerfully organized Celt somewhat resembling the modern Irish with low mental organization', and according to John Pfeiffer in his *The Emergence of Man*, one contemporary English scholar equally mistakenly deduced that the skeleton

> may have been one of those wild men, half-crazed, half-idiotic, cruel and strong, who are always more or less to be found living on the outskirts of barbarous tribes, and who now and then appear in civilized communities to be consigned perhaps to the penitentiary or the gallows, when their murderous propensities manifest themselves.

Isolated finds are not always trustworthy. When the bones of La Chapelle were re-examined recently they were seen to be those of an ageing man, his toothless jaws rotted from septic infection, his body warped with arthritis of the spine and the legs, hardly typical of the majority of stocky, well-built Neanderthalers.

The truth is that these people of a European ice age were the first inhabitants of the world to bury their dead and to care for their afflicted relatives. Their environment was appalling. They lived in a landscape of grey drizzle where only mosses and lichen flourished, overgrown here and there by dwarf birches, willows and stunted crowberries that trailed their bright green leaves along the ground. It was a world of plains and bleak, treeless hills so desolate that people could hardly be imagined in it. Yet it was these wastes that the Neanderthalers inhabited. For much

of the year they hunted in bands across boundless, snow-thick country, tracking down the mammoth, the woolly rhinoceros, the bison. One good kill might provide meat for ten of them for a month in the refrigerating conditions of their climate. One blizzard might starve them to death. Nearly all the women died before they were thirty. A man rarely lived beyond fifty. Yet these people during their struggle to survive accustomed themselves to bury their dead.

From the Shanidar cave in the Zagros mountains two hundred and fifty miles north of Baghdad archaeologists removed seven skeletons, three of them killed by a sudden rockfall that crushed their skulls over 50,000 years ago.[2] One man had been recovering from a wound in his ribs, probably caused by a knife or a spear, much like the Tabun skeleton from Mount Carmel in Palestine with a spear wound in its thigh, perhaps the result of meeting another hunting group desperate for survival in their grudging, thinly provided world. Enmity was inevitable. Self-preservation was imperative. Yet beneath the Shanidar rubble were the bones of an arthritic cripple, blind in one eye, maybe as much as forty years old, his right arm amputated in childhood by his fellows in a crude surgical operation. It was a man who could never have joined in the hunting and the foraging. Unlike the others his teeth were worn almost to their roots because, lacking an arm, he had used them in its place. Despite his uselessness his companions had kept him alive for years probably simply because he was a member of their group.

An even greater surprise lay deep in the cave. Another man had been killed by a savage blow to his head, possibly by the same collapse of rock that had engulfed others there. The survivors had not departed uncaringly. Instead they had gathered branches from pine trees and had made a bed of them on the cave floor, had laid his body on it, and over the corpse they had strewn the bright flowers of Summer— the blue grape hyacinth, hollyhocks, yellow groundsel, as colourful and as reverent as modern wreaths.

Closer to Britain, in the cave of La Ferrassie in France, a whole cemetery of these Neanderthalers was found.[3] A man, his skull protected by stone slabs, lay head to head with a woman whose skeleton was so grotesquely contracted that her dead body may have been tightly trussed with leather thongs, her knees under her chin, before she was committed to her grave. Nearby in individual graves were two children and two infants, quite possibly members of the same family who had been given seemly but straightforward burials. But at the back of the cave was something not so easily explained.

Here a six-year-old child had been placed in a shallow pit. Three flints had been set down alongside the body. But the skull was three feet away under a triangular limestone block on which small hollows had been ground out. These artificial markings must have had a significance but it eludes us. Whether the child had been killed by a predator which had gnawed off the head so that, from some superstition, it had to be placed apart from the rest of the body can only be a matter of speculation. What can be said is that these Neanderthal burials, found so often in occupied caves, sometimes under hearths whose warmth would have percolated down to the cold bones, are the first evidence that people were now thinking of death itself as a continu-

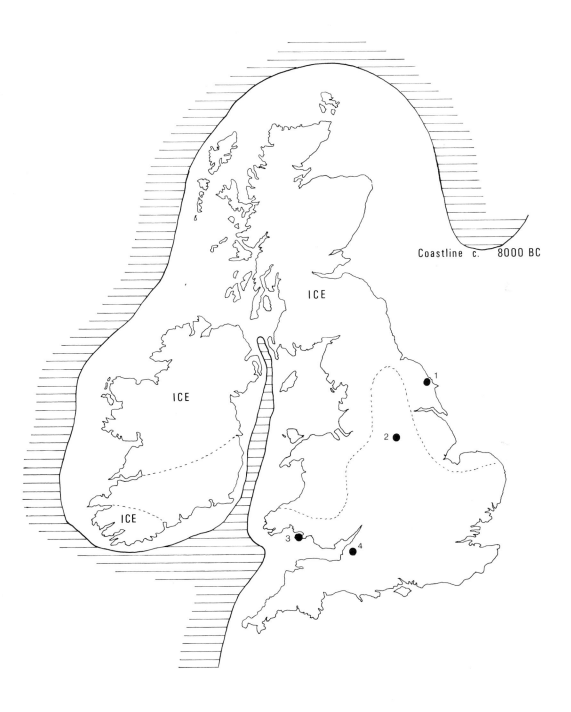

Figure 2 *Some British sites mentioned in Chapter 2:*
1 Star Carr, TA 027810; 2 Pin Hole Cavern, Creswell Crags, SK 533741;
3 Paviland Cave, SS 437858; 4 Gough's Cave, ST 466538

ing part of life, that the dead had not entirely left this world. However vague this belief in spirits may have been and however uncomplicated the ceremonies, limited to burials and without art, they do signify the beginnings of religious thought.

There are also hints of animal cults. In the Lebanon, 50,000 years ago, Neanderthal people solemnly dismembered a deer and buried it, flinging red ochre over its bones in the manner of their own burials. Far away, in north-west Europe, enduring polar conditions at subsistence level, hunters were confronted by ferocious and alert adversaries—the cave bear, the lion, the mammoth—all stronger than themselves. Even as he hunted them for food, attacking them while they hibernated, laying traps, Neanderthal man may have envied their physical perfection and built shrines in their honour, hoping to acquire strength, speed, cunning from contact with their bones. In the French cave of Regourdou the jumbled skeletons of over twenty bears had been jammed into a pit sealed with a thick stone. In the Alps at Drachenloch hunters stored seven bear skulls in a rough chest of stone slabs, their muzzles facing the exit.[4] Other skull fragments were stored behind low stone walls. At Salzofenhohle in Austria three bear skulls were found, neatly ringed with stones and with concentrations of charcoal near them just as at Drachenloch a fire-pit with signs of intense burning was discovered near another cist of skulls with a single skull on top of it. This seems to have been some kind of ritual centre, perhaps a place where offerings were made as sacrifices to a deity, just as the Tungus, hunters of north-east Asia today, venerate the bear and offer skulls and marrowbones from their prey to their god.

Other groups took this cult of the bear to obsessional lengths. Some Neanderthalers in Poland followed tradition by placing bear skulls along the walls of their caves but one band at Hellmich actually kept a brown bear in captivity. In order to render these tons of muscular ferocity less dangerous the men periodically filed down its front teeth, a practice so unbelievable, considering the jerking body and ripping claws, that we can only observe that this was indeed a compulsive religion. The Ainus of Japan also captured young bears, filed their teeth and later killed them ceremonially.

Uncommon though they are such cults show Nenaderthal people seeking for powers beyond their own physical limitations just as the burial of their dead show them acknowledging an existence outside their own bodies.

When they vanished from Europe, perhaps not by coincidence just when our own ancestors, the Cro-Magnons of the Upper Palaeolithic, appeared 35,000 years ago, similar burial customs were practised by the newcomers. The mass interment of twenty people at Predmost, Czechoslovakia; burials of children with shell-ornamented clothing at the Grotte des Enfants, Menton; a hunter at Brno, lying on soft furs and covered with a mammoth's shoulder-blade; all these testify to the careful, thoughtful treatment that some of the dead were given. Sometimes graves were deliberately dug through the charcoal where fires had burned in the cave and the bodies were sprinkled with red ochre to conceal the candle-white of death and protected by stones from the scavenging hyena. Often grave-goods were left with the bodies, snail shells, flints, a bone dagger. As communities became bigger, combining in large-scale hunts, and as settlements along the cliff faces took in more and more people, so ritual also became more elaborate.

It is likely that by then people believed in personal spirits that might travel from the living body in dreams and which left it forever in death; but now religion involved more than just death. Man's intelligence and imagination had populated the whole region of his world with spirits, not only of the dead but of the animals he hunted, the places he lived in, the sky, the weather. Water holes, springs, dramatically standing rocks and cliffs, these might also be invested with spirits by the early hunters, a world in which man and beast, the growing tree, the wind, the rain, the waterfall were all living parts of existence, all with their own powers, an animistic landscape of spirits to be ordered and appeased by meticulously organized rituals.

Now, for the first time, men banded together in ceremonies intended to manipulate the spirits. By careful magic these might be used to provide people with food and to protect them from danger. To this end man became an artist, painting and carving animals for the spirits to recognize. And also for the first time men used holy and secret places for the performance of their intense, very personal ceremonies. Theirs was a world of hunters. Everything that survives reflects this. What is left far down the painted galleries and crevices of caves in the Dordogne and the Pyrenees is a startlingly brilliant palaeolithic world of animals that we may better understand by looking at more modern examples.

Until a few years ago the aborigines of central Australia kept sacred objects in the sanctuary of a rock cleft or in a cave, and before entering that cave they would press the palm of their hand against the wall to acknowledge the presence of the spirit and their identity with it. Hand-stencils which may have had a similar purpose often mark the walls of the painted caves of palaeolithic Europe. In western Australia there are some caves where the natives have painted the totems of their sacred ancestors. Some interpretations of the animal art of the European caves see those paintings as totems representing the spirit of the group, the bison clan, the horse, the deer, man and animal becoming virtually interchangeable in their qualities.

Such identifications may have enriched the minds of palaeolithic hunters and artists.[5] Intermixed with such totems may be the magic of art that was meant to help men catch animals. A rich repertoire of decorated cave walls, moving and writhing in a universe of animals, male and female interrelated, horse and bison and cow and deer, the carnivorous eaters, the lions, the bears kept separate, the animals to be hunted surrounded by dots and lines and patterns and hands, far down the blacknesses of empty, boulder-lain passages, human footprints fossilized here and there in mud 15,000 years old—these paintings and the carvings on spear-throwers all combine to tell us something of this abundant world of the hunters in Europe and of their holy places.

The painters were much concerned with the hunt and with the provision of food for the living. Dying was ordinary. Animals on the walls of these sanctuaries sense the end of their lives, falling in panic over cliffs, pierced by spears, disembowelled, lying lumpish in death. The caves show hunting scenes so vivid they seem to have been still-lifes intended as bridges between the artist's mind and the spirit-world, realistic because they were meant to achieve in life what had already been achieved in the imagination. Such hunting magic is the earliest expression of man's ability to fantasize. Thought and action mingle. The symbol and the reality are one. Only the human beings are unnatural. Men are matchsticks, never shown as they were in life. Women are sexual abstractions without head or arms or feet, symbols of fertility, not to be known as a person, not to be recognized and trapped by the spirits.

In some caves the magic is obvious. Deep in the Tuc d'Audoubert the hunters made clay sculptures of bison for initiation ceremonies. Here boys danced in a gloomy recess lit by the flames of the men's torches in the bison chamber outside. Knee-prints survive by the entrance. Inside are the deep heel marks left by the young dancers and near them the clay phalli that symbolized puberty and the acceptance of the boys into the world of men and hunters.

At Montespan, twenty miles to the west, difficult to reach today because of sub-terranean streams, a crawl along an earthy tunnel brings one to a gallery of clay models and stone reliefs used for similar ceremonies. Hunting magic is explicit here. Once, a bear's skin with skull attached had been draped over a clay moulding of a bear's torso, crouching with claws extended. In the wavering flamelight hunters had circled it, round and round, jabbing and piercing the beast with their spears, pockmarking the clay with the thrusts. Further still into the cave along a sightless, meandering side passage the artists found a panel of clay embedded on the wall. Here men finger-traced a frieze of trapped horses, driven against a palisade, helpless. Into these symbolic victims the people jabbed sticks again and again in a ghostly kill. Nearby, where a river snakes across the gallery, human footprints, many of children, have petrified in the mud.

A further explanation may be given for the choice of these subterranean, lightless and remote locations for the paintings. Among more modern primitives there has commonly been a belief that their ancestors had reached the world only by long and tortuous journeys across lakes or through caves and that it was necessary, for the clan's good, for the living to re-enact these journeys of creation. To this end aborigines painted detailed and complicated maps of the journeys. American Indians made comparable maps. It is very likely that, preoccupied with their beliefs in ancestor-spirits, the palaeolithic hunters chose the twisting darknesses of their caves as appropriate symbols for the living to retrace these mythical journeys, to bring strength and fortune to their people. And by making their paintings in the fearful, unlit dwellings of their ancestors more power might be given to the hunting magic of this art.

Very recently, moreover, it has been recognized that many of these painted caves are close to thermal, mineral springs. At both Montespan and Tuc d'Audoubert, in each of which clay models of animals have been found, a stream flows from the mouth of the cave. Font de Gaume, Pair-non-Pair are but two examples of many other caves which are close to springs. Warm springs which did not freeze even in the most icy weather might well have been regarded as magical and powerful. Caves near them might have gained added potency. Running water in itself has often been considered as pure and living by primitive people, 'more potent, more effective', according to the anthropologist, Levi-Strauss, and the dwelling-place of spirits. Such beliefs about the sacredness of water lingered throughout all the centuries of prehistoric Britain. Some stone circles had avenues leading from water, some megalithic tombs were built alongside streams, the people perhaps believing that the ghosts of their ancestors would be able to control the spirits that lived in the running water. It was in such ways that the dead could be used to help the living.

Even many thousands of years ago palaeolithic man was aware of death, and honoured those who had died before him and who had joined the spirits of the natural and animal worlds that the living had to occupy. Man worked with those spirits to safeguard his own existence and left behind him wordless but eloquent relics of his sensitive mind. It is only at the edges of his world, in what are now the British Isles but which in those times were the freezing outer limits of the land-locked hunting-grounds, that the signs are less, the people fewer (see Fig. 2).

In these lands men travelled reluctantly even when the years of ice and monotonous tundra were declining and when warmer weather was encouraging the growth of a few willows and white, papery birches. Now man could live above the forested valleys in a pleasant, open parkland of grass and trees, where animals searched for plants and for the aromatic juniper trees with their upward-crowding, needled branches, the black berries ripening slowly in the cold winds. Widely dispersed there were horses, reindeer, a herd of bison, mammoths, plentiful food for the hunters. And yet there are only rare signs of habitation. In the fifty or more caves along the river valley that was later to be flooded by the rising sea and become the Gower coast of South Wales little has been recovered. There is, however, a burial.

In 1823 Dean Buckland scrambled into the rough gash of Goat's Hole Cavern.[6] Digging into the floor this cleric and geologist found a human skeleton, the Red Lady of Paviland, that he thought to be the remains of a young woman of Roman times. He also found numerous animal bones that he was convinced were those of beasts drowned in the Biblical Flood. He was wrong about almost everything. The Red 'Lady' was actually a twenty-five-year-old man whose burial had been typical of the later Palaeolithic: a shallow grave, the body laid in it with the dead man's belongings, an ivory armlet, a necklace of bored teeth and shells, a handful of periwinkles for food, some amulets against evil spirits, red ochre cast over the corpse, boulders rolled up to the head and foot of the grave. The mourners may have placed a mammoth's skull nearby.

Other burials from the limestone gorges of Cheddar in the Mendips have the same hunting background. At Aveline's Hole the body was accompanied by sixty seashells for a necklace. Fossils from a source nearly thirty miles distant are witnesses to the wide-ranging territories of these early people. At Gough's Cave a short young man lay crouched as though in sleep.[7] He had been buried when most of his flesh had decomposed. Examination showed him to have been right-handed. From the state of his teeth it was likely that he had cleaned them regularly, a rather unexpected revelation of personal hygiene in the Palaeolithic. With him were some perplexing bones, including a human arm bone. On a rib was a network of grooves, with a series

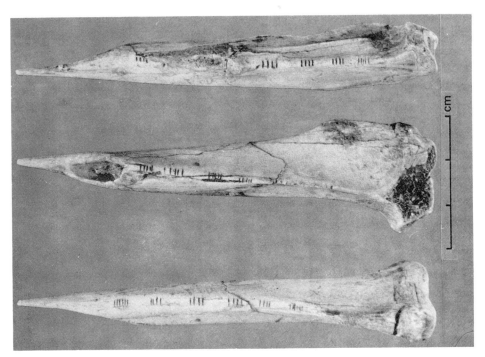

8   *An incised bone of the Old Stone Age from Gough's Cave, Cheddar Gorge. The markings on it have been interpreted as an early attempt to calculate the movements of the moon. It is almost 12,000 years old*

9   *Creswell Crags, Derbyshire. This little fragment of bone from Robin Hood's Cave has a delicate engraving of a horse's head on it. It may have been carved at the end of the Old Stone Age around 8500 bc*

of short strokes on the other side, often in groups of nine irregular scratches rather like a tally-stick. It may have been for counting the herds. The markings may be doodles. They may even be the numbering of nights in a moon-month, an astonishing record of palaeolithic man noting the movements of the heavens.

If burials from this period are scarce in Britain, art is even less common. There is nothing to compare with the caves of central France and northern Spain. It is true that at Bacon's Cave not far from Paviland there are ten vertical red bands about a foot long on the wet rock. They are rather like others at the magnificent Font de Gaume cave in the Dordogne, painted on the side of the Main Gallery near two large bison. There is, however, much doubt about this one example of British cave painting. Darkened and almost invisible today the marks may be palaeolithic or they may, less romantically, be the result of a seaman cleaning his nineteenth-century paint brush on the cave wall.

It is only from the Peak District that art is certain, a bone engraving of a reindeer from the delightfully named Mother Grundy's Parlour in the limestone ravine of Creswell Crags; a horse's head incised on bone from Robin Hood's Cave; and, most important of all, from the Pin Hole Cave another bone engraving, this time of that rarest of palaeolithic images, a tiny human figure, hardly an inch and a half tall, with an animal's mask, holding a bow and with a grossly exaggerated penis.[8]

This half-animal, half-man, is like others from painted caves in France and Spain—the bulging-eyed figures at Los Casares, the bearded and dancing 'sorcerer' high up on a wall at Les Trois Frères. At Le Portel in the Pyrenees someone painted the red outline of a man in a recess of the cave. This alcove may have been chosen because the artist was able to transform a swelling on the rock into the figure's grotesque and raised penis. These half-human pictures are not common but they often have features in common—a stylized body, an animal's head or mask, the torso bent forward as though dancing—painted remotely in the cave, far away from the beasts crowding against each other in a confusion of movement. The sexual symbolism suggests rites of fertility that were expected to lure herds of edible animals into the range of the hunters.

The figures have been explained as priests for the hunting rites, as magicians, as spirits of the sanctuary, as heroic ancestors fused with the clan's totem, even very simply as disguised hunters wearing decoys. It may be that the images are something of all these, linking the spirit of the hunt and of the hunter. Among the Hopi Indians of North Arizona there were symbolic dances mimicking the actuality of stalking the antelope herds. The tribal medicine-man would be elaborately dressed as the Antelope Kachina in a long deerskin over a beaded sash geometrically decorated, over his head an antelope mask surmounted by antlers. Carrying a rattle and a bow he would act hunter and hunted, creeping through the concealing grass, aiming, raising startled head, jerking into flight, dying tongue stretched, prodding the carcase triumphantly.

This acting out of elements of the chase to enlist the assistance of the gods not only has an ancestry deep in the Palaeolithic but was so powerful a part of people's thinking that it endured well into Christian times. Late in the seventh century AD the Archbishop of Canterbury prescribed penances for those who offended against Christian teaching:

> If anyone on the first day of January goes about as a stag or bull; that is, making
> himself into a wild animal and dressing in the skin of a farm animal and putting

on the heads of beasts; those who, in this way, change themselves into the appearance of a wild animal, a penance for three years because this is a practice of the
devil.

St Theodore, *Book of Penances*

Despite denunciations like this there are still some watered-down versions of
these animal disguises in Britain today. There are the six September antlered dancers
of Abbots Bromley in Staffordshire; the black Godiva festival at Southam in which
a participant wears a mask of a bull's head with horns; and the May Day Padstow
hobby-horse festival, one of several, where, significantly, the draped creature deliberately bumps and grabs at women and girls in a custom which must have its origins
in the belief that such a union with the animal effigy would increase the fertility
of the females.

Thus, isolated though it is, the Pin Hole Cave engraving shows our palaeolithic
ancestors already engaged in practices of magic to safeguard the living in a world
infested by indefinite but powerful spirits. Engraved charms and pendants might
give some security. The ghostly presence of mighty ancestors provided extra defence
against misfortune. Living alongside the roaming animals that were his life and his
principal danger man devised yet more protection from the enactment of rites in
traditional places, then ventured out across the plains to the herds of bison, cattle
and horses grazing by the rivers where the trees were most dense. And as the glaciers
continued to withdraw and the climate improved people moved further northwards
into the newly released lands, changing their ways of life as their world changed.

Towards the end of the Palaeolithic period many of the customs suspected from
earlier times become certain. Now not only the burials but the totems and the ancestor cults can be confirmed. And to these was added a new practice, growing out
of the conviction that spirits would help if men pleased the spirits. As the herds
of big game dwindled with the departing snows the paintings and the dances seemed
no longer entirely sufficient. Now gifts had to be made, offered in places where only
the spirits could reach.

The ice was finally going. Crowds of reindeer, horses and giant elks followed
the melting summer snows northwards, south again in winter, always trailed by men
through the trudging days of hunger. In the warmer months groups of hunters would
camp at the very rim of the glaciers where, under the pale skies, reindeer grazed
over the slopes of lichens, heathers and bare rock. Not far from the skin tents by
the lakeside women searched for roots, edible insects and snails while the fur-robed
men, armed with barbed harpoons, tracked the split toe-marks of the deer in the
snow.

At Meiendorf in Germany the remains of a hunting camp of perhaps twenty
people was discovered on a sandy ridge that had overlooked a small lake.[9] Here on
the tundra at the edge of the icefields men had come one summer, hunting the horses,
trapping hares, fowling for unwary geese and swans. A little disc of amber was carried
by one hunter who had repeatedly scratched on it the silhouettes of animals he wanted
to catch, erasing them as the magic worked, animal after animal down to the last
horse's head when the charm was lost in the rushes that bordered the camp.

But it was the reindeer that the people most sought. And when they located the herd, slaughtering and dismembering the animals, they took the carcase of a two-year-old doe, split open its chest, pushed in an eighteen-pound block of sparkling banded gneiss, sewed up the cavity and dropped the weighted offering deep in the waters of the lake, presenting their own gift to the bountiful spirits.

Forty centuries passed. By 12,000 BC pine trees spread across the warming land. Men hunted through the forests with newly invented bows and stone-tipped arrows. A new group of people occupied a sandy rise not half a mile from Meiendorf, coming year after year to this other lakeside, hunting, gathering fruits, berries and roots from the richer earth. Hundreds of bones and antlers of reindeer killed over a period of fifty years show that even at the beginning of the Middle Stone Age man remained a skilful hunter. Other finds show how his beliefs were only slowly changing.

Here at Stellmoor, just as at Meiendorf, young does laden with stones were thrown into the waters, one each year in an offering to the spirit of the lake. The excavator estimated that there may have been at least forty-five of these carcases. It is not unlikely that these were pregnant does chosen for their fertility, potent magic for the increasing of life's richness. We may ask why a lake was chosen for their resting-place. Was it because here they were unrecoverable by man, sinking into regions where only spirits dwelt, or was it because water attracted the reindeer and was therefore considered to contain the very spirits of the animals that were to be supplicated?

Water has been regarded as sacred by many primitive societies. People are aware of its life-sustaining qualities. The dominant nature god of the African Ashanti was the River Tano whose wives, sons and brothers were other streams, springs and watering-places. Tano was honoured in the Ashanti's traditional drum language:

> *The stream crosses the path,*
> *The path crosses the stream;*
> *Which of them is the elder?*
> *Did we not cut a path long ago to go and meet this stream?*
> *The stream had its origin long, long ago.*
> *The stream had its origin in the Creator.*
> *He created things,*
> *Pure, pure Tano.*

It is possible that to the Stellmoor huntsmen the lake itself was the habitation of the spirits. Here men made their offerings. And here they set up their totem pole in the shallows, fixing the skull of an old buck reindeer upon it, the gigantic antlers pointing to the sky. Perhaps the beast was picked out as the oldest, wisest male of the herd and deliberately killed to become the most appropriate symbol of the hunting clan on their seasonal visits. By the pole twelve more skulls lay in the water, earlier totems that the lake had taken. Other finds—antler axes, wooden arrows, bone tools—might not have been accidental losses but votive gifts to the spirits of the sacred waters. At another mere, not far off at Ahrensberg-Hopfenbach, a totem had been put up far from the shore in deep water unaccompanied by any implement or skull or stone-heavy doe. In this lake a willow-trunk had been carved into the formalized figure of a human being with head and arms and legs, a manlike effigy rising from the waters to watch over the living. Two other poles lay nearby.

Religion is born from the needs of mankind. It mirrors their particular hardships and the conditions of their lives. Because the reindeer hunters of northern Europe persisted in the long-established tradition of tracking down the herds of wild game their religion also continued to be based upon hunting magic, more complex after so many centuries, the spirits more personalized, but essentially the same as in earlier times. In other, warmer, easier landscapes the emphasis changed.

Hundreds of miles south of Stellmoor in the valleys, caves and coasts of the Pyrenees other hunters were elaborating cults of their ancestors, still burying their dead in caves but now painting smooth brook pebbles with patterns of points, circles and lines, some in red, others engraved with sharp flints. These motifs may have had something of the same origin as the stylized figures painted on the late palaeolithic rock-shelters of eastern Spain. In those the Levantine artists drew miniature but dynamic hunting scenes of men and animals that existed after the withdrawal of the ice, slim archers warring against each other at Barranco de los Dogues or the famous twisted bulls with onlooking, long-skirted people at Cogul in Lerida. But the painted pebbles from the Mas d'Azil have little to do with hunting magic.

10 *Painted pebbles from the Mas d'Azil in the French Pyrenees. The meaning of the patterns remains obscure*

Thirty miles south of Toulouse there is a forested cliff through which the River Ariége has scoured a vast tunnel. Here at the Mas d'Azil archaeologists have discovered finely carved bones and decorated pebbles which may have been charms or talismen.[10] They have been found in scores in caves and their very plentifulness tells us something about their meaning. The closest similarities are the painted wooden tablets carefully preserved in caves by the aborigines of Australia and Tasmania to whom they represent the souls of the dead. On the central Australian plain each tribe of the Aruntas has its own storehouse for these churingas. In the same way the Azilian pebbles with their stylized human shapes may have been ancestor stones, the embodiment of the clan's origins and the source of its power. We can imagine ceremonies involving the manipulation of these pebbles, the evoking of great spirits, muttered incantations to awaken the sleeping dead who might give protection to these small, isolated communities. Theirs was a religion not greatly concerned with maintaining control over animals because food was more plentiful, living easier in these lusher climates and the people were much more absorbed in their myths of creation, ancestors and heroes, looking back to a hazily recorded time of hunting battles and the overcoming of savage beasts.

It could have been people of this culture who were responsible for the nests of human skulls already mentioned from the Ofnet cave, murdered by blows to the forehead and crammed into packed pits, their spirits destroyed by the removal of skulls from their bodies so they could not molest their living enemies. A painted pebble, safe in its sanctuary, preserved one's own ancestor. A beheaded skull terminated someone else's.

Azilian pebbles have been found as far away from Spain as Bavaria and Switzerland where, in the Birseck cave, no fewer than one hundred and thirty-three were found. Every one was broken, deliberately smashed like those from Ofnet, the work of hostile newcomers who removed the power of the sanctuary by destroying the spirits of the dead.

For century after century the weather became warmer and, relieved of the weight of ice that had crushed down upon it, the earth lifted, unfroze, was fed by freshwater streams and rain, and over northern Europe pine forests spread along the valleys. In the lower country to the east rain and rising seas built vast marshes, the plains were covered with trees and the last of the herds trailed after the snow further and further to the north. Faced with the choice of surviving in polar snows or adapting to the woodlands and lakes men became fowlers, fishermen, gatherers of food, Middle Stone Age or mesolithic hunter-fishers of the forests, beachcombers existing on a diet of shellfish and other seafood along the coasts. Abandoning the caves and rock-shelters, and living in tents or impermanent lean-to huts their traces are few.

In western Europe very little has survived of man's activities from the period between about 10,000 and 4000 BC. Apart from a few burials the migrant people of the Mesolithic left nothing substantial behind them except for some traces of flimsy shelters, the burnt patches of their hearths, and thousands of bits of flint thrown away when they were fashioning their delicate tools and weapons.

In Britain mesolithic sites are not easy to discover.[11] The temporary dwellings have left few traces, and the entire population of Britain may have been no more than about seven thousand people. In the whole one hundred and twenty square miles of Salisbury Plain, then thick with trees, there may have been only one small hunting group, a couple of families tracking along the lonely, wild river banks. At Downton, where the Avon flowed through the forest of oaks and ashes with their undergrowth of hazel and grey-barked buckthorn, the people had lingered for a while on the gravel terrace, digging for flint, sheltering in their flimsy huts. Small cooking pits, a few stakeholes are all that is left. Here and elsewhere relics of superstition and religion are almost nonexistent.

There is, fortunately, one site, Star Carr, that is more informative.[12] Yet even here there is nothing left to see, only the grass of the field and the sunless slopes of the Yorkshire Wolds to the south. The lake has gone. The forest has given way to pastures, suburban gardens, the factories and coastline of Scarborough where the sea surges and swells over an ancient plain across which people once hunted the red deer. Ten thousand years ago two or three families settled here for a winter by a lake where the wildfowl offered an occasional variation from a diet of roots and venison. To reach the water the people cut down a couple of saplings and hauled them through the reeds and the withered, fleshy waterlilies to make a landing-stage for canoes. On the muddy banks they spread branches in a crude platform where they squatted to fashion flint arrowheads and many-toothed harpoons and knives. Behind them, beyond the scattered willows, stretched a forest of birches, spacious, and broken by glades along the northern hills. Timid, elusive, hidden in the silence, deer browsed, stags separated from the does in their winter territories. For miles the trees spread, only thinning where the uplands broke into the limestones and the harsher, thinner soils of the Yorkshire Moors.

There are no painted pebbles or totem poles or offerings of does at Star Carr or at any other British site of the Middle Stone Age but we may assume some form of hunting magic among these lonely families, wandering from summer to winter camp, season by season through the wildernesses of rivers, lakes and woodlands that was their home. But what their ceremonies were is unknown. Almost the only religious objects to survive are skulls of stags that have been hacked into head-dresses, antlers still in place, the interior of the cranium smoothed, the temples punctured for thongs to be passed through. These frontlets have been interpreted as masks worn by hunters while stalking the deer, perhaps as a method of decoying those nervous animals. But they may just as easily have been worn by men in dances intended to increase the fertility of the herds that grazed around Star Carr.

Over twenty antlered frontlets were found near the brushwooded area where the people had worked. It is unlikely that at any time there were ever more than about six grown men among the families, so the group must have returned to Star Carr for several winters, but whether the head-gear was worn for hunting or for hunting magic or both is not clear.

In California the Maidu Indians crept close to the deer packs by using exactly this kind of disguise. One or two braves draped themselves with deer hides, painted

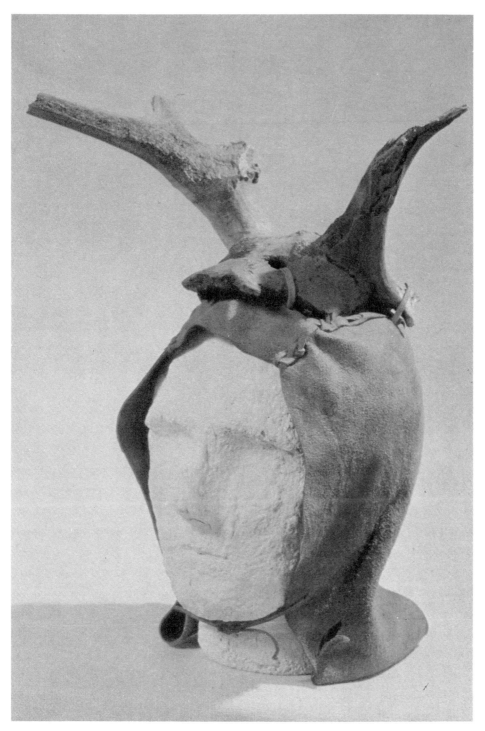

11   *This reconstructed 'head-piece' from Star Carr in Yorkshire shows how these antler frontlets could have been both hunting decoys and also the 'horns' of witch-doctors in the Middle Stone Age around 7500 bc*

their chests white and put on stuffed deer heads. Carrying a pair of sticks, which they rattled together like the clashing of bucks' antlers during the time of mating, they attracted one deer after another, shooting them with arrows poisoned with rattle-snake venom. Tne Star Carr frontlets may have been used like this.

Quite differently, along the Rio Grande the Taos Indians held a winter hunting dance beneath their sacred Rocky Mountain that to them was the Animal Mother. In the whiteness of its snows the dancers, dressed in deerskin and horned head and carrying sticks, walked on either side of the Mother in her graceful white buckskin robes. Some would be 'dead', glassy-eyed with protruding tongue, others would graze peacefully as the stealthy hunters advanced. It was a dance in which the hunted beasts and their Mistress, in human form, came down from the cold mountain sides bringing their helplessness within reach of human beings. The bear-dances in the caves of the Pyrenees may have had the same mimed symbolism. And at Star Carr, as with the antlered 'sorcerer' of Les Trois Frères or the masked figure from Pin Hole Cavern, we are given a glimpse but no more of the customs of these early hunters.

Art has only rarely survived from this period. From Denmark there are replicas of animals carved on bones, a piece of amber shaped in the likeness of a bear from Resen, and from Ryemarkgaard in Zealand another carving on an ox bone which portrays matchstick people shuffling or dancing alongside a mysterious and non-human figure whose significance will never be known. From Britain the art is even scarcer. When mesolithic food-gatherers abandoned their camp near Prestatyn in Wales they left behind them not only a scatter of minute chert tools but also an oyster shell perforated at its centre as though to be suspended around someone's neck.

Year by year through the centuries the cold diminished. The birch forests were replaced by drier woodlands of hazel and pine intermixed on the clays with oaks and elms whose stands thickened and spread as the rains increased. Ill-drained uplands were turned into bogs, streams were changed into rivers that flowed cease-lessly into the rising waters of the North Sea. By 5000 bc the British Isles had been formed, separated from the continent by miles of sea. The forests of oak and elm climbed higher up the hillsides.

Hunting where they could, journeying to highland springs in the Summer, set-ting fire to the bracken to make clearings that would tempt the foraging deer, splitting into tiny bands for the hungrier months of winter by low-lying lakes, the hunter-fishers of the Mesolithic moved from place to place in an unending search for food. Their customs by now were only threadbare copies of the old traditions.

Groups that drifted along the coastlines subsisted on oysters, mussels and peri-winkles, dumping the shells on rubbish tips that made a windbreak against the sea breezes. At Polmonthill near Stirling a family of ten or so people, a small hunting band constantly searching for food and flint, left behind them alongside the remains of their hearths a huge heap of shells—oysters, mussels, winkles, cockles and whelks—the debris of perhaps fifteen years of desultory occupation. Sometimes the dead were buried in these middens. From Denmark down to Spain open-air settlements have been found on low, sandy slopes above a river or the sea. By the Tagus in Portugal the long middens at Muge contained huddled skeletons with a few flints and miserable ornaments of shells and teeth, a thin spread of ochre reminiscent of the great palaeolithic burials but far less ceremonious.

Sometimes the burials do show signs of ceremony. At Durrenberg in Germany the body of a young man was discovered half-sitting in a deep pit. In Poland, at Janislawice, a stocky, middle-aged hunter was stylishly buried with his hunting equipment and with food for his journey into the Other-World.[13] His body had been lowered into a large grave and propped against the wall, his legs outstretched, his spears, bow and arrows alongside him. His flint and bone tools, his boar's tusk chisels were spread around him and near his hand were mussels and joints cut from wild cat and beaver.

A burial like this had similarities to those from the Old Stone Age but it also anticipated some of the practices that were to become commonplace during the Neolithic period when the ideas of crop-growing and cattle-grazing reached Europe. Already, by 5000 BC, in Germany, in the Low Countries and in France the land was being cultivated by farming people whose beliefs were very different from the mesolithic natives of the Atlantic coast. Radio-carbon 'dates' of 4625 ± 350 bc from the island of Teviec and 4020 ± 80 bc from a nearby Middle Stone Age settlement are the approximate equivalents of 5500 BC in real years and show that mesolithic people were living in Brittany long before the incoming farmers reached that area.

Along the Danube large villages had developed, inhabited by agriculturalists whose ancestors had carved small female figurines and worshipped at small shrines in their homes. There is no sign of such cults in the British Isles. Farming reached this country but it was not accompanied by esoteric rituals from the Near East nor does the land appear to have been overrun by intruders. Instead, where these first farmers settled they built monumental tombs in which the burials were in the communal tradition, long established in western Europe.

It has been suggested that the very pressure of eastern farming groups moving across Europe caused the natives along the Atlantic seaboard to draw closer together in self-protection. Their ceremonies also became more organized.

On the little islands off Brittany beachcombers living in the stench of their rotting middens were already giving their dead more formal burial.[14] Ten graves at Teviec contained twenty-three bodies, family burials that were the precursors of similar burials in the tombs of the New Stone Age. Both at Teviec and Hoedic corpses were not merely bundled into the rubbish heaps. Instead, large fires were lit as part of the ceremonies and deep graves were dug. In them the dead were laid. One body was tied up, his legs forced hard back against his loins. Another man with an arrowhead embedded in his spine was carefully interred. Often, children were buried in their parent's arms. In the graves were placed shell necklaces, bone daggers, and over the bodies the inevitable red ochre was sprinkled. Some of the corpses were framed in a setting of antlers. Then the primitive family vault was covered with stones and it is these little cairns that have survived for the archaeologist.

Here were all the trappings of the earlier burials of Old Stone Age people, showing that even in the restless, changing conditions of seven thousand years ago man had retained his burial customs although the art and the remains of cult practices remain elusive. It seems, however, that it was these late mesolithic people, banding together, who adopted the new farming ways without giving up their traditional beliefs. To the contrary, along the 'Atlantic Facade' as archaeologists call it from the way it seems to have acted as a cultural breakwater, family graves like those at Teviec became more and more elaborate, developing ultimately into the monstrous, stone-built neolithic passage-graves and chambered long mounds, some of which still survive. Fifty years ago the great prehistorian, Gordon Childe, remarked that 'The great centres of megalithic architecture in Europe are precisely those regions where the palaeolithic survivals are the most numerous and best attested'. It was the long-established customs of western Europe that were to influence the religious beliefs of the New Stone Age farmers of the British Isles.

3

Good Lands and Bone-Houses

Men lived happy as Gods ...
Always the kindly cornlands, that no man toiled to till,
Brought forth their harvests' bounty. And all men lived at will
Crowned with every blessing, on their own fields quietly.

Hesiod, **Work and Days**, 8th century BC

Hesiod's idyllic vision of life in early farming times was a long way from reality. Even where agriculture had been in existence for hundreds of years and where one might expect the population to be healthy and long lived the evidence is horrifyingly different. Skeletons from the Hungarian cemetery of Tiszapolgar bore signs of paralysis, deformation of the skull, malformation of the spine, arthritis and rheumatism, fractures, head wounds and brain tumours.[1] Only a quarter of the people lived beyond forty-five years of age and as many died before they were sixteen. The picture is no different for neolithic Britain. As Professor Milisauskas remarked of the Hungarian farmers, 'Not only was life short but also various pathological miseries hounded men and women, and there was little possibility of relief. It is doubtful that shamans could cure or relieve the pain of many of these diseases.' With such incurable terrors surrounding them, probably attributed to the malevolence of invisible spirits, these societies turned to ritual for protection.

In the centuries around 4500 BC bands of farming people were settling in the British Isles. Even earlier some mesolithic groups may have found it convenient to corral animals rather than hunt them, feeding them on the succulent leaves of elm, lime and winter ivy, but for thousands of years while these islands remained almost deserted, occupied only by scattered families of these mesolithic food-gatherers, other people on the continent had been growing crops, cultivating strains of the wild wheats and barley that were native only to the lands of the east Mediterranean. Very slowly, as the cereals adapted to being grown in the cooler, damper conditions of Europe, the awareness of land cultivation reached westwards and communities of three or four hundred people searched for the rich brownearths that would nourish their crops.

For the first time men were free of a dependence on the caprices of a migrating herd or upon the chance discovery of a fruitful patch of forest whose roots and berries would sustain a family through the Winter months. Farming enabled them to settle, to build a permanent and warm house, to lay claim to the land that would feed them. Until this time it was an immediate world in which people had lived, existing from day to day hoping to find food, hoping that the wild animals would come within reach of their spears and bows. Rituals and cults had developed to ensure the fertility of deer and cattle. Mimes of hunting scenes, the hunters draped in skins and wearing horns or antlers, imitating the movements of the prey, must have been common.

12   *Neolithic tools. An antler 'pick', an ox shoulder blade for a shovel and a wickerwork*
     basket. Simple equipment like this was used to dig the ditch at Stonehenge and heap up
     the great mound of Silbury Hill

Emblems of pregnant women and male organs modelled in clay reveal the associations in the minds of these distant people between human sexuality and the fecundity of nature.

Even with the discovery of farming these beliefs were not abandoned but, inevitably, they were modified. Planting, cultivating and harvesting were slow and patient processes, very different from the instant world of the hunter where initiative and imagination were necessary for survival. For the farmer tradition was fundamental, each generation repeating the tested, successful patterns of crop-growing that had fed earlier generations. To the hunter land was merely a surface over which he had to travel, offering him concealment as he stalked his prey, providing water holes around which he knew the beasts would gather. Land, to the farmer, was his life-blood, the good earth tilled and tended by human beings, enriched and made bountiful by sunshine and rain, a long-drawn-out existence governed by the changing weather of the seasons. Time and a calendar became part of men's thinking and although cults of fertility survived they were adapted to the new needs for rich earth, for good crops and for kind weather. The climate was milder then than now by 2° or 3° Centigrade, with warmth-loving trees such as the lime growing freely in the warm rains that nourished them and which encouraged the spread of forests high up onto the hillsides.

Although, so many thousands of years later, their way of life may seem almost a Golden Age to us, these early farmers struggled in an environment that was often hostile. Trees covered Britain in a forbidding and unsafe wildwood. In the north and west miles of birch and pine spread unhindered over the hillsides. In Ireland the heavier, darker elms grew, fringed with hazel, wherever there was soil. Even on the southern lowlands of England there were almost impassable forests of broadleaved lime, old, large trees blanketing the chalk uplands, with occasional clearings where fallen trunks mouldered. In the damper valleys sunless oaks obscured the landscape. For centuries travel in the gloom of these forests was dangerous, with no trails to follow, with marshes spreading over acres of the lower ground and with brambles and thorn bushes barricading the higher, drier slopes. Wild animals, boars and wolves, were numerous.

Only a little is known about these early farmers but it seems they avoided the wet clays and instead moved inland along the rivers in a search for chalk country where the wide and flat summits of the downs offered them easily tilled soils, wood for their homes and some water for their few cattle. Separate families settled wherever there was free land, ten or twelve men, women and children who put up sturdy rectangular cabins like that at Ballynagilly in Co. Tyrone, constructed as early as 4000 BC and with a ground-plan the size of a small modern house. Because their farming methods were primitive with little or no manuring or crop-rotation their cultivated patches became exhausted after a generation or so and their descendants moved to another part of the territory, building a new home, their children in turn moving until, perhaps five or six generations later, a group returned to the first over-grown settlement, weeds growing thickly in the clearing and on the rubbish heaps with their remains of hearths, animal bones and broken pottery.

Sometimes such middens, with their associations of magical growth and distant ancestors, became hallowed places and religious structures were built directly on top of them. In one instance, at Ballyglass in Co. Mayo, a small neolithic group, probably no more than six or seven men and women, erected a stone-built court-cairn, a long mound of stones with two burial chambers and a central courtyard, over the site of a rectangular timber house.[2] The cairn was a ritual monument with pits, stone tools and cremated bone in it but the excavator, Sean O'Nuallain, believed that the people had deliberately demolished the domestic building to make room for it even though the cairn could easily have been situated alongside the house. If such a cairn was a shrine as well as a tomb then to build it on the very place where earlier generations had lived would have given it even more sanctity.

This was still a time of spirits. Each family buried its dead to free their spirits,

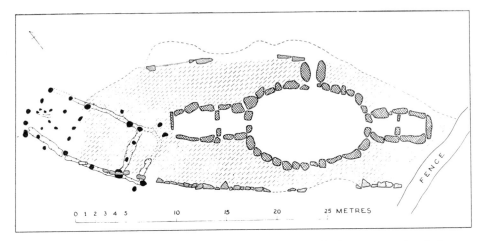

Figure 3 *Plan of house and tomb at Ballyglass, Co. Mayo. Orthostats cross-hatched, kerbstones single-ruled, postholes black*

and in the earth and in every place there were other spirits with whom the living had to share the world. It was a time of personal magic, everyone carrying talismen and charms. At the special times of sowing and harvesting the family would show the spirits what was needed by making offerings to them of good earth, burying it in pits so that it might pass from one world to the other.

13   *Early neolithic pottery. These hand-made bowls with their round bases are typical of the earliest pottery to be made in southern Britain as long ago as 4500 BC*

This was a time when the cult of ancestors was growing. Neolithic people instinctively adhered to the customary ways of farming because the traditional methods of growing crops had been proved successful. Innovation was dangerous. The cycle of agriculture was not amenable to sudden changes of plan if a new experiment failed. It was safer to be conservative, looking back to unknown, godlike ancestors who had discovered the land, cleared it and established the family on it. Within a few generations the people became tied to that land by the efforts they had put into felling trees, hauling stones off the fields, building houses, hampered from moving not only by their heavy possessions of pots and grindstones but by the crops whose harvesting could not be done until the weather was almost too bad for any group to leave its territory and establish a new one in time for next year's planting.

For most people then the world can never have been anything but a small place. A few miles in any direction was all that they ever travelled, and each river, each valley, almost each clump of trees and fall of rocks was a familiar sight. It was also an intense world. A person knew every man, woman and child, knew every stream, every springhead, and these were as much a part of his being as the spirits that inhabited this world, flowing in the waters, dwelling in the hills, living in the fertile soil. It was a fearful world made uncertain by the whims of weather and disease, and held secure only by the ghosts of ancestors who could speak with the forces of nature with whom the living had no direct communication. The world was small, intense and fearsome and in it the dead were powerful.

In *People of the Totem* Bancroft-Hunt has described what affinity a North American Indian had with his environment in which 'everything possessed power or spiritual force, be it a pebble on the beach, a rock, tree, animal or man himself; abstract qualities, such as beauty, had a similar force, as did the sun, moon and stars, and the lakes and rivers'. It was a power that originated in the spirit world but it entered the world of man, on the wind, in the creaking of trees, the sound of water, in the behaviour of birds and animals, in rock formations. Everything had power and everything provided evidence of the supernatural world and its direct link with man himself.

Similar beliefs are to be found in many primitive societies. West Africans thought their giant silk-cotton trees were the homes of spirits. Indians in Guyana believed that all waterfalls were guarded by the spirits of ravenous snakes, and no native would speak the name of a waterfall until he had passed it in case the snake was aroused by hearing its name. Spirits of hills were worshipped in Thailand. There is no reason to think that the early farmers of the British Isles did not also believe in such spirits. In *The Golden Bough* Sir James Frazer devoted the whole of the seventh volume, *The Spirits of the Corn and Wild*, to the role that women played in primitive agriculture as personifications of the corn-spirit. Frazer made four observations about these early rites. Rituals to ensure successful sowing and harvesting required no priest but could be performed by anyone. No special temple was needed. It was not a god but a spirit that was invoked, a supernatural force with limited powers. Finally, the ceremonies were magical rather than propitiatory, acting not through prayer, sacrifice and praise but 'through a physical sympathy or resemblance between the rite and the effect which it is the intention of the rite to produce'.

Rites of imitative magic may have occurred in Britain, men and women mating in the Autumn fields to create a similar mating between Earth and Corn. Sometimes the Corn-Mother, symbolized by the last sheaf, would be ceremonially buried in the stubble of the harvest so that her strength, which would last a full year, would feed the next crop. In the Hebrides as late as the eighteenth century women decorated a sheaf of oats on St Bridget's Day—a saint derived from the Celtic goddess, Brigid, with her powers of fertility—and having dressed the stalks in women's clothes laid the sheaf in bed with a heavy wooden club alongside it. If, in the morning, the sheaf had been disturbed by the club it was a good omen for the coming harvest. Although the symbolism between the female sheaf and the phallic club is obvious it can only be by inference that such practices can be assumed in prehistoric Britain for almost all traces of them will have vanished.

14   *This rock-carving from Litsleby in Sweden shows very clearly the association in the prehistoric mind between fertility, sexuality and the ploughing and planting of the land*

There are a very few objects from the beginnings of the Neolithic period to show how the people's minds did link fertility with spirits and human sexuality. Among the early prehistoric monuments in the British Isles—at causewayed enclosures such as Windmill Hill in Wiltshire with its rings of ditches and banks, or in the long chambered barrows such as the nearby West Kennet, with its masses of human bone—the architecture suggests that the people who built them practised forms of magic. Sometimes this may have been contagious magic whose potency rested in the belief that its practitioners could gain ascendancy over a person or object through something that had belonged to them. In Tudor and Stuart times such spells were widely used in witchcraft as the reports of fingernail clippings and hanks of hair among the possessions of intending witches testify. In earlier times, but still known in solitary country districts today, rags of clothing from invalids were hung on a sacred tree or deposited by holy wells in the expectation that power from the spirits of nature would pass through the personal offerings to cure the afflicted persons. Even dust from the ground where a doomed person had walked would suffice for some witch-doctors.

As late as the eighteenth century it was believed that a sufferer from scrofula could be cured if the king touched him. Shakespeare, in *Macbeth*, mentions

> ... *a crowd of wretched souls*
> *That stay his cure; their malady convinces*
> *The great assay of art; but, at his touch*
> *Such sanctity hath Heaven given his hand*
> *They presently amend.*

It is also recorded that the infant Samuel Johnson was touched by Queen Anne but the scrofula, which he had caught from his nurse, remained with him, leaving him disfigured and blinded in one eye.

A belief in contagious magic is almost impossible to demonstrate from the fragments of antiquity that are left to us, although hints may linger in the legends attached to holed stones that supposedly had the power to cure illness. If from early neolithic times down to the Iron Age the underlying principles of religion remained similar although their outward appearances changed greatly then legends such as these are indications of what people may have believed in our distant past. Where human bones occur in tombs, or votive offerings of precious articles are recovered from lakes we have physical evidence of such beliefs. It is equally probable that even in the mysterious stone circles from which so little pottery or bone or metal has been found the rituals had the same origin.

Easier to detect is the evidence for homeopathic or imitative magic expressed through objects such as carvings of chalk in the shape of male organs that were meant to ensure fertility.[3] Several of these have come from neolithic sites, either with offerings to the earth or with burials as though infusing the bones with new life. At Windmill Hill four such phalli, one with a cup-shaped depression in it, lay at the bottom of the ditches. Their significance is not clear but at Thickthorn in Dorset two others had been placed beneath a long barrow where skeletons had lain. Here they may

15   *This chalk carving of a male sexual organ was found in a ditch at Windmill Hill, Wiltshire. It is about 3 in. long and has a 'cupmark' carved into it*

have been intended to restore life to the dead. Certainly at Maumbury Rings, a circular henge not many miles away outside Dorchester, a huge chalk phallus had been deposited halfway down one of the deep pits that ran around the interior of the bank. It rested alongside an antlered stag's skull. Another skull lay nearby. To the neolithic people who carved these organs so realistically it may have seemed that the act of placing them in the earth with totem objects, which presumably the stag's skull was, or with human bones, would impregnate the earth itself with life, the power of the phallus being passed through the skull or the bones into the spirit of the soil.

Similar reasoning may have caused other people in the south to shape female figurines as faceless and armless as those from the Palaeolithic but also presumably representing pregnancy and fruitfulness. One carving from Windmill Hill was so formalized, or unfinished, that we can only make out the line of the thighs, but an angular slab from the neolithic causewayed enclosure of Maiden Castle near Maumbury Rings is more lifelike, headless and armless though it now is, with skirt, belt and two holes where carved wooden legs once fitted. That such figures were representations of a powerful female spirit is surely demonstrated by the gross, heavy-breasted and fat-bellied woman from the flint mines of Grime's Graves in Norfolk.[4] Here, around 2850 BC, after weeks of quarrying down through the chalk, men discovered that there were only a few thin patches of flint at the bottom of their shaft. To protect themselves from such misfortune again one miner carved the chalk figurine and placed it on a ledge in the wall. The others heaped flints at its feet and laid seven red deer antlers on top of the pile. These may have been no more than their working tools, the levers and picks with which they had hacked and prised out the chalk, but it is as feasible that they were symbols of masculinity intended to generate life within the female statuette, causing the earth to yield abundant flint. This interpretation is strengthened not only by the fact of the proximity of the stag's skull and chalk phallus at Maumbury Rings but also because among the Grime's Graves antlers were several carved balls of chalk. Very similar balls were found at Windmill Hill in pits containing pots, flint axes, scrapers, arrowheads and animal bones, everything broken as though deliberately smashed to 'kill' it and thus enable it to pass into the spirit world. These balls may also have symbolized masculinity. Thirty were found at Windmill Hill, usually in pairs which had been used in some irrecoverable rite before being thrown away. Later in the Neolithic period similar balls of chalk were placed in the ditch at Stonehenge and buried with the body of a young woman by the southern entrance to Avebury. What may have been analogous balls but of stone were uncovered under a mound of sand over several cists at Millin Bay in Co. Down and similar rounded cobbles surrounded a cairn in the nearby stone circle of Ballynoe, all reaffirming their association with death and, by implication, with regeneration.

From the Irish passage-graves, to be discussed in the next chapter, many carefully shaped balls have been recovered, some of them glazed from the heat of the pyre in which they had been burned with the bodies of the dead. Pairs of them from Tara and Newgrange give credence to their identification as sexual symbols. At Newgrange there were balls of chalk, a material that had to be brought from Co. Antrim, many days' journey to the north, where beds of flint in it made the chalk appear a soil with magical powers. To the primitive mind objects carved of such a potent substance would have even greater efficacy.

There are other enigmatic objects made by neolithic people for their rituals. From Windmill Hill and other sites have come small blocks of chalk with circular depressions carved into them, cup-shaped but too small for lamps or drinking vessels, crude lumps in which only the 'cups' are carefully shaped. It is just possible that these represented female organs. Some phalli had cups carved on them, and on top of the 'masculine' antlers and chalk balls at Grime's Graves was one small chalk cup.

In the absence of writing it is no more than speculation to attempt an explanation of such material. Even more perplexing are the tiny chalk 'plaques' with patterns of grooves on them. If these were intended as abstract representations of a 'Mother Goddess' then they are very abstract indeed. They have some likeness to the 'fern' motifs on the splendid Irish tomb of Newgrange but they could as easily be tallies for recording the risings and settings of the sun or moon or even merely doodles though this, considering their recovery from sites such as Windmill Hill, seems unlikely.

It is noticeable that during the New Stone Age such sexual carvings were normally of chalk and have been found mainly in chalk country although it is somewhat strange that none has come from the Yorkshire Wolds where there are over twenty neolithic long and round barrows. It may be that in other districts similar objects were made of clay, earth or wood and have disintegrated. Only from a court-cairn known as the 'Five Sisters' at Ballynichol in Co. Down has a bone object been found that may have been a phallus. If people in the northern and highland areas of the British Isles followed a more pastoral way of life they may have had no use for objects designed by crop-growers to increase the fertility of the land.

To 'understand' how these little chalk objects were actually used is difficult. Leroi-Gourhan, an authority on palaeolithic cave painting, described a group of Australian aborigines squatting in a ring, one of them reciting an incantation.[5] As he spoke his story was accompanied by the exclamations and movements of the others. In the sand he traced a spiral with his finger, its centre corresponding with the end of his sentence, spiral after spiral being drawn until, as the recital came to an end, the speaker joined them together with straight lines in a perfect and completed pattern, concluding the drama of word and picture and audience. These same aborigines 'used' the painted and carved churingas mentioned in Chapter Two. By themselves the patterns on these soft stones are incomprehensible but set down in the middle of a group of men, as the carvings in Britain may have been, they played a part in the same kind of chanted drama, the reciter pointing to them, the audience responding to each sentence with a word, a sound or a movement, everyone involved in this recounting of myth or remembered hunt or spell to bring good to the people. The words and the carvings were inseparable. The figurines and the plaques may remain inexplicable to us because we cannot hear the words of which they were a part. We want to know what the chalk objects 'meant' but, as Leroi-Gourhan commented, their makers may have been 'like a little girl who cannot skip nor even see a skipping-rope without singing in the appropriate tone, "Salt–Mustard–Vinegar–Pepper"', meaningless except to the people of her time. 'What the primitive feels above all is the rhythm of the figurative dramatization', but all that is left of such dramas for the archaeologist is the deserted stage, a few broken props, no actors, no audience and no script. This has led to assertions that it is useless to attempt any reconstruction of something as intangible as prehistoric ritual and that carvings of phalli and female figurines must always remain beyond explanation. This is too pessimistic.

There is, for example, one piece of evidence that reveals, apparently without question, the significance of such carvings. In Somerset as early as 3700 BC people were laying down stretches of trackway across the fens, driving long wooden stakes into the soft ground, fixing beams along them like a railway line and then arranging a mattress of birch stems and branches across them to provide a firm, dry path between the islands.[6] At one place near the present village of Westhay there was a particularly wet spot at the bottom of a slope where the first length of track had proved inadequate and had to be replaced. Before the work was completed someone had taken a piece of well-soaked ashwood and carved an hermaphroditic torso from it. The head is faceless, there are no arms or legs, but from the chest project two breasts and at the base there is an unmistakable erect phallus. This bi-sexual figure, placed upside down in the ground just where the track was weakest, must surely be a foundation deposit. Its implication about the thinking of the people who set it there is clear.

Burials from this early time tell us even more about such thinking because a great deal of evidence has been recovered from neolithic tombs. In many of the southern areas of Britain where the soil was easily dug there are long mounds or barrows of earth and chalk, grass covered and worn down by weather now but once the ritual centres of peasant families who carried their dead to them, each barrow the focus of a small universe, as separate from the others as temples in the Malayan jungle.[7] Despite the discovery of human bones under these barrows it would be an over-simplification to regard them merely as burial-places. The earliest may have been tombs but over the hundreds of years that these earthen mounds were being built their function subtly but persistently changed. It is likely that the latest of them were shrines rather than cemeteries, places from which the bones of ancestors were removed for the rituals of the living.

There were many of these barrows. In Wessex alone, the most densely populated region of neolithic Britain occupied today by Wiltshire and Dorset and their neighbouring counties, there were eight major groups, each with thirty or forty barrows in them, well-built monuments whose material had been laboriously quarried from ditches on either side of the mound. One of the earliest known at Lambourn in Berkshire, raised around 4250 BC, had a spine of heavy sarsen boulders dragged from the cultivated land by the men and women who built this colossal barrow, dumping the stones, piling chalk rubble over them, capping the entire mound with turves. The effort must have been enormous, especially if we are right in assuming that Lambourn, like other barrows, was constructed by the few able-bodied people of a family group.

At the least, weeks of hardship were involved, much of it seemingly unnecessary to our eyes because over three-quarters of any barrow covered nothing but grass and earth. The skeletons beneath them were not laid haphazardly but were always concentrated in a small area at the eastern end, and this was because the erection of such 'burial-places' was not the first but the last act of a whole series of rituals whose nature can only be understood when we realize what a long barrow signified to its people.

A long barrow was a family monument. There were, for example, fifteen of these barrows within three miles of where Stonehenge was to stand, each occupying a 'territory' of about two square miles, quite large enough to support a group of ten to twenty persons who, given the privations of their existence, could expect three or four deaths of the elderly and of infants every five years or so. Many of them may have been buried near the settlement, their graves abandoned when the people moved to their next clearing. Others may have been laid in fenced enclosures open to the sky or exposed on scaffolds where the bodies decomposed until only their collapsed skeletons remained.

Not all of them were forgotten. At some time a mortuary house, turf or chalk-

16   *A painting by the American artist George Catlin of the mortuary scaffolds used by Mandan Indians. The squaw in the foreground is offering food to her husband's skull*

walled and plank-roofed, was put up and some of the weathered bones were brought to it. These little buildings were sturdy, of thick oak posts, and might have endured for as long as two hundred years. They were also carefully planned. Their entrance was directed probably towards the rising moon, one of the first intimations we have that these early crop-growers integrated lunar orientations into their rituals of death. That they should have thought of the sun as the giver of warmth, life and fertility would not be surprising when its obvious associations with Summer, the ripening corn and harvest are considered. Conversely, the moon, darkness and cold may have seemed to epitomize sterility and death. Certainly nearly every mortuary house was built to face somewhere between north-north-east and south-south-east, the outer limits of the rising moon but well beyond the extremes of sunrise which would have reached only as far north as north-east at midsummer and south-east at midwinter. One in every ten of the long barrows was orientated outside this arc of the sun but very few were placed beyond the limits of the moon suggesting that it was indeed nocturnal lunar risings that early neolithic people associated with their dead.

Most of these mortuary structures faced approximately eastwards towards moonrise at the equinoxes in March and September but, interestingly, there were seasonal preferences in different areas. In Wessex some of them faced the Summer moonrise whereas in Kent and along the Chilterns months later in the year were preferred. In Yorkshire the majority were built in the Spring or Autumn. Even the very few mortuary structures facing north or south and apparently not conforming to this lunar interpretation simply reveal variations upon it. The south is the direction in which the moon was at its highest in the sky. The north is the one region of the heavens where it would never shine, so empty an area that the Egyptians thought of it as the home of the dead. The movement of the moon with its regular monthly cycle would have been much more obvious than the slow shifting of the sun along the horizon, and unlike the dazzling sun it was possible for people to look directly at it. It would be quite natural for early societies to regard it as a symbol of death, shining into the newly built charnel-house where they were to place the bones of the dead

> ... in a wall'd prison, packs and sets of great ones
> That ebb and flow by the moon.

> > *King Lear*, V, iii, 8

Although it is tempting to think of women leading the ceremonies of death, moon worship traditionally being linked with priestesses, these lunar associations are no guarantee that society at this time was matriarchal. It is possible that inheritance in neolithic communities passed through the mother and the female line but there is no certainty that this was so. Nor can the myths of a Mother Goddess, widespread on the continent, be used as proof that such a deity was ever accepted in the British Isles. The sad fact is that we know hardly anything about the social structure of neolithic Britain, and the roles of men, women and even of infants remain very poorly defined. We have only their bones and their monuments to guide us.

At Fussell's Lodge, eight miles east of Stonehenge but a thousand years before the first henge there, people built a mortuary house.[8] Salisbury Plain must have been almost empty of people, an expanse of woodland swelling and rising in waves of green shadows across the hills with only lonely skeins of smoke breaking the austerity of the skies. There were perhaps no more than ten or twelve little settlements in the whole three hundred square miles of wilderness, a few families in territories close to one another, enclosed by miles of forest, entirely self-sufficient in their lives, growing crops, working the local flint into tools, making their supple leather clothes and their pots. For the dead there was burial, perhaps in a mortuary house such as the men and women of the Fussell's Lodge site built before 4000 BC.

It faced east-north-east, in a clearing around which dense oaks, hazels and hawthorns reached almost down to the riverside, a big structure, its ridged roof supported by three gigantic oak posts each weighing over a ton. For many years the people brought human bones to it, stacking them neatly inside the gloom, skulls in one place, a heap of arm and leg bones near them, another tidy collection of skulls and long bones at the entrance but, in all this, only one complete skeleton.

Nearly all the people had been unhealthy and short-lived. Almost half the bones belonged to children, most of whom had been poorly fed. The prevalence of rickets showed how ill-nourished they had been. Many jaws had teeth missing. Some adults had healed fractures of arms and legs and had suffered from arthritis. Few of them had lived beyond the age of forty. Very much the same picture of deprivation and disease has come from other long barrows. In one, at Amesbury in Wiltshire, dug into by William Cunnington and Sir Richard Colt Hoare early in the nineteenth century, a skeleton with a grossly deformed skull was uncovered. According to Hoare the man 'seemed to have had no forehead, the sockets of his eyes appearing to have been on top of his head, and the final termination of the vertebre turned up so much that we almost fancied we had found the remains of one of Lord Montboddo's animals'. Monboddo was a perceptive but eccentric eighteenth-century nobleman who believed that men were descended from monkeys and that even modern people were born with tails that were instantly severed by alert midwives. For Colt Hoare to write as he did the neolithic man at Amesbury must have been hideously deformed.

The remains of over fifty bodies—men, women and children—were found at Fussell's Lodge, yet it was impossible to reconstruct more than one fully because

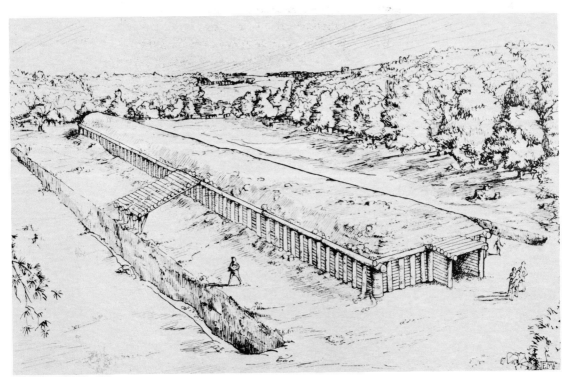

17 *A reconstruction of the Fussell's Lodge earthen long barrow. The burials were all concentrated at the near end under a little mortuary house. This ultimately was concealed when the long mound, over 300 ft long, was raised*

many of the bones were missing. Ribs, bones of hands and feet, other small bones, jaws, all these were frequently absent, and only six of the heavy long bones were not broken. The people must have carried to the mortuary house the remains of bodies that had been buried and disinterred when their flesh had decomposed. The idea that the soul is free to leave the body only when the flesh has rotted is known from other societies. Corpses of Hopewell Indians in Ohio were either exposed and allowed to decay or had their flesh sliced off and it was only then that the chief could be buried, surrounded by grave-goods that had been deliberately broken or 'killed' so that their spirits could accompany the dead man into the Other-World. Closer in time and distance to Britain, neolithic burials in Belgium revealed the same practices. Skeletons at Spiennes had been defleshed. In the Trou du Frontal near Furfooz the bones of eighteen people were mingled together in a rock-fissure, at least fifty of the bones having cut marks where the flesh had been hacked off. Of the same period is the even grimmer site of Dyrholmen in Denmark where human long bones had been split to obtain their marrow. There was also evidence of beheading and one skull seemed to have been scalped with a flint knife.

This may have been an attempt to get at the edible brain, an act of cannibalism which is also implied by the split bones, but at Fussell's Lodge some witch-doctor or medicine-man with a flint had scraped roundels of bones out of the heads of two living people, one of whom, a man of over fifty, had actually recovered from this surgery. In his case the 'scalping' may have been the result of an operation to relieve the pain of some illness that was otherwise incurable. Trepanning or trephination as it is known is recorded from other neolithic and Early Bronze Age burials in Britain and will be returned to.

It is glimpses of the past such as this that bring home the hardships under which these people lived, helplessly turning to the spirit-world for assistance. At Fussell's Lodge an ox hide complete with skull and hoofs had been draped over the roof of the mortuary house, the horned head over the entrance, the skin and legs hanging down the ridged sides. Ox burials are known from other Wiltshire long barrows, the two beheaded skulls from Tilshead being a well-known example, and it could be that these were totem animals whose strength and endurance were prized and respected by people with great need of these qualities.

For generations dead bones were brought to Fussell's Lodge. Then at last the people moved away, but not before they closed the burial-place. At some long barrows such as Nutbane the mortuary house was burned down. At Fussell's Lodge it was buried under a vast long barrow. The men and women dragged nearly two hundred heavy logs to build an enormous rectangular enclosure with the mortuary house inside one end, and into the space they piled a thousand tons of chalk which they dug out of the long deep ditches on either side of the mound. Many of their antler picks, the tines worn down by the scouring chalk, were found on the ditch bottoms. Ten able-bodied people might have felled the trees, transported them, dug the ditches and heaped up the mound in about six months. When it was finished this long barrow, with its timber sides and porch which led only to the vault and the dead bones, resembled an enormous version of the houses of the living and this is precisely what it may have represented, a house familiar to the dead and one in which they could rest comfortably. The very size of these covering mounds indicates that they were intended to be more than just repositories of the dead and that the mound itself was meant to be of enduring importance. As early as the nineteenth century John Thurnam observed that 'from their usually great size, with one end only devoted to interment, they may be quite as much or even more properly regarded as monuments than as mere tombs'.

Fussell's Lodge was an early long barrow in Britain. Despite its trephinations, its stacked skulls and hints of an ox cult it was probably a simple tomb. If so, it was a tomb in which not all the dead were buried. It took at least ten people to build it and in their community there must have been as many again too young or old or incapacitated to help in the work. If a group of that size had only used the mortuary house for a century there should have been the remains of nearly a hundred people in it. Either not everyone was buried there or some of their bones and skulls had been removed. This becomes even more obvious when other long barrows are considered for in them the average number of burials, men, women and children together, is about six. Some three hundred long barrows are known in England and Wales, built over a period of about twelve hundred years. If everyone had been buried in them and no bones had been removed then the implication is that only 1800 people (300×6) died in Britain between 4300 and 3100 BC, three deaths every two years. As the annual mortality rate in comparable primitive societies is about $40 : 1000$ the unlikely inference must be that the entire population of lowland Britain in any one year of the Neolithic was no more than about forty people. This is nonsensical. So few people could never have lifted the heavy stones that cover some tombs or the massive sarsens of Avebury. We must accept that the bones of many people never reached the shelter of a mortuary house.

The rituals that accompanied the carrying of the bones to these tombs can be partly reconstructed. At Wayland's Smithy on the Berkshire Downs not many miles east of Avebury a dense mass of bones had been spread on a pavement of sarsen stones under a wooden 'ridge tent'. Grave-goods are rare in these tombs. There seems to have been little concept of the dead taking food or personal possessions with them into the Other-World, perhaps because the dead were expected to stay with the living and guard them. At Wayland's Smithy, however, three leaf-shaped arrowheads of flint were found, each laid against a pelvis just as they may have hung in a quiver by the hip during life. In each case the tip of the arrowhead had been broken off. This was not coincidence. When John Thurnam, Superintendent of the County Asylum, excavated the Giant's Grave long barrow above the Vale of Pewsey in 1865 he came upon several skeletons but recorded that the other thing he found was a fine flint arrowhead whose point had been broken off. It was a clear instance of the belief that objects can be 'killed' by breaking them and it may explain the broken pottery and smashed animal bones discovered in so many of these long barrows. Thurnam often mentioned from his other Wiltshire excavations how skulls had been shattered. At the Giant's Grave there was a skull which, he claimed, 'had been forcibly cleft before burial'.

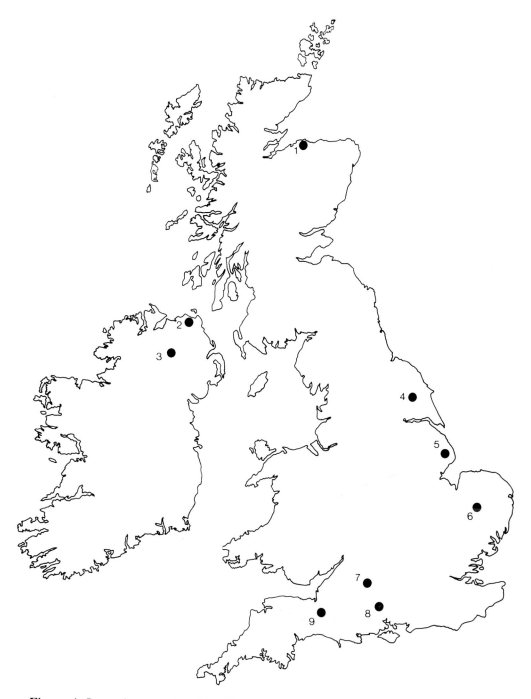

Figure 4 *Some sites mentioned in Chapter 3:*
1 Fochabers Mound, NJ 360592; 2 Goodland, D 197412; 3 Ballybriest,
H 762885; 4 Hanging Grimston, SE 810608; 5 Giant's Hill, Skendleby,
TF 429712; 6 Grime's Graves, TL 817898; 7 Windmill Hill, SU 087714;
8 Fussell's Lodge, SU 192324; 9 Bell Trackway, ST 428422

In other long barrows the bones of animals have been uncovered. Whether these were the remains of feasts or offerings to the dead or totem animals is debatable. The idea of totemism is not unfeasible nor would it preclude these animals from being eaten. American Indians did not hold their totem animals in particularly high regard. What the totem did was to symbolize the social group and its rights and obligations to one another. Any person of the totem had responsibilities to all other members of it, responsibilities which were not always easy to fulfil but which were constantly kept in mind by communal rituals, repeated time after time with the totem animal as their focus. The ox at Fussell's Lodge may have been such a totem. At Bole's Barrow, in which a Stonehenge bluestone lay, there were the skulls of seven or more oxen lying near three human skulls. Another skull appeared to have been beheaded. At Tilshead two ox skulls were discovered, one with axe marks at its base, 'cleanly cleft as if by great violence'. At Amesbury the leg bones and hoofs of three oxen were found in the rubble of the mound, and also a skull. At the unusual long barrow at Beckhampton just west of Avebury no human bones whatsoever lay under the mound. Being built some nine hundred years after Fussell's Lodge this barrow shows how these long mounds changed from being tombs to become the ritual centres of later neolithic people. Along its axis at regular intervals the builders had set down three ox skulls. Totemism seems the most likely explanation.

In some other barrows there were antlers of stags, or in Yorkshire, from the Neolithic to the Bronze Age, pig bones. Although it is likely that many were the remains of feasts not all of them can be explained in this way, not least the three skulls at Beckhampton. Totem activity is probable, the skulls symbolizing the unity of the clan. At the early neolithic village of St Michel-du-Touch where the rivers Touch and Garonne join, the inhabitants of the wattle and daub houses dug several huge pits for their dead but there was one separate grave in which they laid the crouched skeleton of a woman, a tiny vase by her side. In it were the jaws of four hedgehogs.[9] The absence of skulls again suggests that these may have been kept for totem purposes. Outside the entrance to Hetty Pegler's Tump, a chambered tomb in the Cotswolds, two human skeletons had been buried with the jaws of several boars by them. A whole goose was found in the long barrow at Amesbury.

It is possible to visualize these earthen long barrows, weathered and overgrown though they are, as the shrines of families during the New Stone Age, places to which the disinterred bones of the dead were brought, perhaps at times when the moon was full. Incantations may have been uttered around the skulls of totem animals before the bones and broken objects were deposited in the mortuary house, and then bonfires and feasts followed with the recitation of ancestral myths. On other occasions bones were taken away to summon up the spirits of the dead.

After many years, when its posts were decaying, the mortuary house was buried beneath the long barrow. But it was not deserted. People continued to come to it, no longer as a tomb but as a cult centre occupied by the ghosts of long-dead but powerful ancestors, and sometimes these places were so potent that later, more imposing structures were built on top of them much as the tomb was erected over the house at Ballyglass. The small barrow at Wayland's Smithy was covered in this way, about 3600 BC, maybe a century or more after it was built, by the longer, wider mound of a chambered tomb whose tall sarsens still stand by the prehistoric Ridgeway, the monumental façade dark against the northern sky.

Elsewhere in Britain people followed different customs. Along the east coast, in Yorkshire, Lincolnshire, as far south as Kent and as far north as Scotland, skeletons were not simply buried but were often burnt. Although the long barrows of the Lincolnshire and Yorkshire Wolds appear superficially like those in Wessex there were dissimilarities. Erected near the heads of streams these long, east-facing mounds with incurving entrances sometimes covered a mortuary structure that had been deliberately set on fire. The heat had been so intense at Willerby Wold, built around 3800 BC, that chalk blocks in it were transmuted into lime. Others at Westow and Rudston contained the same signs of a conflagration.

Another long barrow on the Yorkshire Wolds was recently excavated at Garton Slack not far away from the famous Iron Age chariot burial that is described in Chapter Nine. Long before that time, around 3900 BC, people had laid bodies inside a mortuary house and, some years later, other corpses had been propped, standing upright, in a barrel-shaped pit just outside the entrance.[10] Air had been fed into this furnace by deep flues so well designed that when the kindling around the bodies was ignited the fire reached a temperature of 900°C. Another long barrow nearby contained the half-scorched skeleton of a woman sitting against the wall of a cremation furnace whose unexpected collapse had extinguished the fire. Burials, not always burned, in deep pits such as this occurred again in Yorkshire during the Bronze Age.

Concealed in these northern long barrows and cairns with their flue cremations there were sometimes standing stones or small mounds that seem to have been symbols of an ancestor cult. The cremation trench at Rudston ended at a circular cairn buried inside the mound, and the traces of burning at Raiset Pike in Westmorland reached up to a tall slab of sandstone hidden in the barrow, a standing stone possibly believed to embody the ancestral spirits who would protect the long mound.

Even as far away as Scotland and northern Ireland people practised cremation but in megalithic tombs whose stone chambers were erected after the burning. Near the village of Edzell in Angus the long mound of Dalladies, now six thousand years old, concealed a light timber shelter roofed with birch bark that had been burnt down. In south-west Scotland a contemporary cairn at Lochhill near Dumfries had been built over a mortuary enclosure with walls of granite boulders, floored with oak planks and bark-roofed. Two thick posts stood at either end. A skeleton had been laid in this vault and the structure was set on fire just as at Ballymacaldrack in Co. Antrim people had filled a similar building with brushwood to make it burn better. Facing the prevailing wind the blaze consumed the bodies of five men and women whose cremated bones were buried in a pit before the stone chamber of Doey's Cairn was built over it.

Burning such as this, drying and splintering the bones, would have been as effective as decomposition in Wessex and the object may have been the same, to liberate the spirits of the dead from their carcases. Breaking the bones in the south, burning

them in the north appear to be variations on the same theme and sometimes they combined. A family near Scamridge in Yorkshire dug up fourteen burials after the flesh had decayed, battered and smashed the bones and then incinerated them in a long trench before heaping a long barrow over them. Broken bones were discovered under the long cairn on Bradley Moor in the same county. Here three standing stones within the mound were thought by the excavator to be phallic symbols but they might be better regarded as guardian pillars embodying the spirits of the dead.

This idea of a stone or post being the essence of a dead person was most apparent at Giant's Hill near Skendleby in Lincolnshire, a long mound that was built very late in the history of these monuments, around 3100 BC. Having laid down a chalk platform at the east people brought the skeletons of eight individuals to it, a man, women and children, and then set up eight tall posts at the west, a correlation of bodies and uprights that could hardly have been fortuitous. In the covering mound were the bones of oxen, sheep and red deer. Before these are accepted as rubbish from funerary feasts the strange site of Hanging Grimston on the Yorkshire Wolds must be considered.

John Mortimer, whose brother Robert had complained about Greenwell's method of digging the Folkton round barrow, excavated at Hanging Grimston in March 1868, less than two years after Folkton.[11] Beneath the barrow, which has recently been dated to about 3540 BC, was the collapsed wreckage of a burnt-down mortuary house, the charcoal of its heather- or rush-thatched roof smothering the floor. Only one leg bone was found of any human being but among the tumbled chalk and ash were four heaps of jaws from young pigs. There were at least twenty of these and Mortimer noted that 'small portions of the points of most of the tusks had been broken off'. Another single pig bone had been carefully buried upright in one of the entrance postholes. If these jaws are all that survived of funeral feasts it is odd that no skulls were left behind. Like the oxen, the boars, the goose, the hedgehogs, it is likely that at Hanging Grimston on its narrow, steep-sided plateau the family had left traces of their totem beliefs, taking the skulls with them, leaving the neatly broken 'killed' tusks and mandibles inside the burning trench.

Smashed objects were not only placed with the dead. Long before the chambered court-cairn of Ballybriest in Co. Londonderry was built earlier people hollowed small pits in the earth, putting into them broken pottery, lumps of potter's clay, burnt animal bones, flints, the shattered collection of things they needed for their everyday living. These were not rubbish pits. All the material was meticulously covered over by a layer of dark rich earth, also with sherds, flints and bones in it, and on this bonfires had blazed before the cairn was constructed. Another great cairn on Lyles Hill near Belfast lay on top of eight other pits with similar contents. They had been dug around the edges of what seemed to be a funeral pyre in an act of homeopathic magic by which the men and women used the bones of their dead to intimate to the forces of nature what it was the living most needed—good soil, flints, animals. Much of the so-called 'rubbish' in these pits may have been brought to Ballybriest and Lyles Hill from nearby, abandoned settlements. Thousands of broken bits of pot, flints and animal bones were found in the cairn at Lyles Hill.

Sanctuaries or cult centres such as these are known as Goodland sites after the place where these rituals were first recognized, on a chalk hillside overlooking Murlough Bay in Co. Antrim.[12] It was one of the first 'temples' to be enclosed in a ring, anticipating the later popularity of henges and stone circles. Work gangs had trenched out eight ditch segments which were joined up to form a crude oval about the area of a modern tennis court. Into the ditch they piled scores of heaps of glacial boulders neatly packed around with sherds and flints, all covered with dark earth in which there were more flints, pottery and quartz. Then the people filled in the ditch, confining the deposits in the earth. For many summers they probably returned to the enclosure, which was near a source of good flint, and each season before they left they dug pits in the interior, putting in them the same accumulation of broken material that the ditch had received.

Study of this showed that although the pottery was broken it had been broken elsewhere for not one pot could be assembled completely. Among the flints there were many waste flakes, discarded when some knapper was striking out his scrapers, knives and arrowheads. Scraps of animal teeth and burnt bone could easily have come from a hearth where cooking and the preparation of food had taken place. The most likely explanation for all this was that the pots, flints and bones had been gathered up from a deserted settlement whose weed-covered soil was rich and fertile after many years of disuse. In it, on middens and in the tumble of rotting timbers, were the sherds and flints which, in the words of Humphrey Case, the excavator of the Goodland site, 'became associated in the mind of early man with fertile soil'. This discarded rubbish was brought to the Goodland enclosure to be buried with the boulders and the quartz 'to promote the subsoil to produce fat nodules of flint for returning visits'. Many of the later court-cairns in northern Ireland had similar fillings of 'rubbish' in the chambers in which there was an inexplicable absence of human bodies, if these monuments really had been tombs. More probably such court-cairns had, like the Beckhampton long barrow, lost their original purpose as burial-places and had become shrines. Case suggested that 'the cairns too seem open to interpretation as exercises in sympathetic magic—less as graves for selected kinsmen' although somewhat tenuous links with a cult of the dead may have survived in them. It is a viewpoint that will be returned to in the next chapter.

It was not until around 3400 BC that people went to Goodland but there is a comparable site in northern Scotland, used four centuries before that, which the writer excavated. It was, moreover, a site which showed a series of occupations from the beginning of the Neolithic down to the Iron Age, an indication of the traditions and myths that must have been attached to many of these ancient places that were respected even three thousand years after they had been built.

At Fochabers near Elgin the side of a tree-grown mound was bulldozed in 1971 during Forestry Commission road laying and out of the disturbed sand tumbled several skulls and human long bones. These had come from a line of burials of Iron Age people right across the crest of the round barrow, all of them with decayed teeth and all buried as corpses, unlike the fleshless skeletons of neolithic people. The bodies had been interred over a period of several years, quite often a later grave cutting

18   *The skull of an Iron Age girl from the Fochabers mound, Moray. An unerupted wisdom tooth can be seen in her upper jaw*

into an earlier, and in some instances a leg bone had been taken from a previous burial and laid across the body of the fresh corpse. In one grave a young man had been arranged so that his left hand lay on the skull of a girl about fifteen years old when she died, perhaps in childbirth. It may well have been her husband, dying not many years after, who was laid so close to her.

These Iron Age people must have used for their cemetery a mound that was already considered sacred. A thousand years before them other people rather amateurishly cremated a young woman and an infant, scooping their bones from the pyre, smashing them and putting them in a small cist whose stones they propped together in a pit at the very top of the barrow. In the absence of other evidence it can be no more than a guess that this was yet another example of the mother and child burials that were quite common during the Middle Bronze Age in the centuries around 1500 BC.

Stretching back into distant times, another thousand years before that cremation, a wandering band of Beaker people had passed along the banks of the River Spey, noticing the mound above them on its terrace. Settling by it they dug a shaft into its core, raising a thick high post there, maybe carved or painted, and concealed one of their finely made pots in a pit alongside the mound. Why they did this, how long they stayed here is unknown. They left no signs of occupation, no hearths, no trace of houses or tents; they simply lingered for a while, performed their rites by the mound and went away.

The excavation revealed all this—the dates, the stain in the sand where the post had stood, the skeletons, the elegant beaker in its pit. These were later intrusions and it was anticipated that the Fochabers round barrow would prove to be yet another of the huge neolithic burial places that are to be found in Scotland and northern England. After six weeks of excavation we learned that it was nothing of the kind.

Around 3750 BC, at a time when Fussell's Lodge may already have been abandoned but long before corpseless barrows such as Beckhampton were to be built, in the early centuries of neolithic settlement a small group of peasants had settled on this sandy terrace in a scrubby oak woodland overlooking the river, cutting down the smaller trees, burning the undergrowth, ring-barking the thicker oaks, letting them dry and lose life. Grains of wheat and barley showed what crops they had grown. They had sheltered behind flimsy windbreaks staked in hollows in the well-drained soil, chipping out their coarse tools, a few made from the finer Buchan flint from the coastlands fifty miles to the east.

These people remained at Fochabers, probably for several years, and before leaving they went through a wearying and lengthy ritual. On the terrace they lit a great fire whose heat was so fierce that it reddened and whitened the sand. In a pit by it they buried three rounded stones. After the fire had died down they raked its ashes over the pit and the working hollows, and they dumped basketloads of flints and broken pottery onto the charcoal and the ash, trampling it down into a thick black layer crammed with sherds, flints and stones.

Had this been all then Fochabers might have been nothing more than a vast rubbish dump comparable to the shell-middens of the Middle Stone Age, although it would have been difficult to explain why the people had bothered to tip not single sherds but whole collections of them onto the fire. This, however, was not all. Having spread the ashes the people then piled up four cairns of heavy stones on top of the black layer. Some of these stones weighed up to a hundred pounds and, as far as could be seen, all of them would have had to be carried and dragged from the river-

19   *The Fochabers mound, Moray, during excavation in 1972. Over a thick layer of charcoal and broken pottery four small cairns were built. Two can be seen under a capping of sand in the sides of the excavation. Neolithic people lived here around 3750 BC*

side, up a long steep slope. It was a hard week's work for about ten people who then covered all the cairns with a thick capping of sand, tons of it, to create a round barrow that concealed not only the cairns but the magical layer of broken objects and burnt soil beneath it.

It is likely that the people returned just as other people in the south returned to their long barrows, long after the mortuary house had been buried under the mound. At Fochabers the barrow may have been their territorial marker, establishing their right to the land. It reveals to us something of the rites of imitative magic such neolithic people engaged in, using not only broken pots but, farther south in Britain, the bones of the dead. These themes converge in the practices of the people who constructed the splendid megalithic tombs of Britain and Ireland.

4

Dead Bones for Living People

Wherefore I praised the dead which are
already dead more than the living which
are yet alive.

Ecclesiastes, IV, 2

All over the western parts of the British Isles where there was fertile soil and building
stone people settled and, once their homes were built and the land cleared, they
raised gigantic tombs of limestone, sandstone or granite whose spectacular forecourts
and dark silent chambers have excited the romantic imagination since Roman times.[1]
These were the counterparts of the earthen long barrows of lowland Britain where
stone was scarce and where timber had to be used. Ironically, these barrows may
have been even more eye-catching than the megalithic tombs, with towering carved
poles, flamboyantly painted; but the posts have rotted away whereas the stones of
the west have survived, only imperceptibly yielding to the corrosion of wind, snow
and rain. To visit Cuween or Porth Hellick Down or Bryn Celli Ddu is to enter
a museum of antiquity, quiet and empty but awesome in its revelation of a people
to whom such a monument was vital and for which, over weeks and months, they
were prepared to haul and manhandle tons of stone into place.

There is a bewilderment of architectural styles in these megalithic tombs that
would be tiresome to itemize. Fig. 5 shows the main regions. There was, however,
one major difference of belief between the builders of these big stone monuments.
Along the central areas of these islands people put up long barrows and in the stone
chambers they laid skeletons, venerating the skulls of the dead in rites of fertility
that involved the same collections of broken objects that have already been described.
Farther west and north round mounds were preferred with long, stone-walled
tunnels that led to a chamber deep inside the barrow, the famous passage-graves
of Ireland and northern Scotland. There were fewer skeletons here, more often cremated bones that had been carried along passages whose stones were devoutly carved
with circles, spirals and triangles, passages that faced not the nocturnal moon but
the rising sun, an association of fire, death and sunrise quite different from the rituals
of people who used the long chambered barrows. Yet in all these different tombs
one creed is common, the cult of ancestors that had grown naturally out of the twin
roots of earlier people—the burial of the dead to release their spirits and the belief
in Other-World spirits with whom the dead could speak. As these ideas merged it
was the ghosts of ancestors that were given even more respect for it was they who
would intercede with the forces of nature on behalf of the living. Gradually, through
the generations, the great megalithic mounds became temples as well as tombs,
shrines where rituals were performed to honour the dead and ask for their assistance.

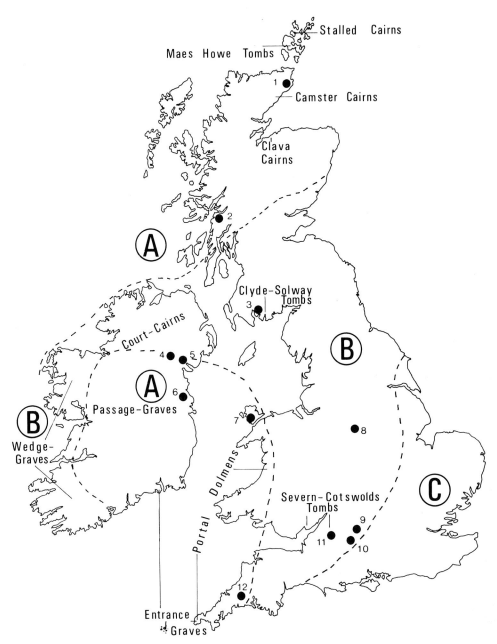

Figure 5 *Some sites mentioned in Chapter 4:*

(A) Major region of passage-graves; (B) of long chambered mounds; (C) of earthen long barrows.

1 Camster Round, ND 260442; 2 Carn Ban, Achnacree, NM 922363; 3 Cairnholy, NX 517538; 4 Annaghmare, H 905178; 5 Slieve Gullion, J 025202; 6 Newgrange, O 007727; 7 Barclodiad y Gawres, SH 328708; 8 Harborough Rocks, SK 243553; 9 Wayland's Smithy, SU 281854; 10 West Kennet, SU 104677; 11 Lanhill, ST 877747; 12 Trethevy Quoit, SX 259688

Despite their colossal stones not all these cairns and barrows are rewarding to visit. Four thousand years of neglect, the recent demands of agriculture and the inflating population of our own century have wrecked many of them. Achaidh by the Dornoch Firth cannot be recommended. Its domed roof has fallen, its skeleton has gone, its mound and square chamber have been overswept by woodland, summer bracken and the sultry droning of flies. Across the sea in Co. Down, Ballyalton court-cairn, from which many splendid pots were excavated, is now hidden behind high fieldwalls and under a confusion of gorse. Nearby, the impressiveness of a dolmen with a heavy capstone is diminished by the rugby posts that shadow it. Nature has taken over the long mound of Cultoquhay in Perthshire. Its mound is lost beneath an undergrowth of woods, bushes and blackening leaves, moss has crept damply down the stones of the chamber, and the tall backslab is green with lichen, as desolate and uninviting as the midnight grave of a vampire.

Others of these tombs, however, have been restored. The cairn of Capel Garmon in North Wales, close to Bettws-y-Coed, has been renovated and one can walk past

20   *Capel Garmon, Denbigh, from the south-east. The deep forecourt of this megalithic long mound can be seen at its front but the entrance to the two ruined chambers was in the middle of the south side. The site was excavated in 1924*

the spot where ritual fires burned near a passage in the cairn's side, inspecting the deep and symmetrical forecourt from which, strangely, there is no access to the chambers. At Audleystown in northern Ireland there are two forecourts, one at either end of the mound, leading to chambers where layers of stones and charcoal, flint and human bone were discovered. The location of this cairn close to a natural harbour reminds one of the travel and the intermixing of groups that occurred later in the Neolithic as trade and the always widening search for land compelled people to move from their homeland. Tombs as magnificent and delightful as Audleystown can be found in the Orkneys, at Long Camster in Caithness where there is a stone platform like a stage built onto the front of the cairn, in the Cotswolds at Stoney Littleton with its cluster of sombre chambers and the impression of a giant ammonite on a portal stone, even as far as Trethevy Quoit in Cornwall, a portal-dolmen whose grey stones tower above the visitor.

Such portal-dolmens may be some of the earliest of our chambered tombs, simple box-like constructions with a great capstone and with a small forecourt formed of two extra stones.[2] The first stone mortuary houses were probably no more than boxes, the capstone easily slid aside when more bones were to be put inside, a mound heaped over it only when the people were to move away. Portal-dolmens are to be found along the shores of the Atlantic in Cornwall, Ireland and in western Wales.

21   *The restored cairn of Long Camster, Caithness. The 'stage' or platform at its front shows up clearly on the right*

Further north in south-west Scotland megalithic boxes set in round mounds have been discovered incorporated into much more impressive long cairns such as those at Mid Gleniron. It is possible that such tiny structures are the stone equivalents of the timber mortuary houses of the lowlands.

As early as the eighteenth century William Borlase, a Cornish rector and antiquarian, was riding out to the prehistoric monuments on Land's End, speculating about their origins and purpose. Although this self-taught archaeologist accepted that Druids had built them—and he could guess nothing else in his uninformed time—he made several sensible deductions about the portal-dolmens.

> It is very unlikely, if not impossible, that ever the Cromlech should have been an altar for sacrifice, for the top of it is not easily to be got upon, much less a fire to be kindled on it, sufficient to consume the victim, without scorching the Priest that officiated, not to mention the horrid Rites with which the Druid was attended, and which there is not proper room, nor footing, to perform in so perilous a station ... it is a Sepulchral Monument.[3]

22   *Poulnabrone, a portal-dolmen in Co. Clare. This neolithic tomb on the Burren was built on farming land of which only the barren limestone remains today. The capstone is over 13 ft long*

In particular Borlase mentioned Mulfra and Zennor Quoits which still survive although their covering mounds have gone. These are splendid sites to visit but whether ruined or not such tombs, obviously old beyond the memory of man and with stones no human could have moved, had mediaeval legends attached to them that provide glimpses of their past use. Some were supposedly the handiwork of giants, a prosaic explanation for their stupendous stones. Others were rumoured to have treasure hidden in them, sometimes as at Maes Howe in the Orkneys guarded by dragons or serpents. Such terrors did not always stop plunderers. The riches of the Sutton Hoo ship-burial of early Christian times were only missed by a lucky chance, and in 1527 it was reported that 'there was iii thousand poundes of gold and sylver in a bank nygh hand to Kettering, and that it is in ii pottes within the ground'. Even the tale that 'a man sprite and a woman sprite did kepe the said ii pottes' may not have prevented someone digging into this 'bank' or barrow. Similar threats did not deter a nineteenth-century farmer from burrowing into the chambers of the Torrylin long cairn above the seashore on Arran. Failing to find gold he did discover that 'these vaults or chambers were filled with human bones ... and strewed them over his field. He selected one of the largest skulls ... and carried it home with him. As soon as he entered his house, its walls were shaken as if struck by a tornado.' The man hastily returned the skull but day and night he was haunted by spectres and he was 'soon afterwards thrown from his horse and dashed to death against the rocks of a stream!'

Other stories link the tombs with fearsome goddesses or witches and may have glimmers of truth in them. Some cairns are said to be composed of stones dropped from the apron of a hag who was both old and deathless. Barclodiad y Gawres, the Apronful of the Goddess, on Anglesey, is one of these cairns and there are others in Ireland and northern England.

These associations with deities harmonize with folk memories of fertility rites. Some forty chambered tombs in Ireland are nicknamed Dermot and Grania's Bed because a young man and his girl who were eloping were supposed to have made a bed of stones every night as they fled. That this story has ancient roots is shown by the girl's name, originally Grainne, meaning 'ugliness', the Old and Undying Hag of many Celtic myths. Dermot or Diarmid may have been Donn, the god who ruled over the world of the dead.

> *Is Death that woman's mate?*
> *Her lips were red, her looks were free,*
> *Her locks were yellow as gold.*
> *Her skin was white as leprosy,*
> *The Night-Mare Life-in-Death was she,*
> *Who thicks man's blood with cold.*   *Ancient Mariner*, 3, 11

This mixture of fear of spirits-beyond-death, of a belief in the Other-World, and of cults of human fertility to promote the growth of crops may have formed the substance of many of the rites in the long timber- and stone-chambered barrows of Britain.

23 *The entrance to the long chambered tomb of Wayland's Smithy, Oxfordshire, flanked by two tall sarsen pillars*

The earliest of these long tombs in the Cotswold and Severn regions of Wessex probably consisted of no more than a chamber of four slabs, three for the sides, one for the capstone, at the eastern end of a long mound. None of the stones weighed much more than two or three tons and could have been heaved and levered into position by a few adults. It was only later when families were grouping together into clans that more elaborate monuments were designed with several chambers either set into the sides of a barrow or leading off a gallery from the entrance, each cell the vault of an individual family. In one case, at Wayland's Smithy, a megalithic tomb with three transepted chambers was built directly on top of a little earthen long barrow at a date well into the Neolithic period.

The orientations of these chambered tombs were just as purposefully chosen as those of the earthen long barrows and presumably for the same reason, that their builders believed it essential to bring the tomb and the dead into association with the moon or the sun. Within the pattern of orientations in the long mounds there were marked regional preferences as a glance at the map shows (Fig. 6). It is interesting to find that in a single cultural group, the stalled cairns of northern Scotland, the people's choice varied from district to district, from Sutherland up to the Orkneys. It is also clear that their kinsmen in Ross and Cromarty, building cairns facing between east-north-east and east towards the rising of the moon or sun, would have

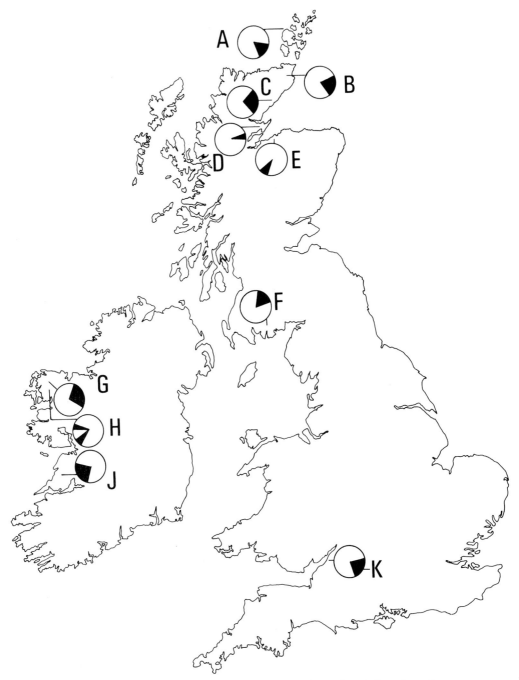

Figure 6 *Some regional preferences in the orientation of chambered tombs:*
A Stalled cairns, Orkneys; B Camster passage-graves, Caithness; C Orkney–
Cromarty passage-graves, Sutherland; D Orkney–Cromarty passage-graves, Ross &
Cromarty; E Clava Cairns; F Clyde–Solway long mounds; G Court-cairns, Co.
Mayo; H Wedge-graves, Co. Mayo; J Wedge-graves, Co. Clare; K Severn–
Cotswolds chambered long mounds

had little understanding of the beliefs of the people of the Clava cairns only a few miles away around Inverness who preferred to have their passage-graves facing south-west to south-south-west, towards the setting of those bodies. This was a fundamental difference and it is such divisions that reveal the idiosyncrasies and antagonisms that could separate communities in prehistoric times. Even in such a small area as the Marlborough Downs near Avebury most of the earthen long barrows faced between east and north-east, whereas only an hour's walk away nine out of ten of the long chambered mounds were orientated between east and south-south-east.

Some of these tombs had entrances through which it was only just possible to drag a corpse and through which, presumably, it was equally difficult for a ghost to emerge except under the control of the living. Trethevy Quoit, despite its size, had one little aperture in the bottom corner of its entrance and this could be blocked. Stoney Littleton had a very low entrance, and on the Isle of Man the only access to Cashtel yn Ard was between two leaning stones, so close together that one had to lie on one's side to squeeze through. The interior of these cairns is often spacious but entrance was rarely easy. In the Cotswolds several mounds had 'porthole' entrances, circular cramped holes chipped out of the solid slab that stood across the front of the chamber. At the Gloucestershire tomb of Rodmarton, now covered over and rank with grass in the middle of a field, short flights of steps led down to the two side chambers whose narrow portholes were the sole means of access to the cells where disturbed skeletons lay, two flint arrowheads with their tips broken off lying beside them. The stones had been tapped away in flakes to make the cavities, the upper half left rough but with a smoothed lower edge over which people crawled with their arms full of bones.

To find how difficult this must have been, particularly when a fully fleshed corpse was to be put inside a tomb, Stuart Piggott and Alexander Keiller constructed a full-sized model of one of the Lanhill chambers and then attempted to get the body of an adult into it.[4] The original entrance was constricted by a slab in the floor and two upright fractured stones, leaving a gap about two feet wide and only just over a foot high. Inside the chamber an earth-covered skeleton had been discovered lying on its back with its knees pressed up to its chest. It was a man of about fifty whose left elbow, wounded in his youth, had remained rigidly flexed for the rest of his life. Other bones and skulls lay tidily around the sides of the chamber. Such an arrangement in a space hardly four feet by three could only have been achieved by someone wriggling into the chamber, lying on his stomach to stack up the bones and clear a space at the centre, and pushing himself out backwards. In turn the corpse, two or three days after death when rigor mortis had gone, was laid in the short passage in front of the entrance, on its back, head over the portal slab, and shoved forward until its shoulders were inside the chamber. Only then could it be swivelled round, its legs tied up to its chest, until it slumped partly onto its side in the chamber. A thin skim of earth was spread over the body, almost like a blanket, leaving the head uncovered.

Rituals in these chambered tombs, especially in Wessex, were much the same as those in the long barrows—skeletons were defleshed, bones smashed, animal bones laid near them, human skulls and long bones removed. People were no healthier. Many of the bodies at Lanhill, whose mutilated barrow once had five or six chambers in its sides, carried signs of osteo-arthritis. Others of these light-boned, slender people had congenital disorders of the spine and had suffered from tooth disease.

It was suggested, because of their physical similarities, that there were family groups in these chambers, an idea which is supported by the evidence from other sites. Several such chambers or cists at Ascott-under-Wychwood in Oxfordshire had collections of bones in them that may have come from separate families, particularly as one cist was empty 'for this suggests that we are perhaps dealing with family groups each of which had its own cist so that when one family disappeared its cist remained unused. The mixture of men, women and children in each cist, apparently completely at random, confirms the suspicion of family groups' (A. Selkirk, *Current Archaeology*, 1971).

Again, there were indications of the dangers these people experienced for one man had an arrowhead embedded in his spine and another had an arrowhead beneath his ribs. To the west, at Nympsfield in Gloucestershire, anatomists discovered that many of the people had suffered from inflamed gums because of bad mouth hygiene and had endured the agony of abscesses and septic teeth. Even at West Kennet, that prince of megalithic long barrows overlooking Silbury Hill, several adults had spina bifida, and others had spondyloschisis, a breakdown in the spinal column some time after birth. There were also abscesses, fractures, one young woman was deformed by scaphocephaly, an excessive elongation of the skull, and virtually everyone over the age of thirty had arthritis, 'the plague of this community'.[5]

Disease, accident and the frequency of death conditioned the rituals of people who could explain their troubles only by attributing them to forces that had somehow been offended and had somehow to be controlled through the spirits of ancestors, a control that might be achieved through the possession of stones believed, because of their unusual appearance, to have magic powers. In several chambered tombs on the Marlborough Downs pieces of oolitic limestone have been found with the dead. The nearest source of this white-pimpled rock was thirty miles to the west around the Mendips where other 'special' stones including Forest Marble could be picked up. Perhaps to give it extra protection the façade of West Kennet consisted alternately of upright sarsens and drystone walling built of this pale oolitic limestone.

Probably several families combined to build West Kennet, a magnificent monument put up on a ridge of cleared land above the wooded valley of the Kennet where one family may have camped at the fringe of the forest. The tomb with its five chambers and its immensely long mound is a testament to the needs and the fears of the community that used it. For centuries they brought the exhumed bones of their dead here, as always arranging them neatly in the chambers. When it was excavated in 1955 and 1956 the remains of at least forty men, women, children and infants were found in it. There were hints of family vaults. Three men's skulls in the end chamber were very like each other and in the south-west chamber a woman's was similar, perhaps the skull of a girl who had been married into another family.

24 *The north-east and north-west chambers of West Kennet long chambered mound in Wiltshire. In these recesses the remains of over fifty skeletons were found. The heavy stones may have been dragged more than two miles from the Marlborough Downs*

Most of the skulls, however, had gone, although their lower jaw was left behind. Also missing were many heavy arm and leg bones. As a large skull fragment and bits of others were found near the entrance it is likely that the people had removed the skulls and long bones for their rituals, speaking to them and invoking their ghosts to assist the living. Excavations at Lanhill revealed the same obsession with skulls, several being found in one chamber. Of three by the wall two were upside down and the other had been put down on another person's jaw bone. There was another by the entrance, and others upside down in the corner with their jaws missing. One individual lacked a skull altogether. At Lugbury, a fine tomb sketched by John Aubrey three hundred years ago, Thurnam's excavation uncovered several chambers in one of which were the bones of four adults but ten skulls. Thigh bones were missing from the chambers at Wayland's Smithy, and whether at Rodmarton, Stoney Little-ton or Ascott-under-Wychwood, where an old woman had been laid to rest with vertebrae that did not belong to her, it is clear that human bones were taken from these 'tombs' for cult practices that were performed in the forecourts.

25 *The monumental façade of Wayland's Smithy megalithic tomb. Between the upright stones is neat drystone walling reconstructed after the excavations of 1962–3. This tomb was built on top of a small earthen long barrow around 3600 BC*

The missing bones at Lanhill had to be passed out through the porthole entrance. Often, later prehistoric holed stones were reported to possess curative powers as if in memory of the times when human bones were passed out through holes for fertility rites. The Long Stone near Minchinhampton once had two large and one small hole in it and may have been the entrance stone to a ruined tomb. Thurnam reported that through it 'not many years since, children, brought from a considerable distance for the purpose, used to be passed for the cure and prevention of disease'. It is another lingering whisper of prehistoric beliefs.

Although it was skulls that were missing from southern chambered tombs the reverse is true in the Orkney tombs hundreds of miles to the north. The people who erected these native stalled cairns changed their burial customs when they intermarried with people who preferred the Irish style of chambers with side cells for the bones of their dead. Formerly, defleshed skeletons had been brought to the cairns and the mourners had broken up the bones into splinters and then thrown burning charcoal onto them. It was a practice also undertaken in several Wessex tombs such as Nympsfield, Sherrington and Tinkinswood, and may have arisen from the belief that before the spirit could leave its body every drop of moisture, the liquid of life, should be removed from the bones. Then earth and stones could be strewn over the scorched remains, sealing them in their tomb. Sometimes provisions were left with these ghosts. Two pots holding food were set down inside Unival in the Hebrides. Other people more symbolically deposited two enormous caches of seafood in the Argyll cairn of Crarae, at least five thousand seashells containing fifteen different varieties including periwinkle. It was a token gesture. Every one of the shellfish had already been eaten.

These customs lost favour as cairns changed from being graves into storehouses from which bones were to be removed. Burrowing among stones and earth for ancestral relics would have been tedious and frustrating and gradually another tradition developed of simply setting the bones down in the chamber, even arranging them into types, perhaps for easier selection. At Round Camster in Caithness, recently beautifully reconstructed, on top of the old trodden layer of blackened earth, ash and burnt bone, there were unburnt bones including two skeletons that were propped up in the passage, covered with heavy stones when the tomb was finally blocked.[6] Neither of them had leg bones. Presumably the bodies had been buried elsewhere and taken to the tomb only when their flesh had rotted. Similar exhumation has been noticed in other cairns.

26 *The chamber and side-slabs of Round Camster, Caithness, photographed during the restoration of this stalled tomb in 1966. The passage is on the left*

It was the way in which the skulls were treated that illustrates most vividly the rites that took place in these magnificently constructed tombs of the Orkneys. At the Knowe of Yarso bones had been heaped in the corners of the compartment but twenty-nine skulls were meticulously positioned along the wall, facing the passage and the entrance, staring down at any visitors. On another island a tomb was erected at Isbister above the steep cliffs of the headland, and to it a family group carried human bones, separating them, putting leg bones in one chamber, a medley of arms, vertebrae and pelvises in another, but arranging the skulls, all of them male, in pairs in the corners and at the cell openings. With them were stone tools, axes, a macehead and a polished knife of orange stone. One thinks of a votive offering for the dead, left for them in a leather bag of which only a fastening button survived.

Many other tombs had arrays of skulls. These may have been removed and replaced many times as the need demanded, the names and exploits of their owners learned by rote by the living, repeated in chants during the rituals for which the skulls were so necessary. Often with them in the tomb were the bones of animals. Blackhammer cairn on Rousay had sheep, oxen, red deer and a flurry of unlikely birds such as gannet, cormorant and pink-footed goose. With the skulls at Isbister were the remains of sheep, oxen, eagle, maybe even a crow. The implications of these Orcadian deposits will be returned to in the next chapter.

Some of these animals could not have been particularly attractive to eat and, just as for southern Britain, alternative explanations have to be found. The three ox skulls along the axis of the Beckhampton barrow and another neatly buried in a pit at Sherrington have been suggested as totem animals. There was another at the chambered tomb of Manton high up on the Marlborough Downs where people buried the poleaxed skull of an ox in the forecourt. The antler of a roe deer had been laid down exactly outside the north-east chamber at West Kennet. The entire skeleton of a calf lay behind the chambers at Notgrove in Gloucestershire and it was in the same county that the quaintly named Hetty Pegler's Tump had the jaw bones of wild boars hidden in the forecourt.[7]

A totem, a person's or a family's bridge between the natural and supernatural worlds, was itself a symbol of *mana*, the acquisition of the power to control spirits. In some societies young men, and sometimes, young women, attempted to gain such power through the dreams and visions that came to them after days of fasting and contemplation, far from their homes, in some lonely, silent place. The revelations were communicated by an animal or a bird or plant which then became the personal totem of the visionary, and it was only those who had *mana* who could take part in the rituals of the community. Others had simply to watch. Only with *mana* could a person have concourse with the spirit-world, and those who possessed the greatest powers, who pronounced the words of the dead through trances or after terrifying convulsions or who could predict with clarity how the following year would proceed, eventually were accepted as priestlike shamans, the natural leaders of the ceremonies of intercession held at the front of the long burial mounds.

Fires were lit and feasts held in these forecourts. Even in those chambered tombs where the chambers were built into the sides of the mound people would construct a neat and imposing forecourt with a false entrance at the eastern end, because in the earlier, simpler tombs this had been where the moon and death combined and where rituals were held. As families grouped together later in the Neolithic the forecourts they built, sometimes after dismantling an original façade, became deeper, almost semi-circular and edged with high pillars. So recognizable as ritual centres are these structures that the focus of the long barrow must have shifted from the chambers to the forecourt where all the people could assemble, squatting around the newly lit fires, chanting their incantations, handling the bones of the dead.

At Belas Knap, finely reconstructed and standing at the rim of a wooded escarpment in the Cotswolds, fires had burned in the forecourt before stones and rubble were piled up against the false entrance. In this blocking lay the bodies of a young man and five children. There had been fires in the forecourt at Notgrove, a seemingly ordinary transepted tomb which is now earth covered but worth a visit by the dedicated pilgrim because it was here that an earlier grave was found, one of the first tombs built by the farmers of the Birtish Isles. The chambers and mound had been put up to cover a dome of earth lined with drystone walling. In it was the stone-slabbed grave of an elderly man and on top of the dome lay the bones of a young woman. We cannot tell from the barrows of Belas Knap and Notgrove whether these young people had been sacrificed but it would not be improbable if some crisis had demanded an especially prized offering to the gods.

27 *Belas Knap, Gloucestershire, showing the 'false' entrance to this mound whose chambers are set in the long sides. The skeleton of a young man and the skulls of several children were discovered when the rubble was cleared from the forecourt*

Dedications were almost certainly made in these places. At Nympsfield there were the remains of many fires, a pit in the forecourt filled with earth in which one bone lay, and in the entrance blocking were lots of pig bones. The fire in Rodmarton's forecourt had been so strong that the stones of the entrance were burned. Here also a pit had been dug and the jaw bones of three pigs placed ceremoniously in it, one at the bottom, one in the middle and one at the top of the filling. Teeth had been scattered all over the forecourt, from oxen, horses, pigs, even boars' tusks and a single human tooth. Here surely, as the fires blazed, people had carried human and animal skulls, laying them down, using the human bones and the animal totems of the group in rites that were designed to bring health and good fortune to the community.

Further north in Britain, in others of the long megalithic tombs, the rituals although not identical had similarities to those of the south. The tall, thin stones of Cairnholy's façade on a hillside overlooking Wigtown Bay curved statuesquely around a crescentic forecourt at the centre of which a single stone stood.[8] As long as the tomb remained open this stone had been the centre of the ceremonies. Around it the earth had been reddened by several fires. Near them were deposits of broken pottery and flints. It is tempting to think of the stone as the symbol of the dead, even of the spirit of the cairn, much like the stones discovered in some of the Yorkshire earthen long barrows and around which skulls were laid during the rituals of evocation.

28   *A rear view of the two chambers and the tall forecourt stones of Cairnholy I long mound, Kirkcudbrightshire*

Eventually, after many generations, it was decided to close the Cairnholy tomb. The people may have believed that they were 'killing' the tomb by shutting it off from the world. Significantly they removed the stone that symbolized its power. They dragged the forecourt pillar from its socket, perhaps jamming it against the entrance. Over the damaged hole another fire was lit and more broken sherds and a flint were laid down near it. Then heavy slabs were heaped up in the forecourt and earth and stones piled over them, completely sealing the entrance to the cairn. Offerings to the dead were left among these stones: sherds, flints, even handsful of winkles, limpets, mussels and whelks. Near them were two small discs of stone, chipped around the edges, one with a diminutive cupmark in it.

Regrettably Cairnholy and its neighbour were robbed of their contents so that we know very little about the people who built them. The same was true of Cuff Hill near Beith where charcoal and human bones were found when the tomb was being hacked into for road material in 1810 and later in 1845. As a local farmer indignantly observed, 'These curious and interesting relics of antiquity the mercenary and boorish labourers are breaking and undoing with the most unfeeling apathy.' A few stones survive of this despoiled tomb that is so representative of hundreds of others.

The stone discs found at Cairnholy, small enough to fit comfortably into the palm of one's hand, are puzzling. Their edges have been roughly flaked but their surfaces have been beautifully smoothed. Yet there is no carving or anything upon them except one little cupmark, no bigger than a baby's fingernail and certainly not deep enough to hold either solid or liquid. By themselves the Cairnholy discs might be ignored but others have been discovered in burial-places, at West Kennet, at Ty-Isaf and Pant-y-Saer in Wales, in Ireland, and not far from Cairnholy at Brackley on the Kintyre peninsula where a sherd of pottery and a small stone disc lay beside the blue-grey stains of bodies on the chamber floor. Other discs have been found in stone circles near human bones and in round barrows of the Early Bronze Age so that their association with the dead is clear.

The Culbin Sands in Scotland were densely populated in prehistoric times. This was once one of the most fertile stretches of land in the British Isles, near Findhorn Bay which looks like a semi-tropical lagoon in summer, and many stone discs have been found there, left behind in the abandoned and crumbled homes of the people. An old man who had been asked to collect as many as he could in the nineteenth century was instructed to hire a donkey and cart to transport them to the museum in Edinburgh two hundred hilly miles away. He did so 'only substituting his wife and barrow for the donkey and the cart'.

One puzzles over these discs. Made of slate, sandstone, sarsen, quartz, anything from one to five inches in size, found with burials, with cremations, in chambered tombs, round barrows, stone circles and in the ditches of enclosures such as Windmill Hill and Avebury, even as far north as the circle-henge of Stenness in the Orkneys, their mystery remains. One suggestion has been that they were pot-lids for vessels in which human bones were stored, ancestral relics kept in the home until the tomb was to be closed. A perforated sandstone disc carved with a fertility scene of humans mating covered a Bronze Age cremation urn in Denmark. Little more can be said. The discs may have been lids but it is as arguable that they were ancestor-stones, or talismen, or representations of the sun or moon. During the Neolithic Age they do seem chiefly associated with the users of long mounds whether in Wessex, south-west Scotland or even with the court-cairn builders of Ireland where, alongside the high cliffs near Mine Head in Co. Waterford, the court-cairn of Ballynamona held not only cremations and broken pottery but one of these little discs.

Perhaps nowhere is the neolithic belief in sympathetic magic shown more clearly than in these elegant Irish court-cairns, and nowhere is the transition from family tomb to open-air shrine more obvious. Well over a hundred of these cairns are known in northern Ireland in the east and right across to the coast of Co. Mayo whose countryside with its lovely limestone hills Thackeray described as 'the most beautiful in the world'. The eastern cairns have deep, crescentic forecourts. Those of the west sometimes have two, one at either end of the mound, or just one so pronounced that it forms almost a complete circle. The cairn at Creevykeel, perched above the sea in Co. Sligo, has an entrance leading to an oval courtyard large enough to accommodate fifty people and with a single inconspicuous burial chamber at the far end. To hallow the open court the people buried a superb diorite axe near its entrance.

It is not difficult to visualize ritual gatherings in these forecourts but what is at first surprising is that only rarely do archaeologists find more than two or three human burials in the cairns. Instead there is usually a mass of broken material, the scraped-up remains of abandoned settlements like that found at the Goodland enclosure in Co. Antrim, and it is probably no coincidence that the earliest court-cairns are found in this part of Ireland. The unhappily named Hanging Tree Cairn at Ballyutoag held no human remains but in its well-preserved courtyard was a low mound with dozens of broken bits of pottery on top of a layer of charcoal. People had spread charcoal in the forecourt of Ballymacdermot in Co. Armagh. Not far away at Annaghmare a fine cairn had several chambers but only four burials were found in them, two cremations, two inhumations. With them the people had placed the teeth of oxen, bear, pig, and sherds, flints and charcoal, all brought together at the same time and carefully laid down in the chambers.

Over the generations several ancient tombs must have been transformed into repositories for potent soil, and the presence of human bone in them became less important. Humphrey Case observed that the cairns 'were built less as graves for selected kinsmen or to commemorate great men or calm their dangerous spirits than to provide by magic rites for the needs of the living ...'⁹ The chambers, emptied of human bone, were filled with the rubbish from deserted and overgrown settlements, preventing anyone from entering them, in a rededication of what had been a tomb and was now a shrine. Henceforth the ceremonies were to be be held in the forecourt.

Far away in the west, where the Atlantic swirls against the high cliffs of Co. Mayo, people raised a huge cairn at Behy with an enclosed courtyard at its eastern end. In the two cramped chambers they threw broken pottery and charcoal but no human bone. On the cobbled floor of the court they left even more sherds, polished stone axes, flint arrowheads and scrapers, the wealth of a community that lived near this cairn four thousand years ago. Signs of other beliefs can be seen at Cloghanmore in Co. Donegal, another great long cairn with an oval courtyard. Off this led galleries and burial chambers in which two stones were decorated with curvilinear carvings, never to be found in other long mounds but very well known in the alien passage-graves of central Ireland. Who engraved the patterns at Cloghanmore is unknown but it is likely to have been someone who had seen and accepted the symbolism and the values of the passage-grave builders and their art.

Outside the north the farmers of the Irish Neolithic did not always think it necessary to raise structures of heavy stones for their dead. There are, for example, very few megalithic tombs around Lough Gur in Co. Limerick where the remains of substantial cabins show that many people lived. The passage-graves around Dublin and Drogheda, therefore, may have been built at the instigation of newcomers although the labour was almost certainly undertaken by natives. These superb circular tombs, edged with ponderous kerbstones and with passages leading to lofty, bee-hive-shaped chambers do resemble others in Brittany, Spain and Portugal and it is possible that it was foreigners to Ireland whose religious customs required such monuments for their dead.

29   *Carved stones in the megalithic tomb of Les Pierres Plats, Brittany. Sub-rectangular motifs with circles and a 'head' are unique to some Breton mounds with sharply angled corridors. The bend in the passage at Les Pierres Plats can just be seen in the distance*

A great invasion of continental conquerors is unlikely. It is equally improbable that people previously content with inconspicuous Goodland enclosures suddenly congregated together to erect such resplendent homes for the dead. Small bands of immigrants with novel but attractive beliefs may be the explanation for the erection of these passage-graves. It is an archaeological problem touched upon because the funerary rites performed in these tombs were very different from those in the long mounds elsewhere in the British Isles.

Over three hundred passage-graves are known, generally in areas well to the south of the court-cairn territories and, unlike those isolated family monuments, clustering in five big cemeteries, two in Co. Meath in the Boyne valley and Lough-crew, two in Co. Sligo at Carrowkeel and Carrowmore, and one in Co. Donegal at Kilmonaster, all fringing the regions occupied by the long mound builders.[10] There are other scattered sites, some across the sea in Anglesey, even the remnants of one near Liverpool where some rearranged stones with carvings of spirals and footprints stand protected under a municipal greenhouse in Calderstones Park, surely one of the most unexpected sanctuaries for megalithic remains in this country.

The builders, native or intruder, normally raised these passage-graves in high places, on knolls or cliff tops or hills. Slieve Gullion in Co. Armagh rises on the summit of a mountain 1894 feet above sea-level. When I first saw it on an August Thursday in 1966 the sign by the country lane halfway up the hillside read: 'Open to visitors, April to Sept. on Saturdays and Sundays. 2 p.m. to 6 p.m. Admission, Adults 6d. Children 3d.' Rejecting the prospect of a fruitless two-mile struggle up the mountain track we returned on Saturday only to find no custodian at the distant cairn and no grille or gate to stop anyone entering.

30   *Bryn Celli Ddu, Anglesey. This passage-grave was built on top of a stone circle and henge whose ditch can be seen in the foreground*

It was worth the frustration and the visit. Even in ruins the tomb is a memorial to its builders. It demands respect for the men and women who had come to this wind-blown peak to drag the kerbstones and the slabs of the chamber upright, slowly but skilfully to construct the roof and then to shoulder basketloads of thousands of stones up the rock-mottled slopes to the cairn. The excavators of 1961 found only a few flecks of cremated bone for, remote though it was, this passage-grave had been robbed. One of the three stone basins where the burnt bone had been set down was cracked and all the grave-goods had vanished. Yet, as it has always been, the view from this cairn is amazing. Facing south-west the passage looks over miles of minute fields, rare and gloomy hills and, in the distance, more countryside hazing away into the mists.

This was a true home of the dead. Professor Michael O'Kelly who directed the excavations of Newgrange, the most exciting of all these exciting passage-graves, remarked that, 'Many tombs were not intended merely as repositories for the dead, but rather were built as *houses* in which the spirits of the dead would continue to live for a very long time ...' The nickname for Slieve Gullion is Cailleach Birra's House. This was the Hag of Berre, of Celtic mythology, who dropped cairnsful of stones from her apron, Mother Goddess and guardian of the land, long-lived and powerful, whose wrinkled beauty epitomized the frailty of man's life. She is heard speaking in a ninth-century Irish poem as evocative as Villon's 'où sont les neiges d'antan' and the Bible's 'the daughters of music shall be brought low'.

> *I have had my days with kings*
> *drinking mead and wine.*
> *Today I drink whey and water*
> *among shrivelled old hags.*

Poetically it was right that her name should be joined with Slieve Gullion for there is a sense of elegy about these abandoned tombs where once the burnt bones of the dead lay, their spirits looking out over the low-lying countryside of the living. This was a cult of the dead, linked with the sun, a cult in which the individual was honoured, his riches placed with him to be taken to the Other-World. To these cairns were brought not the remains of one, two, even a dozen people but hundreds of cremations, and the opulence of their grave-goods was quite unlike the anonymous austerity of the long mounds in which the dead had no personal possessions. Elegance is suggested by these Irish ornaments. There are delicate pendants, fashioned of soft, white-green veined soapstone, or blue limestone, or crystal, jasper, carnelian. Some are shaped like pestles, others are domed, some made like miniature axes reminding one of the solar axe cult hinted at in the wall carvings of the Breton tombs. Others resemble phalli. Occasionally there are double-sphered pendants that imitate the pairs of stone balls found in some of these passage-graves and suddenly it becomes obvious that these are not simple trinkets but religious charms that were as honoured and meaningful as a modern crucifix, expressing those same beliefs in the imitative power of human sexuality noticed among other peasant societies of the British Neolithic.

Stone beads have been discovered with these pendants, to be hung in alternating sizes around the neck. There are bone pins, heads carved into mushroom and poppy shapes for holding the hair in place. Perhaps more than anything else it is these luxuries that are the hallmark of the passage-grave builders who were not concerned to leave utilitarian things of stone or flint with the dead. There are certainly many sherds of rough pottery in these tombs but there are also balls of stone and chalk, many of them burned in the pyre, reaffirming the view that these were sexual symbols, relics of a fervent religion whose followers carried the cremations deep into the tomb, placing them on massive stone basins in the chambers, laying their amulets and talismen with them.

Some of the passage-graves had magic symbols carved into their stones. Knockmany on a wooded sandstone hilltop in Co. Tyrone had three decorated stones lining its chambers, covered with concentric circles, snake patterns, cupmarks, cup-and-ring marks, grooves, crosses, rays, zigzags, triangles, 'eyes and eyebrows' very like those on the chalk drums buried with the child far away on Folkton Wold. Like Slieve Gullion, Knockmany was associated with a Celtic goddess. The tomb is called 'Annia's Cove', the home of the Hag Anu, goddess of fertility and plenty.

The art on these stones was not common. Only one in ten of the Irish passage-graves has such carvings, maybe only one in thirty of the more numerous Breton tombs, but the motifs were undoubtedly of great importance to the people. The two cemeteries of Loughcrew and the Boyne have the richest collections of carvings in Ireland, the Boyne centre with its three monstrous tumuli of Dowth, Knowth and Newgrange and its twenty lesser mounds being a wonder of megalithic art. Here at the first freshwater stretch of the river, in a bend of rich fertile land, people for centuries built passage-graves, the most splendid of them being the quartz-walled colossus of Newgrange.

This was not yet a time of gods and goddesses. A more organized, more hierarchical society with chiefs and priests would have to develop before the spirits of nature were personalized, but centuries later than Newgrange the Celts, who did have deities, believed that this cemetery by the Boyne was the burial-ground of an ancient people, the Tuatha De Danann, and that Newgrange had been built by the good god, Dagda, whose wife was the sacred river, Boann. The idea of the Boyne and other rivers being sources of fertility was an old one, long preceding the Iron Age. Many stone circles and henges of the Late Neolithic were erected near rivers and it may have been the belief that the Boyne was the home of fecund spirits which could bring life back to the dead that caused people to raise the passage-grave of Newgrange alongside it.

A stone circle surrounded this tomb, the earliest yet known in the British Isles, closing Newgrange off from the profane world.[11] Around 3250 BC the long passage and the domed central chamber with its three side cells were erected, the ring of giant kerbstones laid down and the layers of boulders and turves that composed the mound stacked up. A standing stone was set upright on top, above the entrance, like those other stones that watched over the dead in the long mounds of Britain. It was a triumph of devotion and it remains so despite so little having been found

31   *Despite its resemblance to a wartime 'pillbox' this reconstructed mound of Newgrange
with its quartz-faced wall gives a good idea of the passage-grave's original appearance.
Stones of the outer circle stand in front of the kerb-lined mound*

in it. Newgrange had been ransacked centuries before the recent excavations, perhaps
by Norsemen around AD 860, and in 1967 only a few human bones were discovered
together with the expected pendants, pins and balls. This hardly mattered. The glory
of Newgrange is in its profusion of carving on kerbstones and on the stones of the
interior—carvings of abstract motifs, lozenges, chevrons—the face of the stones prepared and smoothed before the outlines were pecked and grooved into them, compositions of triangles, lines and diamonds with the spiral dominant everywhere.

Some have seen in these carvings representations of the Mother Goddess, a
female divinity that was worshipped along the coasts of the Mediterranean during
the early Neolithic period. Figurines and standing stones fashioned in her likeness
still survive in the Greek islands, in Sardinia, Spain, Portugal and southern France,
but if such a deity did exist—for the carved images may be no more than statues
of priestesses—it is unlikely that her cult was ever strong in the British Isles. Few
female figurines have been found here, the best known being the lump of chalk
obesity from Grime's Graves, a statuette that has more in common with the plump
Venuses of the Palaeolithic than with the elegantly dressed Mediterranean goddess
whose arched eyebrows have caused some scholars to refer to her as the Eye Goddess,
an owl-faced and fearsome guardian of the dead.

There are only a few carvings from the chambered tombs of Brittany that can
confidently be interpreted as depicting any sort of woman, and there are even fewer
from Ireland and virtually none elsewhere in Great Britain. In the British Isles, apart
from some strange carvings of hands, feet and axes to be described later, the megalithic art is non-representational. The abstract compositions of spirals, cupmarks,
chevrons, meanders, rays and circles intermingle in a bewilderment of patterns where
the relationship of even one triangle to an adjacent straight line is questionable. To

32 *Megalithic carvings in Gavrinis long chambered mound, Brittany. Some people believe that these are abstract representations of a 'Mother-Goddess'. This style of art is rare in the British Isles*

'see' in this confusion some kind of formalized female figure is fanciful. Some enthusiasts have suggested that the concentric arcs were the hair, the conjoined arcs the eyebrows of the goddess, referring rather optimistically to carvings that resemble nothing so much as a child's drawing of a flying bird. Groups of triangles or lozenges delightfully pocked out on the prepared surfaces of stones in the passage of Newgrange have been interpreted as her patterned skirt. It is true that there are carvings of this 'Eye Goddess' in France that show her in a long skirt, her breasts bare, her eyes staring out from the darkness of the tomb. At Petit Morin in the Marne she stands watchful at the entrance to the rock-cut tomb. Such obvious figures do not appear in the British Isles.

Here the elaborate megalithic art is almost confined to a few passage-graves in eastern Ireland and to our eyes it is almost without meaning. Far from revealing a single, powerful cult of a goddess it differs from one region to another, even between nearby tombs. In the cemetery of Loughcrew there is a profusion of rays, stars and circles that shine like radiant suns from the stones of the chambers, but only a few miles to the east in the Boyne valley tombs of the same design and of the same period bear carvings of spirals, triangles and lozenges. Every district was separate, even every family was different. Hardly a mile away from Newgrange the builders of another huge mound, Dowth, preferred a motif that seldom appears at Newgrange. As Claire O'Kelly has pointed out, 'The lozenge is easier to carve than the concentric circle motif, yet at Dowth, where in general the standard of carving is not as high as at Newgrange, the latter abounds and the former is scarcely represented.'

One wonders what the masons thought as they knelt in the open air by a prostrate stone that had yet to be put in position in the tomb's passage or chamber, grinding and smoothing its face before taking a flint, delicately scribing the perfect outline of a spiral or arc, and then with a hard pebble and sand tapping, pecking and scraping out the sacred symbols for the dead. The work was not art for art's sake, decorating a temple to beautify it, although one should not doubt that these men received an aesthetic satisfaction from the perfection of their craftsmanship. This was not a form of megalithic wallpaper but religious symbolism whose character we cannot comprehend, as much a part of the funerary ceremonies as the passage-grave itself. It was to do with death and, almost as certainly, it was to do with the sun. There is a remarkable carving on a kerbstone at Knowth, another giant tomb near Newgrange, that is almost a replica of the sundials that were set in the sides of Anglo-Saxon churches. The carving is just to the left of the entrance which faces east towards the sunrise at Spring and Autumn. Eighteen rays spread from its central hole which has a second hole above. Another kerbstone near it has several circles, diamond shapes and spirals on it.

Spirals are even more common at Newgrange. Immediately outside the entrance to this, the most monumental of all the Irish passage-graves, is the Entrance Stone, a horizontal slab over ten feet long and as high as the shoulder of the neolithic artist who picked and smoothed the channels of the spirals that swirl over it. Between them a vertical groove points towards the passage and the chambers where the dead lay on great stone basins.

It has been suggested that such spirals were symbols of the eyes of the Great Goddess, watching over the dead, but the fact that these spirals are often joined not only in pairs but sometimes in triplets argues against this. It is more likely that in some way they represented the journey the dead must take before they reached their home in the Other-World. In *The White Goddess*, a book of exquisite poetic insights but questionable archaeology, Robert Graves suggested that a spiral might have been the emblem of the maze the dead had to follow to find that home. The conjoined spirals on the Entrance Stone were rather different. 'Follow the lines with your finger from outside to inside and when you reach the centre, there is the head of another spiral coiled in the reverse direction to take you out of the maze again. So the pattern typifies death and rebirth.'

These interpretations may be mistaken. The Pueblo Indians of the Rio Grande associated the spiral with water, and their traditional symbol for the sun was three concentric circles with a central cupmark; and the double or treble circle, often with a cupmark, is the most common motif in all Irish decorated passage-graves. It is tempting to identify it with the sun. The winding spiral may have had an even more symbolic meaning. Spirals linked with straight lines, rather in the manner of Newgrange's Entrance Stone, were drawn by the Hopi Indians of northern Arizona as a maze, the Road of Life a man had to follow. The two ends of the line were the beginning and end of his life and where the line terminated at the centre of the spiral or maze was the 'Sun Father, the giver of life'. Frank Waters in his *Book of the Hopi* commented that 'It is curious that the symbol has long been known throughout the world.' A spiral is easily drawn and may well have had many different meanings. In Crete and Egypt, however, the mazes or labyrinths were 'maps of the wanderings of the soul in the afterlife until it found rest and rebirth at the Tree of Life in the center...' If the Irish passage-grave builders did have a connection, however remote and attenuated, with Mediterranean cultures then the megalithic spiral may also have possessed such symbolism, a Soul-Path for the dead, overlooked by the concentric circles of the sun.

Many of the kerbstones that surround the base of Newgrange's mound are ornamented with similar magical art. So are the upright stones of the passage to the central chamber with its three side cells. Zigzags, circles, meanders, spirals and cupmarks are abundant. One of the side slabs in the farthest cell has a triple spiral on it as carefully done as those on the Entrance Stone. Another in the West Cell has a peculiar set of raised lines linked at right-angles to another which may signify the keel of a ship. Vessels like these were also carved in Breton tombs like Petit-Mont where the craft has no sail, or in nearby passage-graves in the Morbihan where the boats had high prows and masts. Professor Giot, an authority on these megalithic monuments in Brittany, has suggested that 'perhaps these alleged ships were ceremonial vessels carrying away the souls of the dead'.

It is a suggestion entirely in keeping with the symbolism of the other carvings at Newgrange, particularly where these are also associated with death and the sun. Near the 'ship' carving in the side cell is another which looks like a fern but which is in fact a herringbone pattern of nineteen V-shaped lines. Whether these were a record of the moon's nineteen-year cycle from its most southerly to northerly back to southerly positions on the horizon can only be a matter of speculation, but what is not in question is that the passage of the tomb was precisely aligned on that unique position on the skyline where the midwinter sun would rise at dawn for three or four days around 21 December. Even when the entrance was blocked the sun's rays would still have reached the end chamber because the builders constructed a rectangular aperture, known as the roof-box, above the entrance. It looked like an enormous letterbox and through it, for a few winter mornings, the sun could shine briefly, illuminating the decorated stones and touching the bones of the dead in the farthest recess. A memory of this survived for thousands of years for Claire O'Kelly was told 'that at a certain time of the year the sun lit up the three-spiral figure in the end chamber' which is exactly the phenomenon that was observed by Professor O'Kelly, her husband, when he tested the theory that the roof-box had an astronomical purpose connected with the midwinter sunrise.

Midwinter is the dead time of the year. It is the time when the sun rises and sets farthest to the south, when the days are short and the nights are long and bitter. It is the time that primitive people dreaded, fearing that the Summer would never return and that the sun might continue moving southwards until it vanished, leaving the world in everlasting darkness. Such fears led to midwinter rites to protect the people from this disaster. At Newgrange the sun was for the dead, not the living. Had the builders wished the sun to shine on a priest or a witch-doctor standing among the dead inside the tomb they need only have opened the blocked entrance. Instead, they built the narrow roof-box, fitting it with two quartz slabs that they pushed aside at midwinter. These stones show that the tomb remained blocked, barring the living from entry. Only the dead saw the sun.

There are remarkable stones at Newgrange. A kerbstone at the north-north-east has a pattern on it almost identical with another on a pot from the Orcadian village of Skara Brae to be mentioned in the next chapter. On the Newgrange stone two great joined spirals have pairs of lozenges between them like the spaces between some of the paired spirals on the Entrance Stone. To the north of this kerbstone and exactly on the opposite side of the mound from the entrance is an amazing kerb on which the decoration is divided into two panels, the left having the linked spirals that are the refrain of Newgrange, the right bearing three double cartouches, rectangles with curved corners, each with three deep cupmarks inside them, held apart by little triangles like the sun-symbol of the axe.

Were this a Hopi pictograph each cartouche could be interpreted as a portrayal of spiritual rebirth from one world to the next, somewhat akin to the regular, straight-lined figures drawn by the Malekulan stone circle builders of the New Hebrides, designs that illustrated the journey of the dead. The cupmarks and the 'axes' might stand for the life-giving sun. Such explanations and analogies are seductive but they may be misleading. However satisfying they are it is, regrettably, unhelpful to use the half-understood symbols of one cultural group to interpret the 'art' of another community whose environment and economy were different and who were separated from the first society by thousands of miles and years. Helplessly, we can only gaze

33   *Kerbstone 52 at the rear of Newgrange passage-grave. There is an enigmatic repetition of threes on this magnificently carved stone*

at that enigmatic kerbstone, accepting that its meaning may never be recovered.

This was a kerb that was set up diametrically opposite the Entrance Stone before the mound was built and while it was still possible for someone to sight across the open space towards the midsummer sunset. A circle stone at the north-east, with hidden cupmarks or solar symbols on its base, and with two postholes just to its north, may have been aligned on the midsummer sunrise, the posts used as markers to determine how far along the horizon the sun rose in the north-east. Orientations such as these, impossible to use once Newgrange's mound was built, show how celestial lines could be laid out to bring the sun and the dead together. Other symbolism is less clear. Even though it is clear that three was regarded as a mystical number by the later people of the Iron Age we are left ignorant of the significance of the repetition of threes in this tomb with its three side cells, three stone basins, triple spirals and three cartouches each with three cupmarks in them. We are aware of the cremations, of the amulets, of the art and of the thin winter sunlight creeping up to the burnt ancestral bones, but we never see a person in this still and lifeless world.

Yet these lost people held feasts for the dead near the tombs. Not only have hearths been found near the entrances but bones of oxen, sheep and pigs have been discovered inside the chambers together with the remnants of wild creatures, including the bear, that were hunted down with bows and heavy flint-tipped arrows. Seashells were also placed in the passage-graves and, in one case, as an offering rather than as food.

Barclodiad y Gawres on Anglesey is only eighty miles from the mouth of the Boyne, a day's voyage in favourable conditions in the long, cowhide-lined boats of the time, capable of carrying nine or ten men and easily beached on a sandy shore. Carvings not only in Ireland but in Brittany in tombs such as Mané Lud show these vessels with high, curved prows and sterns, the crew lifting their paddles, and it is in such craft that people travelled the British seas, seeking land and, incidentally, bringing with them new burial customs. One such group settled near the lovely inlet of Porth Trecastell Bay on Anglesey where the seaweed-littered rocks lean, grey and glistening, against the headland where the people built the chambered tomb.[12]

It had a guardian stone in the passage, set lightly upon an unbroken oyster shell that may have been the people's totem. Inside the mound the stones were lavishly carved. Those flanking the entrance to the chamber were covered with zigzags, chevrons and lozenges so well executed that their compositions have been explained as representations of the Mother Goddess herself watching over the dead. Burnt bones

34   *The stone-lined passage of Barclodiad y Gawres, Anglesey. The tomb is now preserved under a concrete shell*

were certainly brought here for the cremations of two youths: the bones, broken after being scraped from the pyre and mixed with sheep bones, were set down under a layer of earth. A weird ceremony followed. A fire was lit inside the chamber and on the flames people placed a water-filled pot into which they dropped oysters, limpets and a winkle together with a nauseating collation of wrasse, eel, whiting, frog, toad, natterjack, grass snake, mouse and shrew, a witch's brew more foul than that in *Macbeth*, 'for a charm of powerful trouble, like a hell-broth ...' When the stew was cooked it was strained, maybe even drunk by the celebrants squatting around the fire, and the dregs were poured onto the glowing ashes. Pebbles, earth and shells were tamped down to quench the last embers. It is a rare, almost unique glimpse of ritual that Barclodiad y Gawres gives us, and one quite unsuspected today by holidaymakers as they take their children to paddle among the rocks beyond the cairn.

During the later centuries of the New Stone Age customs were changing. The climate was drier, forest clearances had opened vast tracts of grassland in the south and cattle grazed where there had once been patches of cultivated ground. Families were banding into societies of scores of people who periodically assembled to trade for the exotic materials that were now reaching their territories. They gathered together to meet neighbouring groups, to feast and to join in communal rites to safeguard the coming year.

Some of these looseknit communities became so large that the long mounds and passage-graves were too small for them. What had been adequate for a single family or even several families could not easily be adapted to the needs of more than a few score people, and now new circular enclosures were constructed, open to the sky, to accommodate them. Some of them—the causewayed enclosures such as Windmill Hill in Wiltshire—may have been settlements and fortifications as well as cult centres, but the rather later henges do seem to have had a mainly ritual function. Other people, keeping to the old ways, sometimes wrecked these novel monuments, burying them beneath more traditional structures. Only eleven miles east of Barclodiad is another passage-grave, Bryn Celli Ddu, 'the dark grave-hill', that some group built quite intentionally on the site of a stone circle. This kind of destruction increased as schisms became sharper during the Bronze Age that was to follow.

In the south no new earthen long barrow had been built for centuries, but near some of their weathered mounds gangs of workers had laboured for months to raise immensely long pairs of parallel banks and ditches known as cursuses (from the Latin 'cursus' or racecourse, which is what William Stukeley had supposed them to be when he first noticed one near Stonehenge). They are among the most mysterious of Britain's prehistoric monuments. Put up quite late in the Neolithic period they are so long that only quite a large and organized society could have constructed them and they may belong to the period of transition from the family to the bigger clan group. One might guess that they were inordinately exaggerated versions of the earlier rectangular mortuary enclosures, in which the dead had sometimes been left to rot before their skeletons were taken to a long barrow. Funerary rituals once performed by families in these small palisades might later have been acted out more

35   *The passage inside Bryn Celli Ddu, Anglesey. In the foreground is a free-standing pillar in the central chamber*

formally and communally in the cursuses by assemblies of people led by priests or chiefs.

The most incredible of all the cursuses, probably the result of two shorter ones being joined together, is in Dorset, six-and-a-half miles long, three hundred feet wide, with two earthen long barrows incorporated at either end of it.[13] Lengths of this cursus are so straight that even before the digging of the ditches and the heaping up of the banks, tasks enough in themselves, people must have hacked down wide patches of undergrowth and trees so that sighting-poles could be set in position.

Just north of Stonehenge is another cursus, nearly two miles long with a long barrow at its east, the body of a single child in it. In Oxfordshire a cursus about a mile long actually passed over the silted-up ditch of what seems to have been one of the mortuary enclosures that these cursuses replaced. There are many more of these strange monuments. Gaps and causeways through their banks would have permitted large gatherings of people to enter them, and they fairly consistently cross valleys where streams now flow and where bones may have been washed before being carried in procession up the slope to the places where they would be buried. At Rudston in Yorkshire, near two long barrows, one of them with the barrel-shaped furnace that has already been mentioned, several cursuses converged on the end of a chalk ridge where the tallest standing stone in the British Isles stood bleakly against the skyline. This tapering pillar of millstone grit, its tip runnelled by weather, still rises twenty-five feet high, over twenty tons of stone that had been dragged for miles from Cayton Bay by descendants of the people who had put up a stone cairn at the end of the cremation trench in their barrow. The Rudston monolith may have symbolized the same embodiment of ancestral spirits as other standing stones associated with the long mounds, watching over the ghosts of the buried dead. Skeletons may have been brought to it along the cursuses, those fantastic avenues alongside older barrows, leading uphill from water. Everything suggests that they were related to the earlier cults of the dead that had now been transferred from the family shrine to these impressive ceremonial paths of death.

The abandonment of the old ways did not occur everywhere simultaneously. In the west and north of the British Isles, wherever the population was small or travel difficult, chambered tombs continued to be built. Low, round entrance-graves in the Scilly Isles, wedge-shaped tombs with Bronze Age pottery in them in the south and west of Ireland, show how reluctant prehistoric groups were to give up their traditions. Around modern Inverness other people were raising circular passage-graves and ring-cairns which, like Newgrange, were surrounded by stone circles.[14] In these Clava Cairns, the first of them built nearer the end than the beginning of the New Stone Age, it is remarkable how few human remains have been

36   *A ring-cairn inside a stone circle at the neolithic cemetery of Balnuaran of Clava, Inverness. In the background is a ruined passage-grave*

found, just a few scraps of bone or the stain of a single body in the sand of the chamber floor. These cairns must also be regarded as shrines rather than tombs. They are of particular interest because their distinctive architecture inspired the design of some of the most intriguing megalithic rings in these islands, the Bronze Age recumbent stone circles of north-east Scotland.

To these Clava Cairns and to some passage-graves magical stones were brought, just as others had been to long mounds such as West Kennet. Quartz, the white crystalline stone that had been used for Newgrange's roof-box and for the steep, brilliant wall of its mound, was sometimes scattered in the Clava Cairns. A lot of fragments lay at the entrance to Corrimony as though protecting it, and quartz pebbles were strewn around a cremation at Druidtemple. In the passage-grave of Baltinglass in Co. Wicklow large quartz stones were so plentiful that they speckled the cairn like daisies. The translucent snowiness of quartz, so like the moon, must have fascinated prehistoric people who frequently laid it with their dead. Achnacree cairn near the waters of the Firth of Lorne in Argyll is a good example.

Carn Ban or the White Cairn, as it is called, was excavated in 1871 and discovered to be something of a mongrel. Part passage-grave, part long mound, its mixed architecture is just what might be anticipated in the later Neolithic as groups drifted along the western seaways exploring the tree-shadowed rivers for clearings where they could settle, encountering and mingling with other families, miles from their homeland and the old beliefs.[15]

People had blocked the long, low passage of Achnacree with stones but, clearing them away, the nineteenth-century diggers crawled and scrambled into a high domed chamber. There were no bodies there. The rains of thousands of winters had dissolved all trace of them but on the floor where they might have lain was a single pot with one pebble of quartz in it. Beyond the chamber was a stone-cluttered cell with neither body nor pot in it, and beyond it another flat-roofed chamber. By the right-hand wall was a ledge and on it were six quartz pebbles, a line of four and then two others. They were so pristinely perfect that one of the excavators remembered that 'they shone as if illuminated, showing how clean they had remained'. Opposite, on another shelf, were two more. Among the rubble and earth on the floor were some pots. One, directly below the four pebbles, contained three quartz stones and the others, although broken, seem to have held one each. The idea that these white pebbles were soul-stones, symbolizing the moon to which the spirits of the dead had gone, is both possible and unprovable. One can simply observe that quartz was believed to have protective powers and increasingly during the Bronze Age, in many parts of the British Isles, pieces of it were placed with the dead.

Everywhere, not only in the south, the chambered tombs, earthen long barrows and passage-graves went out of fashion as larger, more open centres were needed. Even cursuses were being replaced by open-air circles of stone or earth or timber. It was a change that may have been accelerated by years of famine or drought around 3000 BC but, whatever the cause, the change occurred. On the limestone plateau of the Peak District in Derbyshire are the exposed wrecks of eight or nine chambered

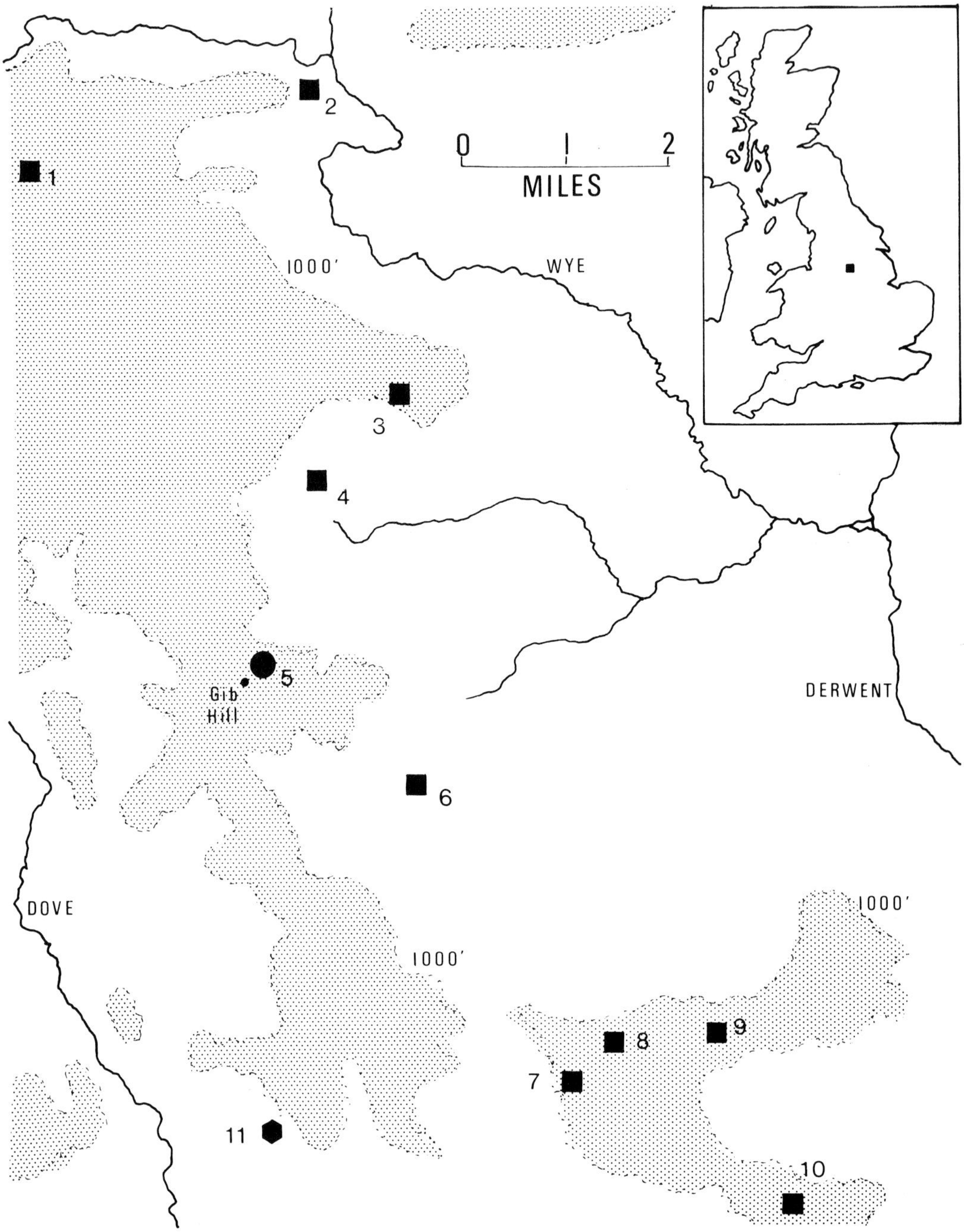

Figure 7 *Some megalithic monuments in the Peak District:*
1 Five Wells, SK 124711; 2 Brushfield, SK 168709; 3 Bole Hill, SK 182676;
4 Ringham Low, SK 169664; 5 Arbor Low circle-henge, SK 160636; 6 Smerrill
Moor, SK 186608; 7 Minninglow, SK 209572; 8 Stoney Low, SK 218578; 9 Green
Low, SK 232580; 10 Harborough Rocks, SK 243553; 11 Liff's Low round barrow,
SK 160566

tombs in a north and a south group, all vandalized, all a mixture of passage-grave and long mound influences, not surprising when it is considered how conveniently the Peak lies for traders from the west and the south, converging on this central upland (Fig. 7). Five Wells cairn in the north had the bones of twelve skeletons in it, the tip of a flint arrowhead lying with them. Bole Hill, Brushfield and Ringham Low nearby are supposed to have had several skeletons in their despoiled cists. 'Low' is derived from the Old English 'hlaw', meaning a hill, showing that these naked slabs were once covered by substantial cairns.

A few miles south is the other group of tombs: Green Low, Stoney Low, Minninglow, Smerrill Moor and Harborough Rocks, built at the southern edge of the plateau. While Green Low's cairn was being heaped up people put the arthritic skeleton of a man among the stones and then buried another pile of disinterred bones mixed with the bones of pig, dog, sheep and deer and some flints close to it. They also scattered quartzite pebbles over the cairn which contained the bones, all of them broken, of at least nine people, half of them children.[16]

At Harborough Rocks a mile or so away another family rested the bones of sixteen skeletons on a pavement in the cairn, putting flint arrowheads with them. The tips of some of these had been deliberately snapped off like those found with the skeletons at Wayland's Smithy, Rodmarton and other Wessex long mounds. The arrowheads from Harborough Rocks clearly revealed one reason why cremation was practised by some people. Those that had not been broken had, instead, been placed

37   *Five Wells megalithic tomb in the Peak District. Its capstone and covering mound were removed years ago*

in a fire, 'and it would seem ... the dead were approached with gifts, which were "killed" by being burnt or broken, in order that the spirits of the things might be set free to join the ancestral spirits'. Smashing bones or flints, or burning them, achieved the same end—of releasing them from this world.

These Derbyshire tombs were probably the ritual centres of ten to twelve families, more than a hundred people farming the land in their separate territories, intermarrying with the others, establishing kinship bonds with them. But as trading networks expanded the need for different and bigger ritual centres developed. Later people gathered together to build the jagged bank, ditch and stone circle of Arbor Low at the centre of the plateau on which the old chambered tombs stood.

This famous circle-henge was no more than a few hours' walk from any of the tombs. It was large enough to accommodate all the people, and its stones were not so heavy that dragging and raising them would have been difficult for these experienced megalithic builders. From its ditch, hacked deep into the limestone, came some four thousand tons of rock, six months' work for fifty labourers, a workforce that would easily have been available from the families in the region. At the centre of the circle, conspicuously placed within the ring of stones, was a Cove, three thick slabs arranged like a roofless sentry-box. This was very probably a representation of the forecourts of the Derbyshire tombs where traditional funerary rituals could be performed, watched by the whole population.

38   *Arbor Low circle-henge, Derbyshire. The stones of the circle have fallen. At their centre is a collapsed Cove, and built onto the bank at the south is a later Bronze Age round barrow whose top has been dug into*

In the centuries after 3000 BC many earthen henges, timber rings and stone circles were erected, some of them actually built on top of cursuses when the cult of the circle outmoded those processional ways. Sometimes a variant of the cursus persisted and was added to a henge or a stone circle in the form of an avenue along which the dead could be carried. It was the circle, however, that was the centre of the ceremonies. The rites performed in it were almost identical to those once enacted in the outdated tombs but now executed in a novel, open-air structure whose stones, leaning, worn and without life, sometimes survive to this day.

5

Rings around the Moon

It is not without some trepidation that we venture on the quicksands of circles and monoliths ...

Magnus Spence, *Standing Stones and Maeshowe of Stenness*

Stonehenge was not the first and certainly not the largest of these new circles but its builders did leave behind them clear evidence of the way in which prehistoric people only slowly, grudgingly, amended their traditions.[1] However unconventional the raggedly circular ditch may have appeared, however strange the chalk bank along its inner edge, the rites acted out within this henge were very similar to those performed in earlier centuries at the earthen long barrows.

There is irony in the name of Stonehenge. First mentioned in the early twelfth century by Henry of Huntingdon as the Second Wonder of Britain, the chronicler called it 'Stanenges', the hanging-stones, because its trilithons, the settings of two tall sarsens capped with a lintel inside the circle, were very like the gallows for mass executions cursed by François Villon in his 'Ballad of the Hanged Men'. 'Stonehenge' it has been ever since, and all the other circular earthwork enclosures of the period have been called henges even though many of them never had a single stone in them.

As always, the population in each region had architectural preferences. The earliest henges had only one entrance but, in Wessex, this was left as a gap through a single, high bank with an internal ditch. In eastern England there were two ditches, one inside the other, with the bank heaped up between them. Sometimes, when the ground was hard and where there were plenty of river stones available, the people did not dig a ditch at all but simply piled up thousands and thousands of cobbles to make the bank. Anyone who has walked around Mayburgh near Penrith, its rampart as wide as a road and high as a house, with the bulky stones jutting through the overgrowing turf, will have realized the compulsions that must have driven these men and women.

In most cases the bank could never have been used for defence, nor was it a gallery for spectators. It merely provided an enclosure for the ceremonies that took place on the central plateau. Few stones or posts cluttered the interior of henges, which were always spacious enough for the assembled population of the district, and one may legitimately imagine families from many miles around coming to these places for communal rites of thanksgiving and supplication, bringing ancestral relics with them.

In other areas people may have erected rings of great posts instead of circular earthen banks but these timber circles have long since fallen and decayed and it

1 *Penrhos-Feilw standing stones, Anglesey*

2 *Cairnholy I: chambered tomb, Kirkcudbrightshire*

3 *Cairnholy I: forecourt*

Figure 8 *Some sites mentioned in Chapter 5:*
1 Mid Howe, HY 371306; 2 Stenness circle-henge, HY 306125, and Maes Howe
passage-grave, HY 317127; 3 Gortcorbies, C 741259; 4 Carles stone circle,
NY 292236; 5 Arminghall, TG 240060; 6 Stonehenge, SU 123422; 7 Maumbury
Rings, SY 690899

is only by luck that we find any trace of them. On the Yorkshire Wolds, where there were at least ten long barrows, only one henge is known. Late neolithic communities there, particularly those who built the gigantic round barrows in the valley of the Gypsey Race, may have erected enclosures of spaced timbers, the posts carved like totem poles, maybe even roofed, but there is no trace of these rings today.

Further south, in East Anglia, another group raised a henge around just such a circle. This hybrid monument at Arminghall near Norwich was constructed around 3250 BC, but five thousand years later the posts had vanished and the henge had been ploughed flat so that it was only from the air that the dark marks of the filled-in postholes and ditches were recognized in 1929. The discovery of Arminghall was made by Wing Commander Insall, VC, who had found Woodhenge near Stonehenge by the same means four years earlier. In 1935 most of the central area of Arminghall and part of its ditch were excavated by Graham Clark.[2]

There are so few long barrows in East Anglia, just two at West Rudham and another at Ditchingham, all of them many miles from Arminghall, that at first it seems that this henge was put up, paradoxically, in an almost uninhabited region; but this is not so. In these bleak wastes of windy grassland and marsh there were several flint mines, not only at Grime's Graves with its female figurine, antler picks and carved chalk objects, but at other centres such as Lynford and at Whitlingham not three miles from Arminghall. In this last mine the skeleton of a miner buried under a fall of chalk in one of the underground galleries reminds us of the dangers experienced by neolithic people and of the need they had for rituals of protection.

These flint mines must have been bustling places with fair-sized settlements near them whose occupants probably dragged the eight long heavy oak trunks down the slope to where Arminghall henge would eventually be constructed. The ramps and the holes where these seven-ton posts stood were laid out in a horseshoe, its open end facing to the south-west. Before erection the posts had been stripped of bark and their bases charred to inhibit decay although, ultimately, they all mildewed and rotted away, and one decayed trunk was snapped off and burnt flints were dropped into its damaged socket. The posts were never replaced.

The bark may have been removed to permit the posts to be decorated. An antler macehead discovered at Garboldisham in Suffolk, the regalia of some early chieftain, had the magical triple spiral carved on it, and in a tiny henge not far away at Maxey in Northamptonshire carved antlers were discovered, incised with geometrical patterns like those in the Boyne passage-graves. Someone had coloured the designs, rubbing soot in to blacken the grooves in one place, reddening them with ferric oxide in another, and it is quite possible that the lost posts at Arminghall had totems and images carved into them, brightly coloured with paints obtained from natural earth pigments, pictorial statements of the people's beliefs in this ritual enclosure.

Arminghall was capable of holding scores of people in its large central arena but the nature of the rites there is obscure. The people left nothing behind them in the interior although the very limited excavation of 1935 did recover dozens of flint flakes from the one short section of the inner ditch that was explored, broken objects tantalizingly like the 'killed' pots and arrowheads from earlier sites, together with sixty more complete flints that had been burnt and some broken pottery covered with roughly jabbed decoration. These waste flakes, the flints that had been in a fire, the shattered pots, conjure up some lines from *Hamlet* (V, 1), spoken over Ophelia's grave:

> *She should in ground unsanctified have lodg'd*
> *Till the last trumpet; for charitable prayers,*
> *Shards, flints and pebbles, should be thrown on her ...*

The Arminghall flints may have come from the pyre in which dead bodies had been consumed. Unlike the majority of the Wessex long barrows those of East Anglia did contain cremations, and the flints in the henge ditch could have been connected with funerary ceremonies in which fire was important. Flint, from which fire could be struck, was a magical stone, vital also for the miners' livelihood, and a stone which according to Laplanders was 'the spark, the emblem of life and animation, ready to burst forth', the embodiment of fire itself. In the Chilterns, at Whiteleaf Hill, the skeleton of an old man was found lying outside a mortuary house by a great pile of broken objects—coarse, whitely patterned sherds, charcoal, animal bones and hundreds of flint flakes—the kind of 'rubbish' used in rites of sympathetic magic that imbued the Goodland rings and court-cairns of Ireland with life-giving force. At Whiteleaf Hill all this was finally buried under a horseshoe-shaped barrow raised at the centre of a circular ditch. It was an arrangement very like the complex of horseshoe and ditch at Arminghall, making it all the more likely that the timber setting there was a representation of a forecourt or even of the barrow itself in which funerary ceremonies and rituals of supplication were held.

It is an interpretation strengthened at Arminghall by the possibility that the henge had been aligned upon the sun which itself was a worldwide symbol of warmth and life. The compass bearing of the causeway is given as 229° which, in the latitude of Arminghall with its flat, open landscape, was just at that position at the south-west where the sun would have set on the horizon at midwinter. Although no priest or witch-doctor could ever have defined it exactly, with only widely spaced posts to indicate the direction of this sunset, the fact that such an orientation was built into the henge suggests that the people there were concerned to include the movements of the sun, shining through the entrance into the centre of their post-lined enclosure, in their ceremonies. The same was true at Stonehenge, put up nearly five hundred years later.

Not unexpectedly, this henge with its unusual outer ditch was very much bigger than Arminghall, enclosing an area five times the space inside the Norfolk ring. There were many more people farming the easy chalklands of Salisbury Plain than lived in the harsher environment of eastern England, and in contrast to Arminghall's three long barrows there were at least fifteen within three miles of Stonehenge, some just to the east of the Avon, most on the slopes and crests to the west of the river.

Many theories have been put forward to explain why people chose to build Stonehenge where they did, including the plausible suggestion that the henge was erected, after long astronomical calculations, at the one latitude where midsummer sunrise and maximum moonset occurred at right angles to each other on the horizon. This is to attach too much importance to Stonehenge. In reality it was seventy-five miles too far north of the exact position: the location for an ideal observatory would have been somewhere in the English Channel. Although astronomical lines were indeed built into Stonehenge it was not astronomical considerations that determined its situation. People built it there because of the presence of the aging long barrows on Salisbury Plain and the more recent cursus only half a mile north of the henge, an area already made sacred by a thousand years of tradition.

What inspired the design of the new enclosure is unclear. The only pottery found was five sherds of Rinyo-Clacton ware, so called because it was first recognized at Rinyo in the Orkneys and at Clacton in Essex. Since then it has frequently been discovered in henges and in some stone circles and it is obvious that its makers must have contributed something towards the idea of these structures. These flat-bottomed vessels have also been called grooved ware, because many of them are decorated with channelled lines, bands and triangles in patterns akin to the art of the Boyne passage-graves, but as the decoration sometimes consists not of grooved but of applied strips of clay and as some other pots are plain the term Rinyo-Clacton seems more appropriate. Quite how these widely spread pots were related to the Irish chambered tombs is not at all certain because they have never been found in those passage-graves and it may have been ideas, rather than architects, from Ireland that influenced the beginnings of Britain's most famous prehistoric monument. Hardly a mile away by the Avon a huge earthwork enclosure at Durrington Walls, put up about the same time, had many large round houses in it. A lot of Rinyo-Clacton ware was found there and it is tempting to believe that this was a settlement in which many of the builders lived.

The countryside around Stonehenge had been widely cleared of forest. Just a few clumps of trees rose among the grassland and bracken where cattle grazed. On a slope falling sharply to the north and less steeply to the east, a round timber hut may have stood around 3000 BC, a mortuary house with a doorway open to the north-east and the midsummer sunrise that shone on the decaying corpses inside.

Whether such a hut, eventually to be surrounded by Stonehenge's bank, ever stood at the centre of the henge is conjectural. Proof could come only from the discovery of its earth-filled postholes but most of these will have been destroyed by the enthusiastic malpractices of earlier diggers: Dr William Harvey, discoverer of the circulation of the blood; the Duke of Buckingham 'out of his real affection to antiquity' who trenched out two holes 'about the bignesse of two sawe-pitts' at the centre of Stonehenge; Thomas Hayward, an eighteenth-century owner of the ring; William Stukeley, antiquarian and Druidomaniac who, on 5 July 1723, removed an area four feet by six feet by one foot deep in front of the Altar Stone; William Cunnington in 1802 who dug 'close to the altar'; and a Captain Beamish who, after a cheerful night in Amesbury around 1839, 'made an excavation somewhere about eight feet square and six feet deep in front of the altar-stone'. Mr Browne, who watched the labourers as they dug up a lot of very modern rabbit bones, 'buried a bottle, containing a record of the excavation'.

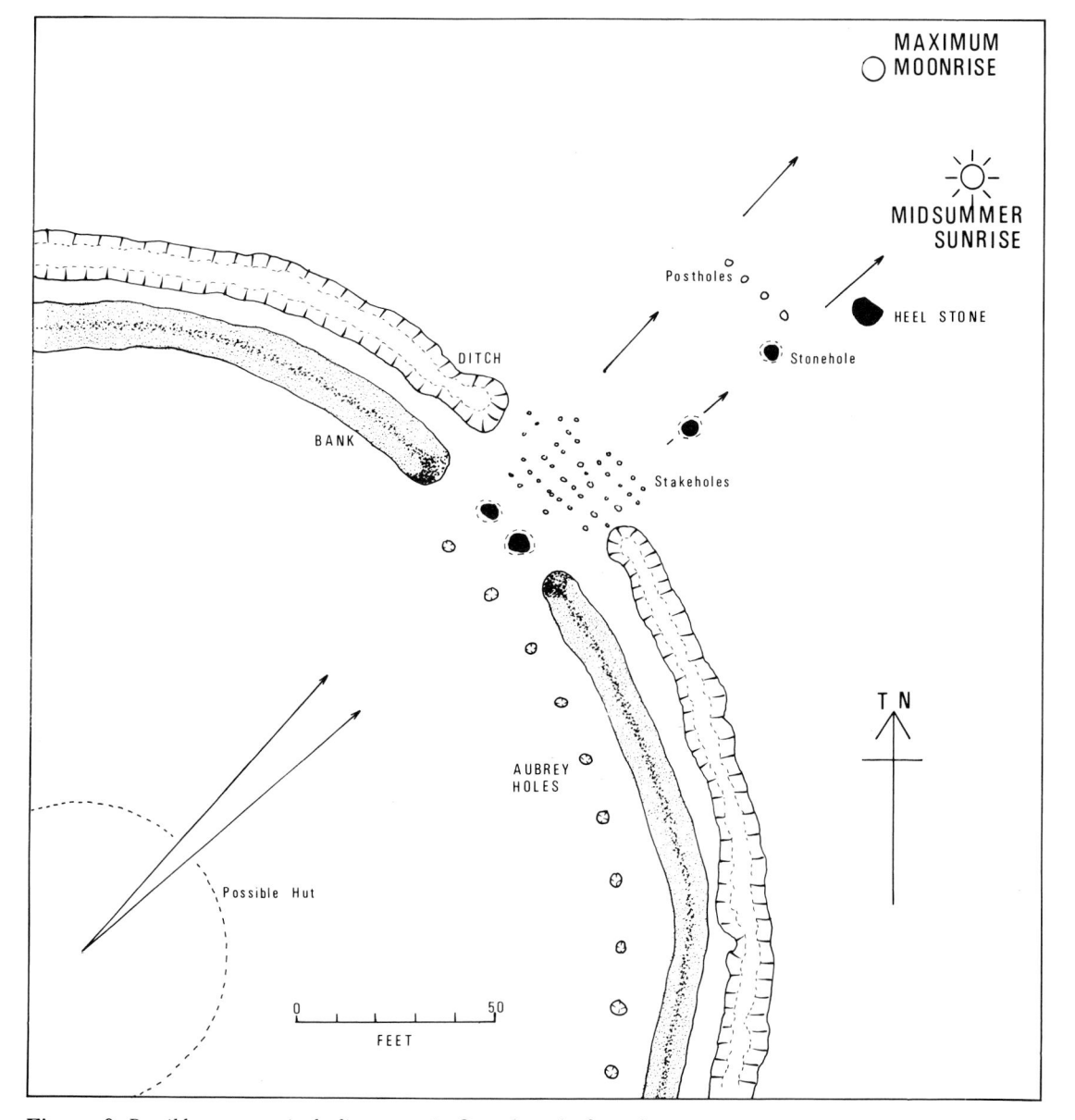

Figure 9 *Possible astronomical alignments in Stonehenge's first phase*

Although skulls of oxen were recovered from these unhelpful pillagings nothing as tenuous as a posthole would have been recognized, let alone recorded, and it is probable that almost every trace of a hut would have been ignorantly hacked away. Just two or three quite big postholes have been located about forty feet south-east of the centre, maybe the traces of a roofed, oak-timbered building the size of the round houses at Durrington Walls.

That it faced north-east is almost certain from the solar and lunar orientations built into Stonehenge, and that it ever existed is made more likely by the fact that to establish these alignments observers would have had to watch the skies at mid-summer and midwinter for years on end, exposed to rain, wind and snow unless a permanent shelter were available.[3] The length of time involved, several generations of those brief lives, once again emphasizes the need these people felt for ritual and safety.

The position on the skyline where the sun rose farthest to the north-east, its midsummer solstice or 'standstill', could easily have been decided within a few years because the solar extremes are constant. A watcher would soon have noticed that during the summer months the sun rose each day a little more to the north until, finally, it appeared behind an inconspicuous hillock on the horizon. For three or four dawns in succession it rose there and then over the following mornings it began moving slowly southwards towards its midwinter rising at the south-east six months later.

This 'mound' position could have been recorded by lining up two posts on it some distance from the hut. Then two massive pillars of the local sarsen, dragged there by the people, were erected like a gunsight on either side of the alignment with a space left between them through which the sun would gleam each midsummer dawn. One of these outlying stones, the Heel Stone, still survives. The unsuspected hole in which the other had stood was discovered in 1979 when a trench for a tele-phone cable nearly cut into it.

Moon observations were much more difficult. Unlike the sun the moon does not have a simple annual cycle but varies in its extreme positions over a period of 18·61 years. One year at midwinter it would rise well up the horizon at the north-north-east but the following year it would not reach as far as that (Fig. 9). Some years later it would be rising no farther north than north-east and, at its minimum extreme, an observer would see it rise near the east-north-east after which, year by year, it would return closer and closer to its maximum north-north-east position, reaching that almost nineteen years after it had last been seen there. Nineteen years was over half a lifetime to most people in the Neolithic and even if someone began to record the erratic movements of the moon when he was only fourteen years of age he might never have lived to see even one cycle completed. Even a man, old beyond normal expectancy, might not have been able to record each rising because in some years rains or mists or low clouds would have obscured the moon. Perhaps accustomed to these lunar vagaries, after centuries of noticing them during the cere-monies held at the long barrows, the people marked each extreme rising that they saw with an upright stake. A single arc of stakes from north-north-east to north-east, rammed into the earth sixty yards from the hut, would signify nearly nineteen years of patient observation. Gaps would show where the moon had been hidden from view by bad weather. At Stonehenge there are six of these arcs, now hidden beneath the grass—fifty-three holes of stakes, accumulated over more than a hundred years, four or five generations—the line at the north-north-east pointing towards the exact midwinter extreme rising of the moon, the other end of the arc terminating at the north-east where it was in line with the midsummer sunrise. It was only then, when the observations were finished, that the henge was built. The stakes were left in the ground and the ditch and the ends of the bank ran up to them. Only when the ditch and bank were complete were four heavier, more durable posts put up near the Heel Stone, lined up on the stakes before those weatherworn poles were withdrawn from the ground.

This tells us something about the purpose of Stonehenge and the other henges with slots and stakeholes at their entrances. It is improbable that any domestic or industrial site would have had such care taken over its construction, and the knowledge that earlier burial monuments on Salisbury Plain were orientated on the moon suggests that funerary rituals were performed inside the henge, bodies left to decompose there and then, when the bones were dry, removed to a funeral pyre. Cremation had become fashionable. This might explain the alignment on the Heel Stone and the sun, and it might also explain the deposits of human bone that have been discovered inside Stonehenge. What it does not explain is the fact that when the people gouged out the ditch with their antler picks and heaped the bank up along its inner edge they left a gap not only at the entrance but also exactly at the south, a cardinal position already noticed among the earthen long barrows of Wessex, and the place in the sky where the sun and moon always reached their highest. One wonders whether it was through this minor entrance that dead bodies were carried.

Professor Alexander Thom, whose researches into the mathematical and geometrical abilities of these primitive societies have stimulated archaeologists to reassess some of their opinions about neolithic communities, observed that cardinal positions were marked elsewhere at Stonehenge. 'Since the position of the first Aubrey Hole is 3·7° from geographical north ... the North point is very nearly midway between two holes and ... all the cardinal points and the four intermediate points (north-east, south-east, etc.) lie midway between holes.'[4] It seems that the henge was no crudely piled-up earthwork but one nicely laid out by people who were aware of precisely what they wished to integrate into its design. This included the pits known as the Aubrey Holes.

They were named after John Aubrey who first noticed these weed-grown 'cavities', fifty-six roughly circular pits around the inside of the bank. It can hardly be more than a huge coincidence that there were fifty-six earthen long barrows on Salisbury Plain, from Brixton Deverill in the west, Shalbourne in the north, Figheldean in the east and Fussell's Lodge at the south, all within eighteen miles of the henge, no more than two days' walking even for the farthest family.[5] It is possible that each Aubrey Hole was the token of an individual group, but what is certain is that these were not graves in which the cremated bones of a relative had been reverently buried. The holes varied in size and depth, and some lacked any burnt bone at all, but all of them had been dug out and then almost immediately backfilled with chalk that was rammed and packed down as though sealing something in the soil. Later the holes were redug and this time earth, some of it burnt, charcoal and ash, scorched bone pins, flints, fire-marked antlers and human cremations were buried, one with a little ball of chalk, others with unburned animal bones. Obviously, the people had reopened the holes, placed cremations there and then filled them with the swept-up remains of pyres, putting in the debris with bones from feasts or from totem

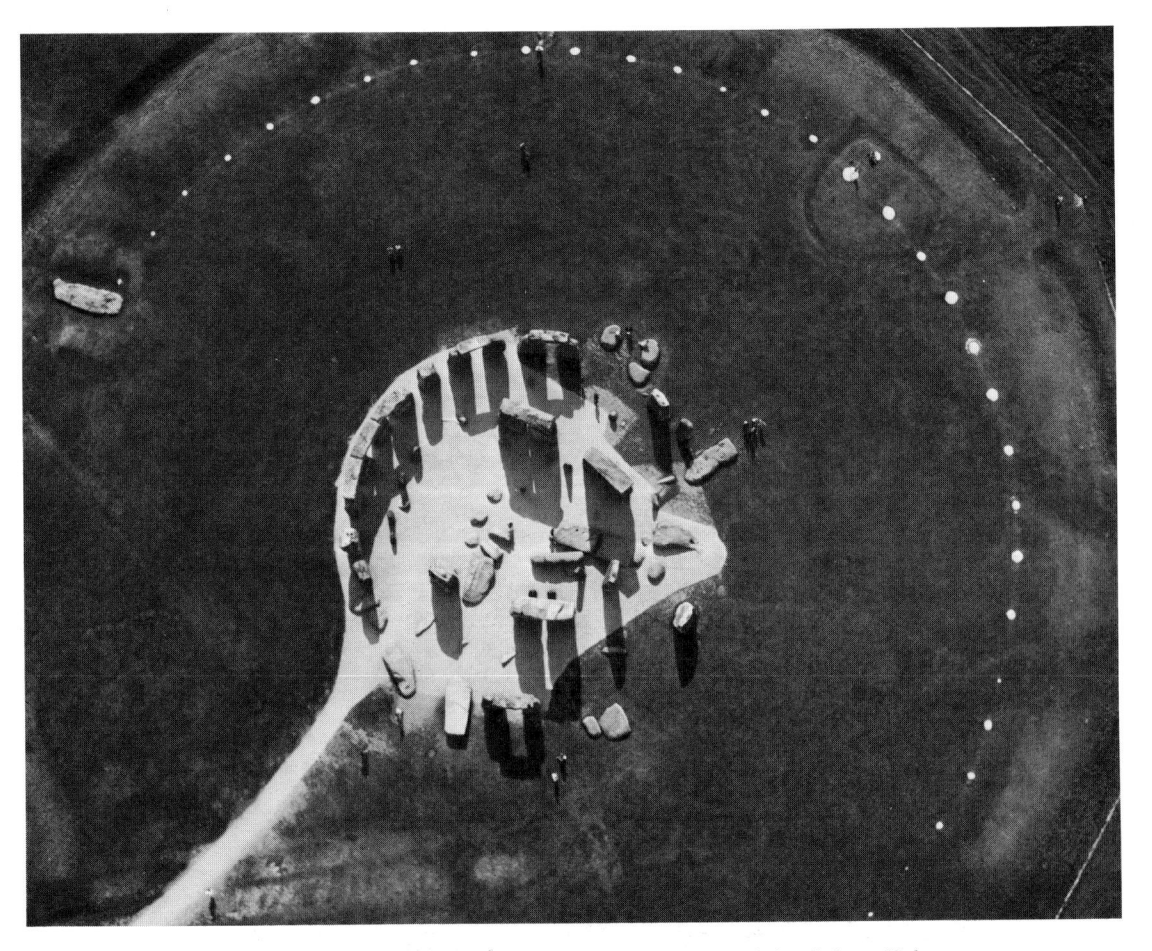

39 *In this aerial view of Stonehenge the white tops of the Aubrey Holes are very conspicuous. The blank area on the left has not been excavated. The fallen Slaughter Stone on the extreme left lies at the entrance through the ditch and bank of the henge*

animals and with fertility objects such as the chalk ball or fingerlength rods of flint that may have had phallic significance. Other cremations were buried in the ditch, at south, south-east and north-east, most of them small and incomplete, 'perhaps of children'. One of them had a lovely macehead, perforated for a handle, shaped like a cushion out of beautifully striped stone from Scotland.

Stonehenge was not a cemetery. Offerings rather than burials were left there. Had there been no more than two hundred and fifty people using the henge—and the number is likely to have been far greater—they could have expected to suffer ten deaths each year and at least five thousand between the time that the henge was built and the years when the Beaker people came to it, changing its architecture. Yet hardly fifty cremations have been found. The same is true of other henges with pits and cremations. There were ten pits outside the entrance to Maxey where the carved antler and bone lay. There were seven in an arc at Cairnpapple near Edin-

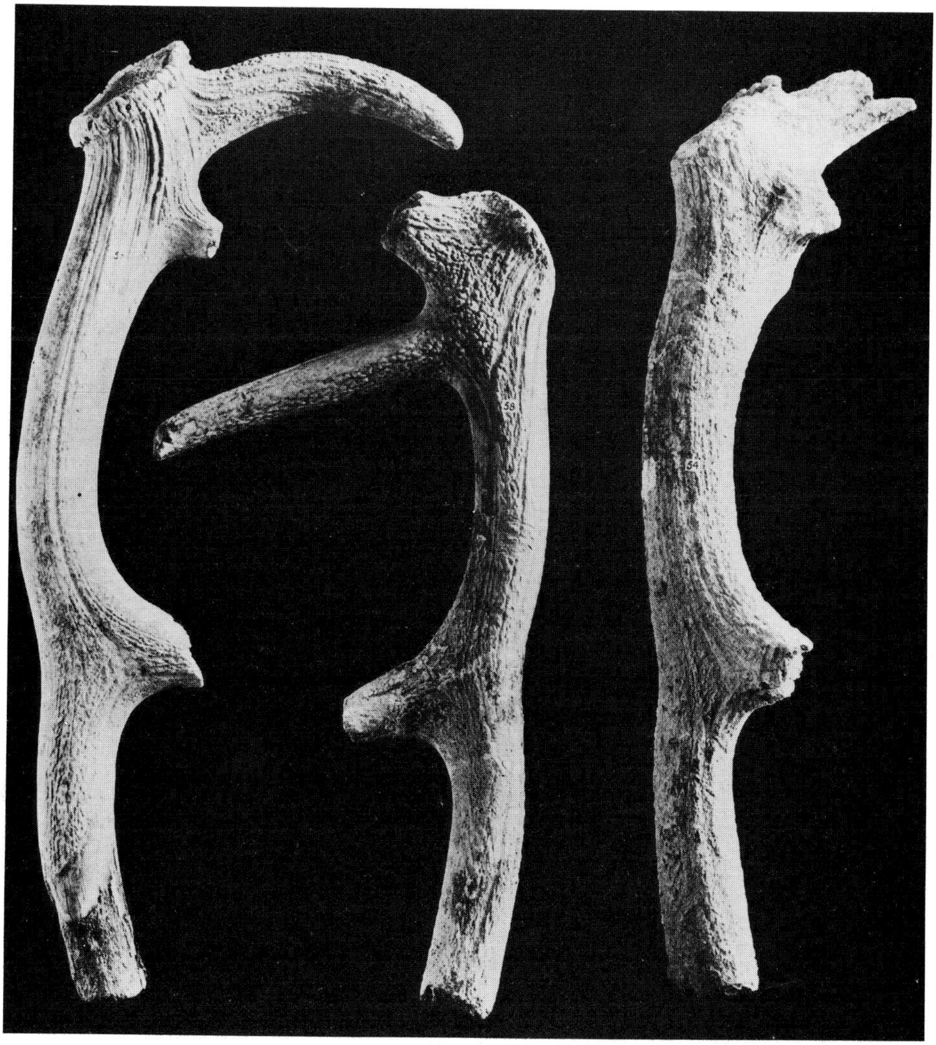

40   *Antler picks from Maumbury Rings henge, Dorset. The tine or branch of the one on the right has been worn down through quarrying*

burgh and with the cremations there were two broken stone axes and a burnt bone pin like those from Stonehenge, 'killed' things buried with ancestral bones that were to live in the henge like mediums between the living and the Other-World. At Llandegai near Anglesey, a henge very like Stonehenge with its external ditch, five pits were arranged in a tiny circle right outside the entrance and, like the stones that guarded the entrances to chambered tombs and long barrows, a small pillar stood in one of them. There may be a more sinister implication in the cremation of a small child in one pit exactly on the axis of the entrance. Sacrifice is feasible. Child burials, strangely treated, were quite frequent in this part of Wales during the Bronze Age, and in Wessex there was a very unpleasant offering of a child at Woodhenge.

41   *A photograph from Sir George Gray's excavation showing the extraordinary depth of the shafts at Maumbury Rings henge. The diggers may have been reaching down to the spirits of the Under-World. Such pits were dug with the simplest of tools (see Plates 12 and 40)*

There has been much astronomical debate about the number of pits at Stonehenge and claims have been made that the fifty-six Aubrey Holes were used to compute the moon's 18·61-year cycle and to predict eclipses by moving markers from one pit to another each year. Yet the number may be fortuitous. It is not repeated in any other henge with pit-cremations, nor can the forty-five shafts at Maumbury Rings near Dorchester have been used for celestial calculations. These pits seem designed for communication with the spirit-world but not for any form of celestial astronomy.

These dedications to the generative powers of the earth were even more obvious at Maumbury Rings, a henge with a colossal bank.[6] Here the people had fanatically delved forty-five precipitous and tapering pits through the bottom of the ditch, some of them thirty-five feet deep and then just as other people had backfilled the Aubrey Holes at Stonehenge, tipped chalk rubble back into them, halfway up their sides. Into these partly filled holes the people put a carefully chosen assortment of objects. Near the bottom there were everyday things, tools of stone and bone, but higher up there were offerings, often burnt, of broken Rinyo-Clacton ware, antlered stag skulls, jaw bones of pigs, carved chalk tablets and grooved blocks, a little drum, plain but not unlike those from Folkton, and a thick chalk phallus laid near the stag's skull. All this the people meticulously concealed under layers of chalk. It was only higher still, covered with tumble from the shafts' sides as they weathered away, that fragments of human skull lay, bits from the forehead and the back of the head, the pathetic remnants of ancestors that had been carried to the consecrated henge for the rituals of intercession there. It is likely that the people of Stonehenge had also brought human bones to their own temple.

Yet in both these henges people had followed the old traditions. Both had pairs of stones flanking their entrances like the portals of chambered tombs, both may have had outlying pillars in the manner of the forecourt stones at Cairnholy, at the Tinglestone in Gloucestershire, and the vast long mounds in Brittany, facing cardinal points. Both contained pits with dedicatory offerings that accompanied the dead in the earlier barrows, both had alignments in them towards the rising of the moon or the sun, although at Maumbury Rings the entrance may have faced only the extreme rising of the moon. In these sacred enclosures the sun and moon were parts of the cosmology of a people who still looked to the earth for protection, handling the dead bones and the skulls of ancestors in the warm days of summer and the frozen nights of midwinter.

Henges were built in many other places, but in the highlands and on the rock-strewn shores of lakes and islands people raised rings of stone, often with features similar to those of the henges. Here, also, were entrances, ditches, outlying stones and relics of death.[7] It is noticeable how much of the interior was left open in the henges, and only rarely did anything more than a small cairn hinder the free movement of people in the earliest stone circles. These marvellous sites—for we do still marvel at them—with their muscular pillars, carry secrets that only whisper by whisper are being prised from them. They lie, quiet and ruined, near older neolithic monuments, large open rings with the merest hint of a worn-down bank that formed a barrier around the stones, low lying in valleys near rivers and streams, and from them have been unearthed the scanty remains of fires, a few broken tools and pots, and slivers of burnt human bone. Some of their stones were aligned on the sun or moon, and methodical examination of their architecture reveals that very often lines towards the cardinal points, north–south or east–west, were built into them. Seemingly plain and uncomplicated, these circles, with no complex geometry in their planning, tease the mind with questions that may never be answered.

If these were ritual centres it seems improbable that we can ever reconstruct their function correctly. In the remote Pacific, twelve hundred miles off Australia, stone circles and avenues of standing stones were erected on islands in the New Hebrides, the natives of Vao and Malekula setting up pillars that embodied the spirits of the dead and of the living, spirits that were essential participants in the labyrinthine dances of death and rebirth within the rings. These headhunters had some things in common with our own New Stone Age ancestors. Living in a semi-barbarous state they made polished stone implements much as our neolithic forefathers did, they were agriculturalists, they kept domestic animals, they performed rituals of their creation myth in rings of great stones.

We cannot, however, expect any close correlation between the ceremonies that took place on the other side of the world, four thousand years later than our own rings, and the rites once to be seen at Avebury, the Rollright Stones or Callanish in the Hebrides. Once we enter the world of symbolic thinking we are faced with tremendous problems of interpretation because the choice of alternatives is so wide.

Often, we cannot be certain whether the ceremonies were held in darkness or daylight, whether they were concerned with water, whether there were offerings of flowers, fruits or cereals. We do know that fire was essential in many of the rituals, but we are not sure whether the rings were designed for the use of dancers, the enactment of myth or for the initiation of the young, although we have hints of the answers.

There are traces of fires on Dartmoor, at Fernworthy, Brisworthy and the Grey Wethers, and at the Stripple Stones on Bodmin Moor. There may also be half-lost remembrance of fertility activities in some of the legends attached to rings such as Stall Moor, sometimes called 'Kiss-in-the-Ring'; or Stanton Drew, nicknamed the 'Weddings'; or at Er Lannic in Brittany where barren wives would rub themselves against the potent stones. There are suggestions of dancing in the names given to the rings: the Trippet Stones on Bodmin Moor, reputedly maidens turned to stone for dancing on the Sabbath; at Stanton Drew where the avenue stones are known as the Fiddlers; at Stall Moor again, known as the Dancers; at the Hurlers in Cornwall where a pair of outlying stones are called the Pipers; at the Merry Maidens with their own Pipers. Other Pipers are to be found in Co. Kildare at the Broadleas ring. Even as far north as the bleak Shetlands there is an irregular ring named Haltadans, the 'limping dance', and in the same area are other cairn-circles, the Fiddlers Crus (crus, according to a native of Shetland, 'being stone circles where young girls danced and made merry'). Almost unbelievably, being so far from the regions of other stone circles from which such folklore may have spread, there are also 'superstitious

42 *The paired stone circles of the Grey Wethers, Dartmoor. Traces of fire have been found inside them*

stories such as "That the stones were those who had been dancing who were caught by the rising sun"'. There are other legends in Britain of stones that are supposed to move at midnight or dawn, and it is worth recalling that Stonehenge has been known as Choir Gaur, the Giants' Dance. There is a drawing in the sixth edition of William Camden's *Britannia* showing the stones in semi-human form.

Stone circles present many problems. At first it seems impossible to tell whether they were for one, several or many people; for a family or a kinship group; for a tribe; for men or women or both; whether their ceremonies were seasonal or annual. We wonder exactly what the symbolism was behind the scattering of quartz fragments in many Neolithic and Bronze Age burials and in the recumbent stone circles of Scotland. At Gortcorbies, a small and late concentric circle in northern Ireland, people had lit a great fire inside the ring, throwing branches of oak, willow and hazel into the flames around the carcases of pigs, sheep and oxen, flints strewn around them, the black soot and ashes swirling in the air and settling thickly over the circle.[8] When the fire died down the men and women constructed a cist of slabs near the middle of the ring and filled it with fine soil which they also spread all over the interior of the ring, a statement of their need for fertile earth, covering their offerings of animal bones and flints in a rite of sympathetic magic.

Later people heaped up a cairn with a central cist across the perimeter of the outer circle. In it they placed several pots, one a tiny food vessel. Inside this they heaped up a pyramid of seven pebbles around an upright stone whose sharp point projected above the rim. Around the pot they scattered fragments of white quartz.

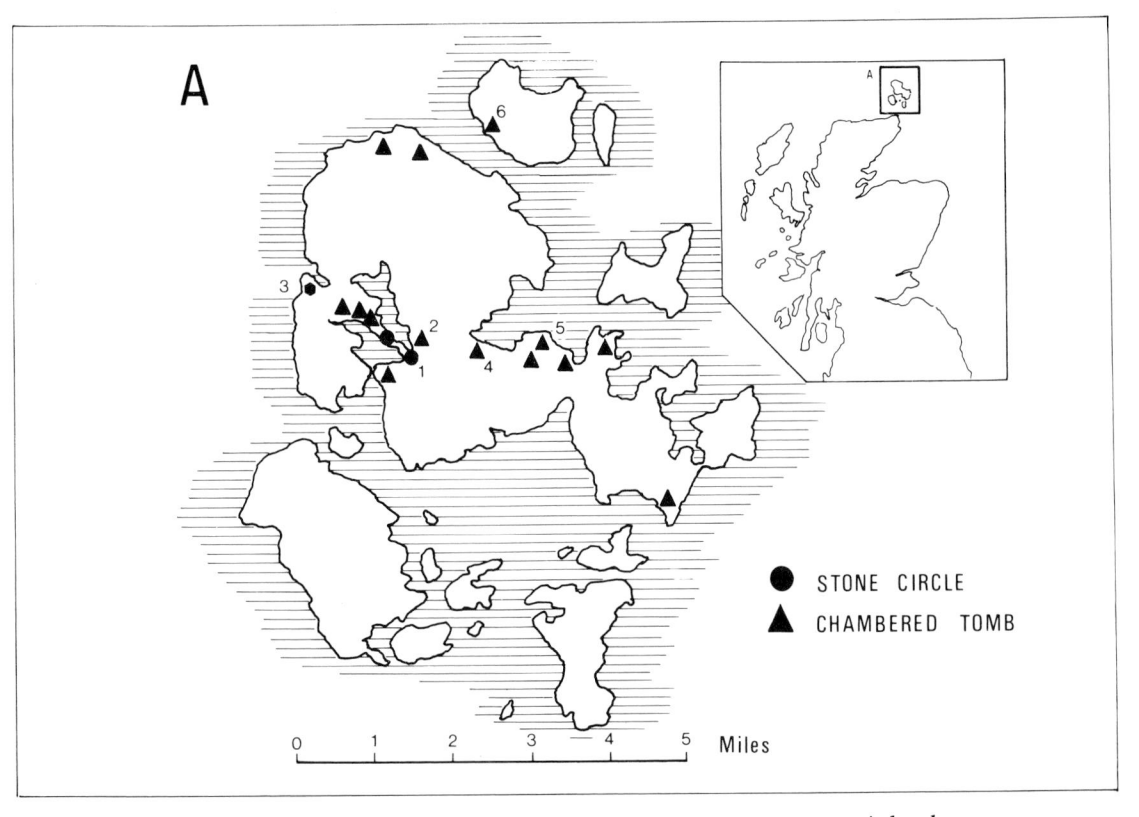

Figure 10 *Stone circles and chambered tombs on Orkney mainland:*
1 Stenness circle-henge, HY306125; 2 Maes Howe passage-grave, HY317127; 3
Skara Brae village, HY230187; 4 Cuween passage-grave, HY364127; 5
Quanterness passage- grave, HY417129; 6 Mid Howe stalled cairn, Rousay,
HY371306

Fire, quartz, soil, animal bones recur time and again in the British stone circles. Although we are mystified by the exact nature of the rites we can reconstruct some of the ceremonies more particularly than some pessimists fear by looking at one of the earliest of them, the Standing Stones of Stenness in the Orkneys. The ancestors of the builders had lived on the islands for centuries and an understanding of their traditions illuminates the rituals that were performed in the stone circle. There are neolithic settlements on the Orkneys, the sand-covered Rinyo, the early houses on the Holm of Papa Westray whose plans are duplicated in the stalled cairns as houses of the dead, and only six miles west of Stenness is the famous Skara Brae with its stone furnishings and reeking, worm-writhing middens whose contents have told us so much about the food and livelihoods of the inhabitants of the village.

Thirty or forty people lived here, using tools of bone and stone, storing grain in bowls of Rinyo-Clacton ware, seven or eight families of leather-clad peasants who kept cattle, some sheep, a few pigs, who fished, hunted, lived as best they could off the miserly land. The Orkneys were almost treeless in prehistoric times, as they are today, low and undulating islands of heather moorland, blown by ceaseless

43   *The stone-built furniture inside Hut 7 at Skara Brae, Orkney Mainland. Stone-slabbed beds stand on either side of the central hearth. In 1928 two skeletons were found under the right-hand bed, both of old women who had suffered from arthritis*

winds that permitted only rare hot days. Although the rainfall was never high it came most heavily at the very time of year when the crops had almost ripened so that the harvest was always endangered. It was an uncertain world in which the families of Skara Brae and the other islanders lived. Inevitably, many of them died young as the bones from Quanterness will show.

The tombs on the Orkneys are especially rich in their revelation of the rituals enacted in them, and by good fortune there were a few centuries when the settlements, the aging tombs and the new stone circle were in use together (Fig. 11). It is possible to take the evidence from Skara Brae and from stalled cairns such as Mid Howe to bring light not only to some of the rites that took place in the ring of Stenness but also to show how these ceremonies were derived from traditions that were already many centuries old. The tombs are wonders of prehistory. Many of them have been reconstructed and the visitor can stoop along passages, peer into cells, stare up into the darkness of a tall, vaulted roof and touch the stone benches where the dead were laid thousands of years ago.[9]

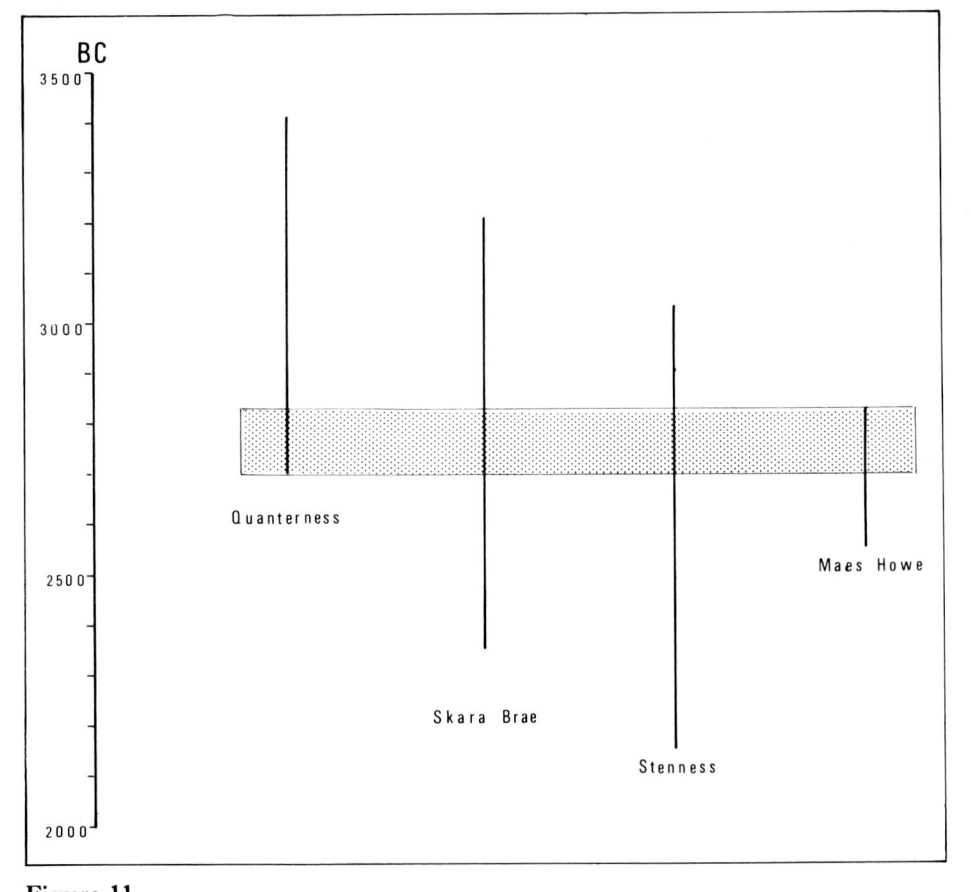

Figure 11

Carbon-14 dates from the neolithic Orkneys. A diagram to show how chambered tombs, Stenness stone circle and Skara Brae village were in use together around 2800 BC. The line from each site indicates for how long the monument may have been in existence. The stippled rectangle illustrates the period of overlap

On Orkney Mainland most of these tombs belonged to the Maes Howe group with passages leading to a central chamber, its corbelled roof a triumph of architecture and beneath which, in the sides of the chamber, are small cells that remind one of the plans of Irish passage-graves. It may have been settlers from the south who brought the concept of such transepted tombs to the island, journeying sporadically northwards, working their way up the Atlantic coasts towards the Orkneys.

The tombs on the outlying islands, however, were quite different, obviously the handiwork of settlers from northern Scotland who divided the long passage into stalls by means of upright slabs jutting from the drystone walls. Their ancestors had built the passage-grave of Round Camster in Caithness with its layers of broken, scorched bones over which there were undamaged skeletons, two of them propped upright in the passage.

Customs intermingled. Six miles east of Stenness the floor of the Maes Howe

4 *Duddo Four Stones circle, Northumberland*

5 *Poulnabrone dolmen, Co. Clare*

6 *Dowth passage-grave, Co. Meath: stone basin*

44   *The projecting slabs of Unstan stalled cairn, Orkney Mainland*

tomb of Quanterness was buried under an eighteen-inch-thick pile of fire-crackled, smashed bones, earth, stones and charcoal, the bones of some four hundred men, women and children, nearly all of whom had died before they were thirty years of age.[10] This was a family tomb. Quanterness was used for at least a thousand years, from about 3400 to 2400 BC, and with five short-lived generations to a century a group of ten people would have produced just such a number of deaths. Yet in other Maes Howe tombs such as Cuween there were no broken bones—they had probably been cleared away—and instead there was an emphasis upon skulls and animal bones. There were five skulls on the chamber floor together with the skulls of twenty-four dogs, just as in the cairn of Burray, where the seven stalls each had the skeleton of a dog in it, the stall facing the passage also containing 'the skull of an animal with horns about nine inches long'. Here there seems to be very much the same interest in ancestral bones and animal totems that has been perceived in the long mounds of southern England.

    On Rousay, the island half a mile north of the Mainland across Eynhallow Sound, there were thirteen cairns, each apparently in a family territory of a square mile or so of good arable soil. No tomb, however, was built conveniently on this farmland because it seems the builders were not bothered about it being close to their settlement. They were far more concerned that it should stand close to the sea, at the head of a steep slope from which it could be seen for a good distance.[11] As a conspicuous landmark it was a statement both that the land was owned and that the territory was guarded by the powerful spirits of the dead who themselves lay near the waters over which their own ancestors had passed on their way to the island.

One of the cairns, Mid Howe, close by a coastline of black, sea-wet rocks, had an immense range of twenty-four stalls, some of them with stone benches on which unburnt skeletons were laid, three of them with skulls set upright against the other bones. Fifteen other individuals lay near them or underneath the shelves. Only six had skulls. On the Holm of Papa Westray, the skulls of six skeletons were removed from the tomb. When they were returned the people put them down some distance from their skeletons.

This surely is evidence of an ancestor cult. It is difficult to explain the removal and return of skulls unless this was done in the belief that the people would be able to communicate with their ancestors if certain rites were performed with these skulls outside the tombs. The families appear also to have had totems. The twenty-four dogs at Cuween suggest this as do the remains of twenty-four sheep as well as some oxen, deer, gannet, cormorant and a pink-footed goose at Blackhammer. Some of them, like the revolting concoction at Barclodiad y Gawres, must have been inedible. One could explain away as the remains of funeral feasts the ox and sheep bones found at Mid Howe, even perhaps the bream, wrasse and the heap of limpet shells for bait, but it would have been a desperate community that chewed the oily and tough skua, cormorant and guillemot, and only the starving could have fancied the scrawny flesh of buzzard, eagle, gannet and crow whose bones also lay in the tomb. Some of the birds may have flown in by accident but this would not account for the indigestible otter found a quarter of a mile from the sea in the cairn at Lower Dounreay. Nor could feasting have been the reason why a pigeon's egg was placed under the armpit of one skeleton at Mid Howe. The most likely explanation for such a variety of bones is that the people named each other after animals as American Indians did—Swift Running Horse, White Eagle, He Who Swims Like a Fish—each person with his own totem that was taken with him to the grave. Other evidence from the Orkneys—the little whalebone dishes holding red, yellow and blue pigments found in the houses at Skara Brae—suggests that the inhabitants painted their faces in patterns of magic for their ceremonies, much as American Indians did, and it is likely they they had totemistic beliefs similar to those of the Indians.

In later centuries the tombs, side-celled or stalled, became shrines for the same reasons as the long mounds of the south, erected by people whose existence was just as hard and brief. The men and women at Cuween had suffered from arthritis. So had the family at Mid Howe whose teeth, moreover, were worn down and infected. It was people like these—short, lightly built, long headed, respectful of ancestors, their clan identity and kinship expressed through totems, some of them living in

45   *The sidestones of the long chamber in Blackhammer stalled cairn, Rousay, Orkneys. As well as human bones, sheep, ox, red deer, gannet, cormorant and pink-footed goose were found in this tomb*

the snug and gloomy village of Skara Brae—who raised the tall stones of Stenness.

The location was dramatic. Here, around 3000 BC, on a plain that had once been cultivated but where weeds and grass now reached down to a thin neck of land between two lochs, twelve slim pillars of sandstone were dragged upright in a perfect circle perhaps thirty-six body-yards across.[12] These were elegant slabs, split from the laminated flagstone of a distant quarry, stones twenty feet or more in length but so slender that a score of people could have put them up before turning even more obsessively to the task of digging out a wide ditch around the ring, over a man's height into the solid bedrock beneath the turf. Technical data can be tedious yet when stating the religious compulsions of prehistoric people it is worth noting how much effort they went to, splitting, levering and lifting twelve hundred tons of sandstone at Stenness to make a bank outside this ditch which was not perfectly circular but was a ring of straightish arcs, presumably the segments allocated to different families to dig out. There were thirteen tombs on Orkney. Even if every one of them was still being used as a shrine by a family, and if every family had been able to send as many as five able-bodied workers to Stenness, the construction of the ditch and bank, and the quarrying, transportation and erection of the stones must have taken them at least three months of continuous, exhausting labour before the circle-henge and its internal settings were completed.

This was organized work. By the Late Neolithic, as families banded together for greater security and for communal ceremonies, even if there were not yet chieftains there were most probably headmen, the forerunners of the leaders and priests of the Early Bronze Age, richer, more powerful than other men, ready to plan the work and provide food and shelter for the workers. It was probably under the guidance of such a man that the people built the temple of Stenness. They left a single entrance at the north. Just inside it they put up a broad stone with two others in front of it in an arrangement like the two sideslabs and backstone of a stalled chamber before the drystone walls were built.

In the south of Britain three-sided settings like the one at Arbor Low are known as Coves and were, probably, imitations of the burial chamber in the megalithic tombs of the Peak District and Wessex.[13] There were others at Avebury and at Stanton Drew in Somerset, both circles that were put up in areas where there were so many tombs with stone-built chambers that it would have been natural for later people to imitate them. A drawing by William Stukeley of the embanked circle of Meinigwyr in south-west Wales shows just such a 'Cove' to its north (Fig. 12). The fact that we do not now know whether he had drawn the ruined chamber of a megalithic tomb or a Late Neolithic free-standing Cove only makes the connection all the more firm. In the same way, the Cove at Stenness was probably a representation of a burial stall in an Orkney tomb, erected for traditional funerary ceremonies that would now take place in the open. Several hundreds of years later it may have been replaced by a little wooden mortuary house.

Beyond this Cove or 'chamber', which faced eastwards, two other stones stood. Beyond them, a short stretch of paving led to the centre of the stone circle where the people had set out a rectangle of four thin slabs, laid flat, around an area where

46   *The end of the rock-cut ditch at Stenness circle-henge, Orkney Mainland*
   (*see Plate 12*)

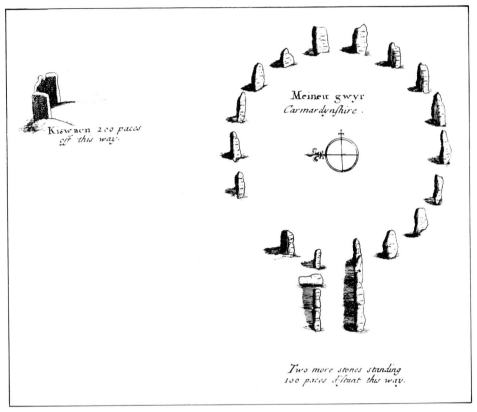

Figure 12 *A drawing of Meini-gwyr by William Stukeley*

a tall post stood. Just as the setting near the entrance resembled a stalled chamber so this rectangle looked very like the hearths in the Skara Brae houses.

If these architectural features were all that survived at Stenness one might speak rather despairingly and vaguely of funerary rituals that included the use of fire, admitting reluctantly that little more could be said. Fortunately, there was more. The meticulous excavations by Graham Ritchie in 1973 and 1974 recovered much material from the ditch and from the interior of the ring which makes it possible to flesh out the scraped architecture of the stones. At the west, the ditch was found to contain decayed thistles, weeds, buttercups and nettles mixed with twigs and with bones of wolf, dog, foot bones of oxen and jaw bones of calf and young ox. Above them, when soil had begun dribbling down the sides of the ditch, people had dropped two human bones and some burnt animal bones. Nearer the entrance, sherds of a Rinyo-Clacton ware bowl lay alongside the teeth of an ox. Above them, in the weathered silt, were dog and cattle bones, two human hand bones and an arm bone. On the other side of the causeway were more burnt animal bones and a slate disc, its edges chipped like those other discs found with human burials. From the middle of the stone circle, in the 'hearth', were even more burnt animal bones, black earth, charcoal, little scraps of Rinyo-Clacton ware and small flint flakes. No fire had burned here; the stones were not reddened or cracked. Over this deposit of 'killed' things was a thin and rotted layer of what may have been seaweed. Outside the circle-henge, in line with the entrance, was a tall stone put up on a rise in the ground, with a head-sized hole at knee height through it. In Viking times it was called the Hole of Woden, significantly the god of death, and for a long time in Orkney this perforated outlier was known as Odin's Stone.

Although the rituals at Stenness cannot be recovered with certainty an imaginative reconstruction can be attempted which does not distort or omit any of the facts. Even the realization that several different interpretations are possible does not excuse the archaeologist from a duty to enliven the stones and the artefacts with people, a reincarnation controlled by the known facts. Without people history is no more than a compendium of annals and rolls, and without people prehistory is little more than stones and sterile statistics. Despite the cautionary advice of that great prehistorian, Gordon Childe, that 'Motives are in fact hardly capable of genuine historical study', it is as well to remember what another great prehistorian, Mortimer Wheeler, wrote about archaeologists that 'Too often we dig up mere things, unrepentantly forgetful that our proper aim is to dig up people'. All that our ethics and principles demand is that we should be 'content to do what we can with the material vouchsafed to us, in full consciousness of its incompleteness'.

47   *Five sandstone pillars, two of them broken, of Stenness circle-henge. Inside them is the Cove, its rear slab fallen backwards*

Let us imagine, then, families approaching Stenness at the appointed time of year, men, women and children, carrying bundles of bones collected together from the skeletons of disinterred corpses—skulls, mandibles, long bones—carrying also the skulls of totem animals, herding a beast that was one of several to be slaughtered for the feasting that would accompany the ceremonies. On the night of the full moon over a hundred people assembled around the hillock where the outlying stone stood. Beyond it, directly south through the henge entrance and silhouetted against the moon, they could see the tall post at the centre of the ring, and when at last the moon was at its highest in the sky, shining above the post, they passed the wrapped human bones through the hole in the outlier, bundle by bundle, chanting spells to bring life back to the dead.

It was a ritual symbolizing the withdrawal of the body from the earth, animating the clean, washed bones that were now free of their corroding flesh, preparing the ancestral spirits for the rites that were to follow. The people, faces painted, squatted around the stone, their finest, soft leather clothes patterned with symbols of moon, sun, life and death. It was the first, formalized act of a pageant of mimes, dances and incantations that lasted for nights. Four thousand years later legends persisted of the curative powers of this holed stone. 'If when they are young, they pass their head through this stone, they will never shake with palsy in their old age', just as other holed stones were supposed to cure children of rickets.

Significantly, the stone also had lunar associations. Early in the eighteenth century, John Toland in his *Critical History of the Celtic Religion* said the natives called Stenness the Temple of the Moon. A far older story about a Viking recorded that 'For nine moons, at midnight, when the moon was full, he went nine times on his bare knees around the Odin Stone of Stainness. And for nine months, at full moon, he looked through the hole in the Odin Stone . . .', hoping for a vision of the future. Nine years was the time it took the moon to pass from its maximum to its minimum risings and settings, a journey known and probably imitated in dance around the ancestor-stone, which no longer exists today. Having survived, hallowed and visited, for five thousand years it was utterly smashed by a tenant farmer less than two hundred years ago.

After the bones had been symbolically disinterred they were taken to the 'burial chamber' in the same way that excarnated bones had been taken to the chambered tombs. One can visualize an excited procession, torches flaming, carrying them through the entrance into the sacred enclosure, putting them down in the Cove, and it was at this time that animal bones and the stone disc were laid with them as offerings had always been made. The funeral rites that followed are lost forever but there would have come the moment when the skulls were to be removed, leaving the other bones behind, and this was when the dead could be angered if every action and every word were not ritually perfect.

Some people carried the skulls. Others took bags filled with the broken things and the sweepings of hearths and cooking fires that were to be offered to the spirits of the Other-World. All were taken along the paving to the central hearth, the great stones of the circle black in the moonlight around the people as they scattered the flints, the sherds and the charcoal around the post.

The Orkneys are islands of stone and trees are scarce. It would have been easier to find a pillar of sandstone than to seek out and drag a log, probably of driftwood, from the seashore, and we can only guess that wood was chosen because it could be carved and because human and animal skulls could be suspended from it. This was the place of spirits, of ancestors and totems, the offerings placed around them, and it was now that the people spread seaweed over the hearth, asking for good soil and good harvests in a land where the growing of food was hard.

Seaweed had medicinal properties. It could also be used as fodder for animals that would otherwise have starved in the winter. Even today on North Ronaldsay, an island only forty miles north-east of Stenness, sheep are fed exclusively on it. Probably it was most valued by neolithic farmers for its marvellous enrichment of the soil, improving good earth when allowed to rot into it and, more miraculously still, producing crops where nothing had ever grown before. Mixed with sand or sandy soil it could even be spread over bare rock to make 'lazy beds' of rich and fruitful compost. When laid over the broken things inside the rectangle, a totem pole looming over them, so magical a plant imbued the rites with great power, and the spirit of any skull set down on it within the sacred hearth would surely be awakened, attentive to the pleas and incantations of the living. Dancing and chanting as each offering was set down, the names of ancestors recited and their virtues praised, the people circled the post with its leprous-white skulls.

It is possible that they also mated inside the circle in the expectation that the fertilizing of human beings would, by sympathetic magic, encourage the earth to be fruitful also. As late as Victorian times, every New Year's Day, young people gathered at Stenness bringing food with them, and for four or five days they would dance and eat in the church. Meetings like this often led to betrothals and 'The parties agreed stole from the rest of their companions, and went to the Temple of the Moon' where they made promises of marriage to each other. From the circle they went to the holed stone, the Stone of Odin, holding hands through it, a ceremony 'so very sacred ... that the person who dared to break the engagements made here was considered infamous and excluded all society'. Frequently, it is said, after this troth-making at the stone the man and girl 'proceeded to Consummation without further Ceremony'.

For how many centuries the rites of fertility continued is unknowable but even late in the Iron Age people were coming to the stone circle. Beyond the hearth several little pits had been dug. They contained nuts, twigs, fruits, cereals, grain and broken pottery, offerings derived from the same belief in homeopathic magic held by the earlier Neolithic society. Charcoal from one pit gave a date of AD 519 ± 150, only a few decades before St Augustine landed in Kent, bringing with him zealous missionaries who were to preach with passion against these pagan customs.

When the ceremonies were done the people returned to their homes, taking the bones with them to be placed in the family tombs. Some bones, overlooked, rotted in the grass or were scavenged by animals, others were thrown into the ditch, but there was never a skull with them. For hundreds of years the assemblies continued at Stenness. One by one the old passage-graves and stalled cairns were closed, their passages blocked with stones and rubble. A new chambered tomb was built, for the whole community but in which, maybe, the bones of headmen, the leaders and priests, were placed.

Only three-quarters of a mile east of Stenness, erected there three hundred years after the stone circle had been built, Maes Howe is one of the wonders of the prehistoric world. This magnificent passage-grave, set on a low platform, enclosed inside an oval, rock-cut ditch, is incomparable in its combination of graceful architecture and ritual symbolism.[14] Under its round barrow, composed of neat layers of peat, clay and stones, all held securely in place by concealed walls, the long passage led to a high, corbelled chamber whose corners were buttressed by strong but well-proportioned pillars. Small side cells, hip high from the floor, contained the bones of the dead before Vikings pulled the blocking stones to the floor in their search for treasure. Even after this despoliation a fragment of a human skull and some horse bones and teeth remained for the excavators of 1861 to find, simple evidence that the traditional rites of ancestors and of totemism were practised here in this late prodigy of megalithic tomb-building.

Maes Howe was prodigious, and it was different. Unlike almost any other neolithic tomb in the British Isles its passage faced south-west, a direction which was to become more popular in the Bronze Age when many of the Irish wedge-graves were directed towards the west and the setting of the sun and moon. As a group, only the Clava Cairns of Inverness-shire shared this interest in the western sky with Maes Howe. The reason may have come from a fusion of creeds. If it is true that the builders of the long mounds looked towards the moon in their rituals and that the people of the Irish passage-graves looked towards the sun then a compromise would have had to be accepted unless the cults were to remain separate and hostile, something which does not seem to have happened in the Orkneys where the intermarriage of families led to the mingling of passage-grave and stalled cairn rituals. The solution may have been simple. Only rarely was the moon visible during the day but the sun, at its setting, could be seen, burning and resplendent, in the western sky as night and the moon were entering the world. To build a monument with an entrance towards the west permitted both sun and moon to be seen by the dead within a few hours of each other, reconciling beliefs, merging them into a creed acceptable to the larger societies of the Early Bronze Age.

As long ago as 1893 Magnus Spence suggested that people had aligned the entrance of Maes Howe towards sunset in midwinter, kinking the passage slightly to allow only a few evenings when the sun could glow straight along it into the chamber. Local legends claimed that the sun did shine down the corridor on the shortest day of the year, a powerful indication of the value of these folk memories, especially when the similar stories told about Newgrange are recalled. A decade after Spence that earnest investigator of megalithic astronomy, Sir Norman Lockyer, expressed doubts about the theory, commenting that Spence's article had 'no pretension to scientific accuracy'.[15]

There is, however, one telling piece of evidence, seemingly never commented

48   *The symmetrical perfection of the chamber of Maes Howe passage-grave, Orkney Mainland. The blocking slab of the little cell in the wall lies on the floor*

on in this context, that suggests that Lockyer was mistaken. The men who erected Maes Howe were masters of building in stone. The squareness of the corners, the rectangularity of the chamber, the perfection of the drystone walling, demonstrate their skill everywhere in the tomb. They even constructed a recess on the left-hand side of the passage into which the blocking stone of the entrance could be pushed whenever people wanted to get into the tomb. This stone still exists and can be seen, filling the recess exactly as one would expect from the craftsmen who measured and shaped it.

Yet when it was dragged from its recess to close the tomb, although in width it fitted precisely across the entrance, its upper edge was fully eighteen inches lower than the lintel, leaving a wide rectangular gap between its top and the roof of the passage. It can hardly be thought that this was incompetence. Instead, we should remember Newgrange to which Maes Howe is so similar, and the roof-box above the entrance, a megalithic 'letter-box' through which the midwinter rising sunlight poured onto the burnt bones of the dead. At Maes Howe a comparable aperture had been left at the entrance and, despite Lockyer's calculations, the rays of the midwinter setting sun did enter there. On 21 December 1972, the evening of the winter solstice, George Mackay Brown went to Maes Howe in the company of several other people. 'The sun made a cloudless descent. The interior of the chamber was full of crepuscular, whispering figures. Then the sunset flowered on the stone—the last beam of light of the shortest day—and it glowed briefly on a wall that at every other time of the year is dark.'[16]

Maes Howe, the tomb and shrine, Stenness, the circle and ceremonial centre, stood close to each other as symbols of changing customs that were being adapted to new ways of living—of societies with leaders, of pastoralists whose increasing herds demanded that people move constantly from grazing-ground to grazing-ground, a life in which the permanent tomb and the handling of human bones were becoming anachronisms. Yet death, the sun and the moon continued to be part of the rituals in monuments whose plans, time and again, were based on the cardinal positions of the landscape.

6
Fine and Private Places

Great circular henges were being put up in many parts of Britain, from Maumbury Rings near the Dorset coast to Broadlee henge a few miles from the Solway Firth, always close to water. Where there was stone people put up spacious megalithic rings. There was Avebury in the south, its ditch littered with human jaws and bones, and not far to the west was the enormous ring of Stanton Drew, a Cove well outside its circle of rugged, pebble-dashed stones. Stenness stood hundreds of miles to the north, and in Ireland other rings such as Ballynoe in Co. Down showed how widely the cult of the open-air circular enclosure had spread. These rings of earth or stone, perhaps even of timber like Arminghall, differed in size as could be expected in regions and populations so distant from each other but they were consistently similar in two respects. People had put human bone inside them and their builders had laid out the ring from an axis that pointed either east–west or north–south, the four corners of the imagined world.

In the Lake District there was Long Meg and Her Daughters with two cairns at the centre of the vast ring and two cumbrous blocks at the east and west. A pointed pillar stood outside the entrance in line with the midwinter sunset. In the Orkneys, on the opposite side of the isthmus from Stenness, the rather later Ring of Brodgar with its wide, rocky ditch and delicately tall stones was set out on an axis within a degree or two of true north. Circular, low lying, near water, these rings with their unnoticed and forgotten cardinal alignments brought the past and the future together, the traditions of death being acted out in assembled dances through the novelties of chiefs and priests.

That most evocative of rings, the Carles at Castlerigg outside Keswick, as grey and silent as the tendrils of mist that curl up from the River Greta, has two monstrous stones on either side of its northern entrance. Faint traces of a cairn can just be made out inside the circle, and there is a perplexing rectangle of slighter stones at the south-east jutting into the interior of this megalithic temple. When Kinsey Dover dug into the peculiar setting in 1882 he found nothing except a pit at its western end filled with black soil and stones and, near the bottom, 'a few pieces of burned wood or charcoal, also some dark unctuous sort of earth'.[1]

The rectangle is unique to the Carles but it may have been a representation of a burial chamber just as Coves were. Thirty miles to the east under the long barrow of Raiset Pike near Crosby Garett in Westmorland was a rectangular trench lined

49   *The Ring of Brodgar circle-henge, Orkney Mainland, one of the largest stone circles in the British Isles*

50   *The Carles, Castlerigg, Cumbria. Two tall stones flank the wide entrance at the north. The much lower stones of the 'rectangle' can be seen between them. This may be one of the oldest of the British stone circles*

with limestone, comparable in shape and size to the Carles' rectangle. Inside it was a pit which was 'full of burnt earth, burnt stones and charcoal', very like the Carles' pit.[2] A tall stone stood at the end of the trench. It is noteworthy that the tallest of all the circle stones is at the eastern end of the rectangle in the Carles set at right angles to the circumference, its axis pointing towards the midsummer sunset. This combination of sun, stone and fire suggests that, as in other stone circles, Late Neolithic people had constructed an open-air version of a burial chamber for their rituals.

Some of these Coves, whatever form they took, may have been erected before the circles themselves during the flux of centuries when chambered tombs and long mounds were being abandoned but before the erection of circular enclosures was widespread. The Cove at Stanton Drew is not inside the great circle but stands at the edge of a low ridge several hundred yards to the south-west. The Beckhampton Cove near Avebury was also a long way from where the circles were to be built and it was probably only later that a second Cove was erected inside the concentric ring of stones at Avebury itself. Another Cove, now destroyed, at Cairnpapple, a circle-henge with many features in common with Arbor Low but two hundred miles to its north near Edinburgh, may also have been put up before the enclosing bank and circle there. Very little has been found from the desultory and dreadful digging around these Coves, just a few scraps of human and animal bones, but no carefully laid offerings. It is likely that the ceremonies at these great stone settings were mimes of bringing corpses to the tomb, laying them down and then removing the skull or long bones to another place for the rituals of intercession with the dead. If this interpretation has any truth then the Cove at Avebury may have been the counterpart of the three-stone arrangement at Stenness. The centre stone of the South Circle at Avebury, Stukeley's Obelisk, would be comparable to the tall post inside the 'hearth' of the circle-henge on Orkney. Pits filled with good earth have been discovered near the Obelisk just where the people may have gathered for the climax of their rituals, the time when the spirits of their ancestors were to intercede on their behalf through rites of sympathetic magic that symbolized the needs of the community.

Whatever the truth of it few Coves survive and maybe only a very few were built. With the decline of the chambered tombs and the growing popularity of round barrows containing the bodies of a privileged Bronze Age caste, rituals changed. There was no entrance to these new barrows and no means of withdrawing skulls and bones for ceremonies. Coves themselves became archaic, overtaken by an age of fire and sacrifice, of peasants and a warrior aristocracy whose personal wealth could not have been imagined by neolithic people. It was an age of axe cults and water cults. Between 2600 and 2200 BC there were many changes in religious activities caused partly by the climate, partly by the introduction of metalworking, partly by Beaker people from the continent, probably most of all by a change in the structure of society.

There seems to have been a crisis in Late Neolithic Britain, perhaps because of over-intensive farming.[3] For many years grass spread over abandoned farmlands. Some people turned to herding but as the families recovered, generations after the famine or whatever disaster had disrupted society, they worked even harder to

51   *The Cove inside the North Circle, Avebury, Wiltshire. The missing stone to the right of the wide rear sarsen fell and was broken up in the eighteenth century*

52   *'Adam', the one surviving stone of the Beckhampton Cove outside Avebury. 'Eve', the only stone left of the Beckhampton Avenue, stands beyond it. Avebury is hidden behind the trees in the distance*

produce more food. In the warmer, rather drier climate at the end of the Neolithic these efforts seem to have been successful but, inevitably, they led to the creation of what anthropologists call 'Big Men', who persuaded other people to work hard for them by the promise of lavish communal feasts when the year's work was done and the harvest with its excess food was gathered in. Whether it was grain, cattle or the sheep that were now grazing over immense tracts of southern Britain the rewards were similar: a huge celebration in which the Big Man or chief gave out food and gifts to his followers, keeping little for himself. It was prestige rather than wealth that he valued although, over the years, wealth too would come to him.

The emergence of these leaders resulted in other changes. The chief displayed and maintained his superiority over his people by wearing elaborate apparel and by carrying rare and impressive regalia—the antler macehead, the stone battleaxe, or, best of all, the new axes and daggers of bronze. The discovery of ways of working copper and, later, bronze provided leaders with exhilarating possibilities of increasing their status through the acquisition of metal weapons, and the demand for these objects led to trading links between a whole network of petty chiefdoms. Exchanges of gifts to keep the peace between chiefs, gifts of cereals, tool-making stone, cattle and women, the purchase of bronze and even gold ornaments, created even greater necessity for surplus production. Warriors were needed and had to be fed. Great earthworks and enclosures were erected—Silbury Hill, Durrington Walls, henges at Thornborough in Yorkshire, the gigantic defensive stockade at Meldon Bridge in northern Britain—built over generations by hundreds of willing peasants whose rewards were the feasts, the gifts and the proud ostentation of their leader. These enormous structures were declarations of their chieftain's power and wealth. Government, trade and religion blurred and overlapped in them just as the roles of chief and shaman did. The axe, symbol of authority, was also a religious device that seems to have signified the sun.

Beaker people must have contributed something towards these changes.[4] A few humble bands of farmers entered the country from the continental mainland around 2600 BC in the last centuries of the Neolithic, settling along the eastern coasts but soon infiltrating along the rivers, bringing with them a knowledge of prospecting for the copper ores that were already being exploited on the continent. Slung across the men's backs were fearsome bows. By their sides hung quivers of arrows tipped with finely chipped flint heads. These dynamic people stimulated the search for copper, extending trade-routes across the seaways to Ireland, making alliances, travelling like Canadian trappers from one local encampment to the next, staying for a winter here, moving on again in the spring, canoeing watchfully along the unknown rivers. Some of them lingered for a while in the shelter of Newgrange's mound, squatting in the rubble of its collapsing wall of quartz, the tomb shabby and green with weeds, talking warily around their fires with natives about barter, asking which trails to follow to the west. Other explorers reached as far as Lough Gur in Co. Limerick where the people had raised a massively embanked circle by the lakeside. Ceaselessly, dangerously, the Beaker prospectors searched for ores and when they returned to their homes they brought back tales of weird customs and remote peoples in whose

53   *Beakers from Oxfordshire. In front of the pots can be seen (left to right): flint arrowheads, gold 'basket' ear-rings, an archer's wristguard, copper knives and a bone leather-working tool*

land gold might be discovered.

Impressed by the monumental temples they had seen, the great stone circles, the henges, some of these Beaker people, who after two centuries may have become overlords on Salisbury Plain, decided to replace the mouldering hut at the centre of Stonehenge with a double ring of stones from the Preseli mountains in south-west Wales. These famous bluestones may already have been on Salisbury Plain, brought there by natives who for years had been trading in axes from the same source. The stones may have been moved many miles eastwards from Wales by glacial action. It may even have been the Beaker people themselves who brought them to Stone-henge, sailing and paddling pairs of canoes with a four-ton stone lashed between them along the Welsh coasts and moving from river to river deep into the heart of Wessex. Whatever the truth, the work was begun and would take years to complete. A great avenue lined with earth banks was thrown up from the henge's entrance down to the banks of the Avon nearly two miles away. The entrance itself was narrowed and a ditch and bank were dug around the Heel Stone, keeping it secure inside the avenue along which the dead would be carried past the ancient sun-stone. Inside the henge the old timbers were dragged away and people laboured to raise two concentric rings, one inside the other, with extra portal stones aligned on the entrance, to emphasize it. It has to be assumed that the circle was concentric in order to duplicate the hut which had been constructed of two rings of posts just as the wooden Sanctuary near Avebury was replaced by a concentric stone circle that piously reproduced the spirit of the traditional building.

Figure 13 *Some sites mentioned in Chapter* **6:**
1 Cruden cairn, NK 075368; 2 Carles stone circle, NY 292236; 3 Duggleby Howe,
SE 881669; 4 Knockast cairn, N 245435; 5 Lligwy dolmen, SH 501860; 6
Dorchester, Oxfordshire, SU 570957; 7 Woodhenge, SU 150434; 8 Mere Down
round barrow, ST 811345

54   *Barbed-and-tanged flint arrowheads often found with Beaker burials. Elegant and deadly, their barbs were sometimes deliberately snapped off before being placed in the grave*

The Beaker newcomers also persisted in giving their dead individual burial, believing that the spirit could take with it its own unbroken ornaments and weapons. Almost for the first time in Britain the dead were given grave-goods. Many men, and women too, had single graves in which beaker pots were placed, beautifully made vessels holding up to a litre of what may have been the first alcoholic drink in these islands, a form of mead. With the bodies were other possessions—a bow and a quiverful of arrows, a copper knife, very occasional pairs of gold earrings, bronze leatherworking tools and gold-capped wooden buttons decorated with the cross-symbols of the sun because these people venerated the sun. In their earliest graves, simple pits with no barrow above them, Beaker people in northern England often arranged the body to face the sun, men with their heads to the east, women to the west, but both of them facing southwards to where the sun would be highest in the sky. In Wessex men had their heads to the north and faced the east, women were reversed and looked westwards towards the sunset. Gradually in the turmoil of these changing centuries Beaker beliefs merged with those of the natives, sometimes disappeared or became dominant, often blended to produce local forms of architecture and ritual. Round barrows or cairns were heaped over the graves, carefully sited on the upper slopes of hills from which they could be seen from below.

Today these mounds, so characteristic of the Bronze Age that followed the Neolithic, are to be found in all parts of the British Isles, many of them ravaged in the nineteenth century by enterprising but destructive antiquarians. Even the estimable Wiltshire pair of diggers, Sir Richard Colt Hoare and William Cunnington, were

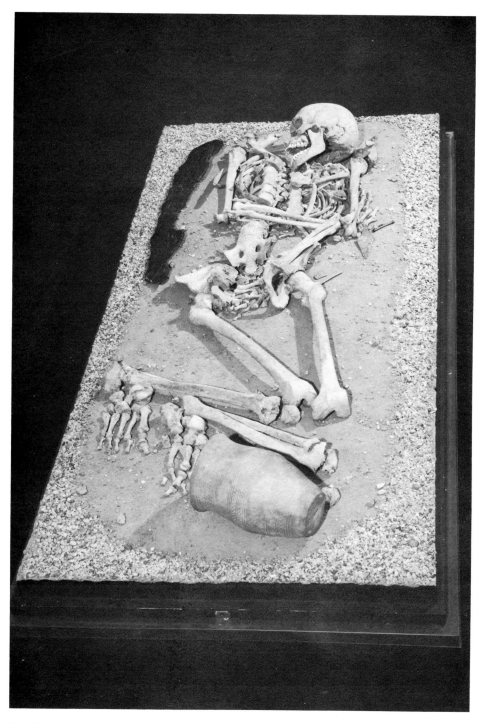

55   *The reconstructed burial of a Beaker man from Barnack, Cambridgeshire. By his hip is a greenstone wristguard, a bronze dagger lies by his elbow and his enormous beaker has fallen over by his feet*

not blameless for they opened nearly five hundred barrows and although they did record many of their finds they did not always treat them gently. Quarrying into one round barrow near Stonehenge they came across two superb beakers and three skeletons, one of them nearly six feet down in the chalk. 'When throwing out the bones of this skeleton, we had a strong proof of how well they are preserved when deep in the chalk, as they would bear being thrown for a considerable distance without breaking.' One of the skeletons had had his skull trepanned during life but had died of the operation, for the roundel of bone had never healed. Hoare commented that it 'had apparently been sawn off, for I do not think that any knife could have cut it off in the manner in which this was done', and one winces at the thought of prehistoric surgery by a medicine-man scratching and scouring through the scalp and skull with his serrated flint.[5]

Some of these Beaker people assumed the role of chiefs, intermarrying with native women, lording it over the peasantry. Their burials reveal the wealth and prestige these leaders were acquiring. Twenty miles west of Stonehenge Hoare and Cunnington dug into a small, low barrow on the slopes of Whitesheet Hill, and beneath it they found a long grave cut into the chalk, neatly set out east–west.[6] Two skeletons lay in it, a well-built man with a younger, slighter person by his side. 'From the position of their heads, they seem to have been placed in the affectionate attitude of embrace, as the two skulls nearly touched each other.' By the bodies were a splendid beaker, a copper knife whose prehistoric value it is impossible to assess, a slate wristguard to protect the archer from the whiplash of his bowstring, and a broken bone spatula that may have been used for leatherworking. There were also two button cappings of thin Irish gold. About the size of a fifty pence piece but of incalculable worth they were decorated with the cross-patterns that are usual on these buttons. Made in Ireland around the Wicklow mountains, by Irish smiths who may still have adhered to the sun-religion of the earlier passage-grave builders, these buttons with their crosses may have represented the sun itself. Only one of the gold buttons has survived from this Beaker burial at Mere Down and is now in Devizes Museum. What was not even removed from the end of the grave was a mass of charred wood. It was possibly an attempt by the living to keep the ghosts of the dead secure in their grave. The belief that spirits would not move past a fire is known from other societies.

56   *Found with a beaker in a round barrow*
     at Mere in Wiltshire, this gold button-cap,
     about 1 in. wide, was one of a pair.

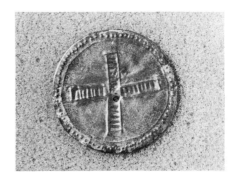

One wonders if both the people under the Mere Down round barrow had died together naturally or whether the younger person had been killed to keep company with her (?) master. With the blending of Beaker and native customs, however, it is possible that the first corpse had been stored in a mortuary house, or even buried somewhere, until the time of the second death. A cist at the bottom of a deep, stone-filled pit at Cruden in Aberdeenshire contained two beakers, a wristguard, the remains of a quiverful of arrows and the incomplete skeletons of a young man and a child, both of whose bones had been put there long after the flesh had decayed. Other instances of excarnation from England and Wales show that whatever rituals Beaker people introduced into Britain they did not eliminate aboriginal traditions, although their insistence that the dead person needed to take his property with him may have persuaded some natives logically to sacrifice young servants and warriors as part of their own chieftain's possessions.

Despite the Beaker people communal burial did not disappear from the British Isles, it merely took on new forms. Mass burials in pits near Avebury show how the local inhabitants held on to their old ways even when they knew of Beaker beliefs. As far away as Anglesey, near Red Wharf Bay, people had battered out a pit in the bedrock at Pant-y-Saer, erected an odd imitation of a megalithic tomb in it and, over the years, buried more than fifty bodies there, unknowingly including nine un-born infants, a harsh reminder of the perils of childbirth in prehistoric times. It may have been for rites to fend off such unpredictable dangers that some skulls had been removed from this tomb.

A capstone, grotesquely large, covered these burials and an even heavier one was dragged to a similar grave two miles to the north near Lligwy Bay, this time over a natural fissure in the ground.[7] Casual though they were the excavators of 1908 noticed the different layers that had been heaped up in this cavity in which a man could have stood upright. Under the upper depth of wind-blown earth there was a thin packing of red clay in which limpet shells had been liberally scattered. Then came a band of black earth speckled with human and animal bones—ox, sheep, pig, deer, fox, fowl, dog, otter—and broken sherds, some clumsily decorated like beaker pottery as if a native woman had tried to copy it. Under this layer was a crude paving of flat stones on top of more black earth and human bones laid over a wet, sticky scatter of mussel shells. The bones, including those of a newborn infant, had been broken into minute pieces but it was possible to reconstruct three excep-tionally wide jaws whose owners may have belonged to the same family. Over this cemetery, in which at least thirty people had been buried, the living had hauled the ponderous capstone, many tons of awkward limestone, propping it on eight squat pillars that surrounded the edges of the pit.

Across the sea Irish people clung just as stubbornly to their ways. On the summit of a lonely hill near Lough Ennell some of them dug out three pits into which they crammed charcoal, ox and sheep bones and a pig's tooth.[8] Around these offerings they built cists and other graves, burying over forty bodies, most of them cremations under a cairn. The objects found with them at Knockast in Co. Meath show that these people had lived in the Early Bronze Age but the hilltop situation of the cairn

*57, 58   This long-necked beaker and the highly polished hammerstone for copper-working came
from a round barrow at Amesbury near Stonehenge. The beaker was decorated using a
wooden comb, fingernails and a reed. The stone, a siliceous hornstone, is about $4\frac{1}{2}$ in.
long*

and its mass burials belonged to a tradition that looked back to the years when passage-graves were being built in this part of the British Isles. Another of these multiple-cist cairns with a passage leading to a cremation trench was found very close to Fourknocks passage-grave in the same county, and its builders, like those at Pant-y-Saer and Lligwy, seem to have retained some memory of the megalithic tradition of their forefathers. Similar continuity is revealed at Moneen in Co. Cork where one of these cairns was actually put up on top of a Goodland site with its ritual pit offerings. There are many others, one of the most interesting being on Topped Mountain in Co. Fermanagh where the memory that these shrines were centres of fertility magic lingered on into the twentieth century, courting couples traditionally going to the cairn late in July at the time of the ripening harvest.

Perhaps because the use of megalithic tombs went on longer in Ireland than elsewhere in Britain these multiple-cist cairns were not built until the Early Bronze Age, but in lowland England the transition came earlier. At Dorchester in Oxfordshire, a long cursus passed over the site of an earlier rectangular mortuary enclosure. In turn this cursus was interrupted by a series of circular family cremation cemeteries.[9]

59   *Lligwy dolmen, Anglesey. The enormous limestone covering slab measures about 18 × 15 × 3 ft, weighs over fifty tons and must have required scores of people to manhandle it into position*

Cremation, practised for centuries in eastern Britain, was gradually being adopted in the south, maybe because the burning of the body more certainly liberated the spirits of the dead. Now that skulls and bones were less frequently needed, cremation seemed preferable. Even when bodies were not totally burned charcoal and ash were sometimes buried with them to trap the ghosts in their graves. In Sweden people from remote times would throw live coals and charcoal after a funeral procession to frighten the dead man's spirit from returning. Frazer in *Taboo and the Perils of the Soul* recorded that Australian aborigines put burning coals in the ears of a corpse to keep its ghost imprisoned until the people could travel a safe distance from it.

Cremation removed the ghost for ever, freeing it from this world to travel easily to the land of the dead. This was particularly necessary for the spirits of powerful people, chiefs and magicians, whose wraiths might maliciously cause much harm to the living. A few bits of charcoal or some burning torches might suffice for the common peasant, scaring off his feeble timorous spectre. Cremation also protected skulls and bones from misuse by enemies, especially by the sorcerers and witch-doctors that were emerging as distinctive members of society at this time. In *Urn Burial* Sir Thomas Browne expressed the fear and the solution well:

> To be knav'd out of our graves, to have our sculs made drinking-bowls, and our bones into Pipes, to delight and sport our enemies, are Tragicall abominations escaped in burning Burials.

It is ironical that Browne, who died at Norwich in 1682, was disinterred in 1840. His skull was taken to Norwich Hospital Museum.

The Late Neolithic people at Dorchester may have shared his fear that their bones might be tampered with. In the light woodlands that fringed the Thames some families settled, no more than about forty people, hunting with dogs, keeping cattle and sheep, their lives no less difficult than in former generations. Seven out of ten of them died before they were twenty-five. Their corpses were burned on top of stacked pyres that disintegrated the bodies, leaving only spikelets of bone and marble-sized brown clinkers that had formed when the hair and fat melted together. When the flames were dying down and the bones had slumped into the glowing ashes the people threw the dead person's ornaments and tools into the fire—bone hairpins, flints, a stone macehead. Then, when the ashes had cooled, they raked out as many bones as they could find, washed them clean of charcoal, broke up the larger pieces and put them into a leather bag together with the charred trinkets. The bag was taken to a small circular enclosure where it was buried in a pit.

Except for its size the ditch-ringed circle was very like Stonehenge fifty miles to the south-west along the Ridgeway that had become one of the major tracks for traders and travellers. There were segmented ditches at both Dorchester and Stonehenge, and there were pits, at Dorchester dug into the ditches but very like the more famous Aubrey Holes. The cremated bones were buried in the open central space, sometimes near offerings of animal bones. At Dorchester there were at least six of these circular cemeteries, none more than about twenty paces across and perhaps measured out in multiples of five 'body-yards' of two feet nine inches. They seem to have been put up one after another over several centuries and it is probable that everyone who died was given burial in them, except for infants. This was not unusual. Many primitive societies believed that until a child was weaned and could walk and talk it was not properly a member of the community and could not be buried with real people.

At the middle of one enclosure which was surrounded by a squarish ditch there was the crushed skeleton of an adult, little more than white powder by the time it was discovered in 1946, but as all the other burials at Dorchester were cremations, over a hundred of them, this individual may have been the first to be buried here, his spirit guarding the cemetery. Only two hundred yards to the south-east of the little settlement there was another enclosure about the same size as the others, its ditch encircling a little rectangular mortuary platform. The only finds inside this ring were a single cremation, an axe of Cornish stone and a handful of seashells.

Such rings were ideal family cemeteries but for those occasions when groups assembled for communal ceremonies greater and more impressive structures were needed. The mortuary platform was dismantled and the people replaced it with an enormous henge built in the eastern tradition with two great ditches and an intervening bank. This site, known as Dorchester Big Rings, stood at the extreme south-

60 *King Arthur's Round Table henge, Westmorland. This delightful picture was taken in the 1930s before the site was damaged by road-widening*

west corner of the eastern region, separated by the Thames from the 'Wessex' henges with their single internal ditch. Westwell, as big as the Dorchester henge, is only twenty-four miles to the west, and the Devil's Quoits, once with as many as thirty great stones standing in a ring inside it, was only a few miles across the river. These spacious henges, built by scores, perhaps hundreds of people, were probably settlements as well as temples, the centres of day-to-day life, trade and ritual. They also reveal some of the changes in society, no longer free and classless but becoming stratified with a few people possessing power and riches, others accepting a lifetime of working for their leaders.

Despite the examples of Dorchester and other great earthworks it was more common to keep settlement and sacred precinct apart, although at Avebury not many miles to the south-west stone circles rose in the very heart of the enclosure. Usually stone circles or earthen rings were built well away from the ordinary houses of the people. Many of these temples were to be built in the Early Bronze Age, some of stone, some of timber or earth. The rituals in them were becoming more savage than those of neolithic people as the unsettled times of a growing population and land shortage demanded more personal, more valued offerings to appease the spirits. Among the chambered tombs of the New Stone Age there had been infrequent hints of a sacrifice but in the centuries of the Bronze Age such dedications became commoner. The young child at Folkton, buried with the carved drums of chalk, may have died of disease but her grave, isolated from all the others, suggests that she may have been killed to sanctify the round barrow with its central burials.

This interpretation is likely because there was sacrifice earlier than the Bronze Age on the Wolds. Three miles south of Folkton along the valley of the Gypsey Race three hill-sized round barrows, Willy Howe, Wold Newton and Duggleby

61   *The large round barrow at Wold Newton, Humberside. In 1894 John Mortimer discovered many skeletons in the mound, including one whose skull had been smashed into small pieces, but there was no burial at the centre of the barrow*

Howe, were erected close to the magical stream that flows only when there is a drought. From them has come evidence of changing burial rites, of leaders and, almost certainly, of the killing of children who were to go with their chief on his journey to the land of the dead.

Under the five thousand tons of chalk that men and women broke and packed firmly into the brilliantly white round barrow of Duggleby Howe bodies of old men with their regalia were accompanied by the burials of a youth and a child.[10] Into a dark shaft that anticipated the deep pits of some Bronze Age burials on the Wolds people laid the corpse of a strongly built man in a cramped wooden mortuary house like those in the earlier long barrows. Near the body they set down a locally made pot and nine flints. Rotted haematite beside him had probably been used for body-painting when this petty chieftain prepared himself to lead the ceremonies in his lifetime. Into his grave-pit the people tumbled lumps of chalk, but halfway down they left the jawless skull of a youth who had probably been killed at the time of the man's death. Mortimer, who excavated Duggleby Howe in 1890, remarked that 'there is a large, suspicious-looking circular hole' in the skull. At the top of the shaft's filling the people placed the skeleton of a two- or three-year-old child.

The pattern was repeated in a shallower hollow to the east of this central shaft. Here, half-sitting in his grave, were the remains of a fifty-year-old man, his tools and trinkets around him, flint arrowheads, flakes, a knife, ox bones, two beaver's teeth, a bone pin and twelve boars' tusks. A small mound was heaped over his body. In it were the skeletons of a boy and a very young child. The one exception to this sinister pattern of man, youth and child came with the discovery of a very tall, seventy-year-old man whose body had been arranged so that his head overhung the edge of the shaft, looking down into it. In his left hand he held a cushion-shaped wafer of pellucid flint, holding it up to his face as though gazing into a crystal ball.

If these men were leaders, as their age and possessions hint, then it may have been fifty years or more after the first burial that a fourth man, about sixty years of age, was buried in the mound of clayey earth that had been heaped over the graves. With him the people placed his fine flint axe, a lozenge-shaped flint arrowhead and an antler macehead, weapons that can be recognized as symbols of his authority. Above him in the mound were the skeletons of a boy and, at the top of the little barrow, the bones of a child. Four collections of mixed animal bones near these burials—ox, roebuck, red deer, fox, sheep or goat, pig—intermingled with broken human bones show that offerings were still being made to the dead, all of them male at Duggleby Howe, buried in this little barrow.

In following decades people piled a further layer of chalk grit over it, in which they buried over fifty cremations. On this in turn even later people packed a layer of blue Kimmeridge clay and finally completed the barrow by covering it with chalk rubble to create a monstrous pile, forty paces across, as high as a house, white and monumentally conspicuous along the valley. It was a proud memorial to those dead chieftains but even as we admire their handiwork we remember the children who had been killed to travel with the spirits of their masters.

Far to the south on Salisbury Plain, just outside the entrance to the settlement

62   *Despite several excavations at Silbury Hill, Wiltshire, no burial has been found in this gigantic barrow which was erected around 2700 BC. It was constructed in drumlike tiers and the steps between them were filled with rammed chalk*

of Durrington Walls, there is even less doubt. Not two miles from Stonehenge, around 2250 BC, when the Aubrey Holes were overgrown and the ditch was half-filled with weeds and crumbling chalk, people erected dozens of massive posts in six concentric ovals whose long axis pointed to the midsummer sunrise. At the very heart of the structure, which archaeologists jokingly called Woodhenge, there was a great open space surrounded by twelve oak columns.[11] At its far end, near the south-west, was a shallow grave lying across the central line of the oval. In it was the skeleton of a three-and-a-half-year-old child, probably a girl, lying on her right-hand side, facing the entrance and the rising sun. At first the excavators thought an extra skull had been put in the grave with her, but they were wrong. It was the girl's skull they were looking at, split completely in half by one blow from an axe.

7
Graves for the Rich

Some dark priest hales the reluctant victim ...
Percy Bysshe Shelley, *Prometheus Un-bound*

Woodhenge is an enigma. Stonehenge, Stenness, Avebury and a thousand other rings also are enduring puzzles whose solution is not to be discovered inside their own banks and stones. There are many paradoxes in British prehistory and one of the most formidable is that for anyone to learn the purpose of henges and stone circles it is necessary to turn away from these monuments which are notorious for the meagre and almost meaningless bits and pieces of the past that they yield to the excavator. However romantic their images are today they are merely the ribs of antiquity whose flesh dropped from them when the assemblies of people departed.

Conversely, the dead do tell us about the living. From burials of the Early and Middle Bronze Ages come flecks of information about amulets, body-painting, totems, hints of superstition and of a belief in an after-life, dots and stipples that like a pointillist painting compose themselves into recognizable and persuasive impressions of a society in which death, sacrifice and rites of fertility were commonplace. Before one can understand the living one needs to unearth the dead. This chapter is much possessed with death, like John Webster who

> *... saw the skull beneath the skin,*
> *And breastless creatures underground*
> *Leaned backward with a lipless grin.*

T. S. Eliot, *Whispers of Immortality*

The girl at Woodhenge was not alone. Other children were sacrificed as the needs and fears of society became fiercer. The banding together of families into larger communities had led to the emergence not only of chiefs but of shamans, sorcerers, wizards, medicine-men, who became the central figures of the gatherings. Claiming an intense and personal knowledge of the spirit-world, and being able through charms and spells to cure illness and avert disaster they slowly gained more and more power over the generations, demanding from a community which had become so large that individuals were less important, that in times of crisis a human life should be given. What in a family was almost unacceptable became in a clan or a small tribe a dreadful but not tragic necessity. At Loanhead of Daviot, a stone circle with a recumbent stone in north-east Scotland, people dropped fragments of skulls, many of them from children, at the centre of the ring. Child-cremations were discovered in pits at the heart of the Druids' Circle on a headland overlooking Conway

63   *The Druids' Circle near Conway Bay in north Wales. The stones stand in a low bank. Cremations of young children were found inside this ring*

Bay. Across the Irish Sea, on a hillside at Castle Mahon, other families burned the body of a child inside a circle of stones and then buried the ashes in a cist alongside the smouldering pyre. All these, like the Woodhenge girl, may have been sacrificed as dedications when the rings were built, extravagant offerings that added power to these new enclosures.

Sacrifice should not be equated with our modern attitude to murder. In the same decades that Woodhenge was being erected Abraham was prepared to sacrifice his own child. 'Take thy son . . . and offer him there for a burnt offering upon one of the mountains which I will tell thee of.' It was the imperative of his god rather than a free willingness to kill his own son that left Abraham without choice and forced him into filicide. Nor could it be considered murder when the victim herself went voluntarily to her death. Nearly two thousand years after Woodhenge Euripides described how the Greeks sacrificed the daughter of their leader Agamemnon, to Artemis, goddess of the moon, to gain favourable winds to Troy. It is the response of Iphigenia that is remarkable to our western minds.

> *. . . Listen now!*
> *I will choose death, and freely will I choose.*
> *Fear I have banished wholly from my heart.*
> *Artemis asks my life. Can I refuse her?*
> *Then let my life be given.*
>
> **Iphigenia at Aulis**

Sacrifices, the strongest and most precious of all man's gifts, have been made in many societies for many reasons. Hiel of Bethel sacrificed his oldest and his youngest sons as foundation offerings for the walls of Jericho when the city was rebuilt in the ninth century BC. Not long afterwards several kings of Jerusalem, Ahaz and Manasseh among them, had their children burnt alive in honour of Baal whose shrine was in the nearby valley of Hinnom. At the funeral of a Ugandan king hundreds of his people were seized and killed to provide his ghost with servants. Flesh from sacrifices was scattered in fields in Ecuador to encourage the growth of crops. The Pawnee Indians sacrificed a young girl at their Morning Star ceremony, painting the left side of her naked body red for the day, the other side black for night. After she had been tied to a wooden frame one medicine-man held a burning torch against her, another killed her with an arrow while a third cut into her skin to drain away the blood. All the braves then shot arrows into her corpse which was cut down and taken to rot in the fields where the newly sown seeds would absorb strength from it.

Men have even been hunted down and killed to obtain their skulls so that their spirits would watch over the crops. Sir James Frazer in his *Spirits of the Corn and of the Wild* quotes the creed of tribesmen in Burma:

> Without a skull his crops would fail. Without a skull his kine might die. Without a skull the father and mother spirits would be shamed and might be enraged. If there were no protecting skull then other spirits, who are all malignant, might gain entrance and kill all the inhabitants ...

In Iron Age Britain, hundreds of years after Woodhenge, the historian Strabo reported that the Druids held a great sacrifice of criminals every five years. 'The more there were of such victims, the greater was believed to be the fertility of the land.' In a strange way a sacrifice was almost impersonal for it was not the object given but the act of giving it that was significant. Today when we put flowers on someone's grave we are not expecting the dead person to see or smell them. Instead, we are performing an act of communion that expresses our love and respect for that person whose spirit will sense it. Similarly, a sacrifice symbolized some need in society, the urgency and necessity of which was more keenly stated if the chosen symbol was a human being.

Needs would vary, sometimes coming at times of prolonged drought, famine or the horror of an epidemic, sometimes from the erection of a new ritual enclosure because it seemed that the stones or timbers demanded an offering to give them vitality. When the weathered posts of the Sanctuary, the timber ring near Avebury, were being replaced with stones during the Early Bronze Age just such a human offering was made.[1] The stone circle was destroyed in 1724 and now one finds only modern markers to show where it stood alongside the Ridgeway, round barrows greenly fringing the track across the Marlborough Downs. It is dull now, spiritless and wire-fenced, often with a grimy lorry in the layby and with cars speeding up the hill, distracting contemplation. Yet from this place one can see Silbury Hill, the tree-covered East Kennet tomb and, across a valley, the great stones of West Kennet staring out to where the circle had risen on its hilltop.

64   *The Sanctuary, Wiltshire. Concrete markers now show where posts and stones stood in these rings. Corpses may have rotted inside a timber building here before the bones were taken to long chambered tombs such as East Kennet in the trees on the left*

Stained rectangular blocks show where stones stood in two concentric rings. By the easternmost block of the inner ring there is an ugly blob of concrete. It marks the place where a girl was buried. Before they put up a heavy sarsen the people dug a hole and crammed her body into it, head to the south, looking towards the rising sun. Over the corpse they scattered burnt animal bones and by its knees they placed a beaker pot perhaps filled with some drink to solace her ghost. Then they hauled the stone upright, tight against the body, ramming the earth and chalk back over the remains, sealing her in the ground. No other bodies were found inside the Sanctuary and it is very likely that the girl had been killed on the occasion of the stone circle being built.

Even the newly discovered techniques of metalworking, a craft introduced into the British Isles around 2500 BC, may have required sacrifices to ensure that this craft mystery was to be practised successfully. During the later Bronze Age a bronze-smith had lived for a while in the damp, gloomy misery of a cave at Heathery Burn near Durham. His tools, broken pots and fires close to the stream that trickles through the cavern show that he had stayed here, and a burial near a hearth suggests that his stay might have been a long one. But, as Gordon Childe pointed out, 'Broken human skulls near by remind us that in barbarous societies metallurgical science is still bound up with mystic rites for which human blood may well have been required.'[2]

Sacrifice, for whatever reason, also implies more elaborate rituals than those expected from single families. The beginnings of formal religion were attended by the emergence of men or women who would conduct the ceremonies according to the rigidly accepted patterns. Neither the words 'priest' nor 'witch-doctor' are very apt terms for such people. 'Priest' suggests a ministry and an organized religion with a god or gods, concepts that seem hardly developed in the Early Bronze Age. A 'witch-doctor', one who professes to cure disease and combat witchcraft by the control of natural forces, offers perhaps too limited a role for the people who were becoming the organizers and chief performers of rites in the stone circles and henges. 'Shaman' might be more appropriate, akin to the medicine-men of American Indians, a 'priest' who could influence the spirits of the Other-World, who could converse with them and whose incantations could bring health back to the sick and give safety to the wandering souls of those who had just died.

Skilled in the occult arts of the supernatural, feared and yet wanted, their powers so terrifying that these men were almost shunned by ordinary tribesmen, the need for such shamans could only arise when societies were large enough to free them from the day-to-day work of planting and herding. This was true among the Tungus, the nomads of north-east Asia. A seventeenth-century traveller noticed that 'If five or six of these ... families happen to live near one another they maintain betwixt them a Shaman, which signifies as much Sorcerer as Priest' (A. Brand, *Muscovy into China*).

In a world still rabid with spirits, as early prehistoric Britain was, shamans are likely. Their vision of the world was very different from ours. In western civilization today man is a separate object, detached, as though he were the sun around which all other things revolve, as though these other things were two-dimensional pictures on a screen. When James Joyce asked whether a rose growing in an endless desert, never be seen by man, could be beautiful he was asking a question not only of the young artist but of modern, western man. A so-called 'primitive' of thousands of years ago not only would not but could not have asked such a question. To him a rose or a stream or the swirling smoke of a cloud was not dependent on man for life, it was part of existence itself, and would live whether man was there or not. The late lark singing in the quiet skies, the sun, a leaf falling, the gibbous moon were all realities of life and were mirrored in the world of spirits, all of them with senses that were as aware of man as man was of them. Each thing lived.

The world of prehistoric man was a complete one, wondrous and awful, and to survive in it he needed the protection that shamans could give. They could predict the future and they could control the present. To cure illness the medicine-men of the American Indians would lay magical objects around the sickbed—a figurine, a skull, woven strands of birch bark, a box filled with miniature totems, misformed pebbles—and then, with painted face and flamboyant head-dress, would prowl around the patient muttering spells and incantations. To the student of Stonehenge or a visitor to Stenness or Newgrange this may seem an alien, even unacceptable picture of the way of life in Early Bronze Age Britain. It may be wrong. But before we dismiss this Hobbesian view of prehistoric existence

> No arts; no letters; no society; and which is worst of all, continual fear and danger
> of violent death; and the life of man, solitary, poor, nasty, brutish and short
>
> *Leviathan*, I, ch. 13

it is as well to acknowledge that, grossly overstated though it is if applied to the
Early Bronze Age, it is more in tune with the surviving evidence than believers in
a prehistoric Utopia like to accept. There is evidence for sacrifices, there is evidence
for shamans and there is evidence for body-painting.

Medicine-men of the Winnebago Indians carried a variety of equipment: bear-
paw bags with herbs in them; otterskin pouches with hollow bones; whistles; snake-
skins; vertebrae; cormorant heads; wooden figurines; eagles' claws; dried leaves and
grasses. This is very little different from a collection discovered at Hvidegard in Denmark, buried with a Bronze Age man whose body, wrapped in a soft skin shroud,
had been laid in a stone coffin.[3] In his leather wallet, preserved by a fluke of geology
that only too rarely occurs in Britain, were a piece of amber, a shell, a wooden cube,
a flint, dried roots, bark, a snake's tail, a falcon's claw, tweezers, a knife, the jaw
of a squirrel and some herbs. Hardly a score of miles to the west, at Maglehøj in
Zealand, with the cremation of a woman, a bronze box designed for being carried
on the back held two horse's teeth, weasel bones, the claw of a wild cat, a deer bone,
part of a bird's windpipe, snake vertebrae, bits of burnt bone, probably human, aspen

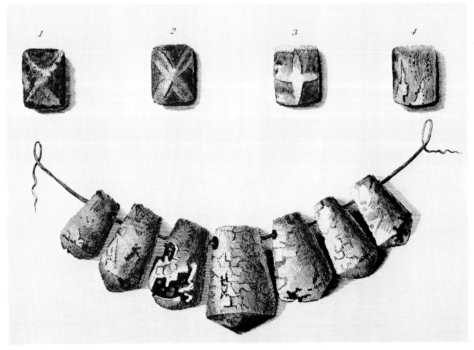

65   *A necklace of pendants and some fingernail-sized bone tablets from a round barrow in
the Lake cemetery near Stonehenge. The tablets may have been part of the apparatus
of a shaman or a witch-doctor in the Early Bronze Age*

and ash twigs, quartz pebbles, lumps of clay, pyrites and a wire hook. This surely, was the apparatus of witchcraft, as repellent as the brew at Barclodiad y Gawres or the 'consecrated wine, powdered goat, human bones, skulls of children, hair, nails, flesh, and wizard's semen, with bits of goose, female rat, and brains' with which Sister Marie de Sains attempted to conjure up the devil in the seventeenth century.

The chances of organic materials like those from Hvidegard and Maglehøj surviving in this country with its warm, seeping rain are small but there are a few hints that shamans may have been known here. Under a Bronze Age round barrow at Upton Lovell in Wiltshire the skeleton of a heavily built man had rows of thin, perforated bones across his neck, thighs and feet. These may have hung in fringes from his leather tunic and trousers, very like the costumes of shamans in Siberia, and it is notable that the Upton Lovell man also had an attractive battleaxe of dolerite, undamaged and probably some kind of insignia. Buried with him were some boars' tusks, some broken white flints and some pebbles which were 'not of the neighbourhood'.

It is quite possible, as the Maglehøj cremation suggests, that some of these spiritual leaders were women. There are many rich female graves from this period including a burial on the Sussex Downs to the north of Brighton. Investigated in 1872 by the pioneer of scientific excavation, Augustus Henry Lane Fox, better known by his later title of General Pitt-Rivers, the Black Burgh round barrow covered the crouched skeleton of a tall, well-built woman with a necklace of shale beads, a bronze pin, a fine bronze dagger that displayed her social importance, and, perhaps significantly, a pot decorated with eyebrow motifs similar to those on the chalk drums from Folkton. Such art may have symbolized a goddess of fertility who watched over the dead, and the presence of the food vessel in the dead woman's grave indicates that she may have had a special role in her community. Knowing as we do of queens such as Boudica and Cartimandua in the Iron Age and of the many goddesses venerated by the Celts it does not seem at all unlikely that 'priestesses' existed earlier in the Bronze Age, accorded as much wealth and respect as the male shamans.

Other, rather similar burials from Cambridgeshire and Yorkshire may also be the last traces of shamans or medicine-men. As long ago as 1821 William Bateman, a Derbyshire antiquarian, digging into a round barrow on the moors near Youlgreave uncovered two skeletons lying side by side, one of them a well-built man with worn-down but healthy teeth.[4] Near him were many quartz pebbles and by his side was a heavy basalt axe. A circular amulet of bronze rested on his chest. A triangular piece of porphyry lay near it and behind his head were the teeth of a dog and a horse. Whether he was a shaman we cannot tell but in an age when chiefs and magicians were not necessarily separate people it is quite possible that his authority, symbolized by the axe, was as much spiritual as temporal.

That body-painting was known in Britain long before Julius Caesar's woad-decorated Celts seems certain from the many finds of colouring pigments with burials, particularly from the Bronze Age. The late neolithic whalebone pots at Skara Brae have already been mentioned, probably the personal paint jars of the inhabitants of the village, and over the following centuries many groups in the British Isles buried lumps of ochre with the dead.[5] Even during the Neolithic, in the Cotswold chambered tombs of Nympsfield and Rodmarton, pieces of haematite had been left with the jumbled skeletons, of no use inside those megalithic shrines except to allow the ghosts to adorn themselves with red and black patterns of magic. People had brought the pigments here specially for there is no haematite occurring naturally within twenty miles of either tomb.

It was during the Early Bronze Age, however, that such colouring material was more commonly placed with the dead. Red ochre was dropped at the Sanctuary, maybe lost during funerary preparations. At the small Gretigate stone circle in Cumbria there was a rounded piece of haematite with the cremations. To the south, by Morecambe Bay, under the rough paved interior of another circle, the Druids' Temple, where a sandstone disc was found with some cremations, people had left a bit of 'raddle' or red ochre with the ashes. Earthy clays like these with much iron oxide in them are common in these islands. They can be red, yellow, even a rich tawny brown, and mixed with animal fat can be as easily applied to the face or body as modern-day cosmetics. Chalk and charcoal, treated in the same way, would provide contrasts of white and black.

Two Yorkshire round barrows at Goodmanham, dug into by Greenwell, covered skeletons with balls of ochre by them. Under one of the mounds, lying on a wooden floor, was the skeleton of a seventeen-year-old girl, hands to her face and with a beautiful necklace made of over a hundred tiny jet beads around her neck. Near her were several bits of yellow ochre. Another round barrow at Garton Slack, not far from the long barrow with its cremation furnace, contained the bones of a youth who had two quartz pebbles in his left hand, a pork joint by his elbow and two boars' tusks in front of his face. A clay disc lay behind his head. This magical collection of food, amulets and totems had been supplemented by two walnut-sized lumps of ochre, the sides and corners of which were 'clearly rounded by use' according to John Mortimer who excavated this barrow in 1865. The burial was all the more remarkable because the youth's jaw had been removed and into his mouth the people had pushed a diminutive pot with the bones of a small animal in it. This, presumably, was intended as a meal for the dead person. Near the pot were the skull and teeth of a sucking pig.

Ochre has been found in Bronze Age cists at Poltalloch in Argyll, in the remarkable Nether Largie North cairn with its axe carvings in the Kilmartin Valley and in Carnasserie cairn to the north. Showing that it was not just meant for the dead other pieces have been noticed in the Dalrulzion hut-circles of Perthshire. In England one of its locations was in Liff's Low cairn, a Bronze Age mound not far from the southern group of megalithic tombs in the Peak District. When Thomas, the son of William Bateman, opened the cairn in 1843 he came to a cist of eight limestone slabs, half-filled with stiff clay.[6] In this was the crouched skeleton of a man with 'a fine and intellectual skull'. He had an impressive panoply of articles with him. There was an odd but well-made miniature pot, two fine flint axes, a knife, a saw and two perfect oval arrowheads, all of flint, and a macehead fashioned out of antler which was probably similar in purpose to the ceremonial battleaxe from Youlgreave.

Figure 14 *Some sites mentioned in Chapter 7:*
1 Collessie cairn, NO 288131; 2 Dalgety cemetery, NT 178842;
3 Tillicoultry, NS 925971; 4 Nether Largie North cairn, Kilmartin, NR 831985; 5 Ardmore stone, C 473264; 6 Gristhorpe barrow, TA 093832; 7 Garton Slack cemetery, centred on SE 953600; 8 Calderstones, SJ 400869; 9 Liff's Low round barrow, SK 160566; 10 Burgatia stone, W 303355; 11 Rollright Stones, SP 296308; 12 Soldier's Grave, SO 794015; 13 Sutton round barrow, SS 957720; 14 The Sanctuary stone circle, SU 118679

66   *Objects from the cairn at Liff's Low in the Peak District. As well as the flint axes there is a perforated antler macehead—presumably the regalia of a chieftain—two oval flint arrowheads, a strange little pot, and one of a pair of fearsome boar's tusks, 'trophies . . . perhaps, of his last sylvan triumph', according to the excavator*

Alongside the man was a pair of gigantic boar's tusks. Three bits of red ochre had been left with his body.

This round cairn, now sadly mutilated, is less than five miles south of Arbor Low, and it is easy to imagine the chieftain/shaman in his lifetime, proudly carrying the regalia that proclaimed his importance, clothes garishly coloured, face painted in cabalistic patterns, preparing to lead the ceremonies of life and death inside the circle-henge. Some of these rites would have been funerary, acted out at the Cove when a corpse was borne to the enclosure by one of the mourning families in the district. Decayed fragments of a sledge on which a body may have been dragged to its grave were found with a Beaker burial at Dorchester, suggesting that the dead person had been brought there from some distance away.

There were other rituals in the ring, however, held at special times of the year to ensure the growth of crops and the continuing health of the community. The unsatisfying tatters of evidence left to us indicate that by the Early Bronze Age ceremonies of burial and fertility had become separate and that tomb and ritual centre were quite distinct, people with their dead sometimes travelling many miles to the circle for the funerary rites that would be conducted there by a shaman or a chief. There are very few instances from this period of megalithic rings or henges being used as cemeteries, but there are many circles erected close to earlier neolithic long mounds and with many Bronze Age round barrows in their locality.

There was a long and dreary trackway between the Yorkshire Wolds and Salisbury Plain, much travelled by traders and wandering groups of smiths who crossed the Humber and then followed a thin, low ridge tangled with copses and wild bushes, day after day shouldering their packs along the rough trail before hurriedly crossing a forested wilderness up to the hills east of modern Leicester where the trees were fewer and where men could move more easily, less fearful of the lurking boar and wolf, hunching round fires at night, coming to more uplands that twisted into the Cotswolds and then veering southwards along the banks of the Evenlode, past the stones and earthwork of the Devil's Quoits and onto the cool grasses of the Marlborough Downs and the Ridgeway, by the land mark of Silbury Hill, trudging around the reedy muds of the swamps in the Vale of Pewsey, at last climbing up the scarp that rose onto Salisbury Plain and the heartland of Wessex.

On this trackway, near the place where another meandering route from Wales joined it, some families put up twenty or more stones in a perfect circle, the tallest probably standing on either side of an entrance at the north. The people had chosen a spot where the ridge narrowed to a neck of heathland that any traveller had to cross. Where the slope dropped sharply to the north they erected a gnarled pillar of limestone, visible from lower down even though the ring itself was hidden. This circle, the well-known Rollright Stones, was built on hallowed land. A few hundred yards to the east, in full view from the stones, was the chambered tomb of the Whispering Knights. The two immense portals at its ruined entrance have been

67   *The Ridgeway near Avebury, Wiltshire. To the north are the banks of Barbury Castle, an Iron Age hillfort*

likened to a Cove and it seems probable that it was only when the stone circle was constructed that funerary ceremonies were abandoned at the tomb.

Even today, when the rich soils of this part of England have been ploughed for centuries, some round barrows survive within four or five miles of the stones, at Sarsden and Spelsbury Down, Barter's Hill, Chastleton Hill and elsewhere. These mounds still hold the remains of men and women whose corpses may first have been carried to the Rollright Stones for the rites of the dead. In Stukeley's time there were even more barrows. 'Upon this same heath eastward, in the way to Banbury, are many barrows of different shapes, within sight of Rowldrich; particularly, near a place call'd Chapel on the heath, is a large flat and circular tumulus, ditch't about, with a small tump in the centre ...', an acute observation of what is known as a disc-barrow. There are several, covering the richly accompanied cremations of women, in the vicinity of Stonehenge.

The dead were taken to the Rollright Stones, carried past the outlying King Stone that watched over the land. Here, inside the ring, traders haggled, safe in the

68   *The weatherworn limestone fragments of the Rollright Stones, Oxfordshire. Most have broken away from stones and the circle originally had only about a quarter of the number now to be seen*

sanctuary of the stones. Here too came people for the rites of fertility, rituals so strong and persisted in for so many centuries that their memory is preserved in wisps of folklore.[7] The stones are supposed to go to drink at a spring at midnight at the New Year; young men and girls went to the ring on special days to eat, drink and enjoy themselves; drovers from Wales would chip bits from the stones as charms against sickness; and, up until the eighteenth century, barren wives visited the circle during the night, each going 'in the hope that by baring her breasts and touching the Kingstone with them' she would be made pregnant. Legends of the fertilizing powers of similar stones are widespread in the British Isles, hardly by coincidence, and it is difficult to explain such a pagan belief unless it were truly a vestigial memory of the earlier, sexual activities that took place inside these stone circles.

The Rollright Stones have attracted witchcraft and legends. The village at the bottom of the hill was reputed to house enough witches to drag a wagonload of hay up Long Compton Hill, and anyone happening to pass the ring when the church clock was striking midnight was supposed to see the stones leave their places and dance. Dancing, water, fertility, moonlight and nocturnal rituals—all of them combine in the mysteries of this ring—and it is clear that circles such as the Rollright Stones were not only for the dead but were also for the well-being and fecundity of everyone who went to them.

Stukeley sensed this but in the limitations of his knowledge he could add little more. He called the Rollright Stones 'the first kind, and most common of the Druid temples, a plain circle; of which there are innumerable all over the Britannick isles'. There were once perhaps six hundred or more such 'plain circles', evocative rings such as Boleycarriggeen in Co. Wicklow, a worn-down bank encircling the stones; or Tregeseal in Cornwall, the battered survivor of a pair of rings, the other finally destroyed only recently; or Guidebest at the very tip of Scotland, cut into by the river that has scoured at its side; or the Trippet Stones on Bodmin; Gors Fawr near the Preselis; Mitchell's Fold in Shropshire, lovely in its amphitheatre of hills. All of them are plain, empty rings representative of scores of other simple circles of stones with 'round barrows and cairns, singly or in groups, in their neighbourhood.[8]

Around Stonehenge, in some respects the apotheosis of the funerary cult in stone circles, there are at least a dozen of these barrow cemeteries, the mounds often arranged in lines starting from an older neolithic long barrow.[9] These may have been clan graveyards for groups of families who carried their important dead there for burial at special times of the year. As some of the long barrows were built as early as 3700 BC and the latest of the round barrows contain burials of the Middle Bronze Age, around 1500 BC, these cemeteries apparently represent an astonishing two thousand years of continuous use, eighty or more generations. People must have returned year after year to the sacred place that held the bodies of neolithic men and women, Beaker people, Wessex chieftains of the Early Bronze Age who helped in the building of Stonehenge, right down to the peasant communities of the mid second millennium BC who were to prefer other forms of burial and who put the cremated bones of their dead in flat, unadorned urnfields.

69　*A remarkable aerial photograph of the Normanton Down barrow cemetery. Among this group of embanked round barrows Bush Barrow is the third from the left just south of the bend in the long, diagonal farm-track. Its top, mutilated by Cunnington's labourers, shows clearly. Stonehenge is on the middle right of the photograph*

Some of these Early Bronze Age burials, cremation or simple inhumation, were very rich. There was the Bush Barrow man, buried under a plain round barrow but laid to rest with his bone rings and his macehead of rare limestone, its shaft adorned with bone mountings. His belt was fastened with an exquisitely patterned belt-hook of hammered gold, and two gold lozenges, also delightfully and cunningly decorated, were attached to his tunic. Yet this was not the finery of a popinjay. With these trinkets was a metal axe, by his head was his studded leather helmet, and beside him were three copper and bronze daggers, dreadful weapons with blades a foot long, kept safe in wooden sheaths, one dagger with a pommel inset with thousands of minute gold pins.

There are other burials around Stonehenge containing articles of bronze, gold, jet and amber that show how wealthy some people had become. Beads of powdery

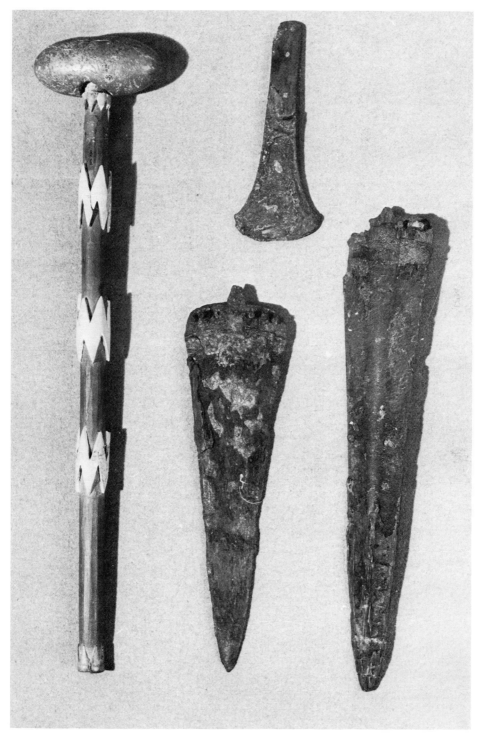

70   *The axe, daggers and macehead from Bush Barrow. The larger dagger is over 12 in.
long*

blue glass known as faience lie in some of them. Others in East Anglia, Wales, Scotland and Ireland give the same impression of a rich, ruling class from which women were not excluded. It would be wrong, however, to dismiss these as no more than opulent, straightforward burials of leaders, warriors and shamans. The rituals attending them were more protracted than those of previous ages and involved a great deal of superstition and fear of the ghosts of the dead. The dead were given riches, it is true, and with them were laid an assortment of discs of stone, totem objects, broken articles and foreign stones but their corpses were imprisoned inside rings of stones, posts or earth from which they could never free themselves. Once the burial circle had been constructed—sometimes a ditch, sometimes a timber or stone ring—funerary ceremonies took place that may have taken days or even months to complete and it was not until the final rite that the corpse or its cremated ashes were placed at the centre of the ring and the barrow heaped over its remains. An understanding of their funerary customs is vital for anyone interested in the ritual practices of people in Bronze Age Britain because from the round barrows and cairns, far more than from the henges and stone circles, vivid illustrations of the beliefs and values of that remote society emerge both in the structure of the burial mounds themselves and in the objects that were left with the dead.

When Collessie cairn in Fife was excavated in the 1870s the workers were dismayed at the labour in which they found themselves involved.[10] Even with a gang of labourers it took eight tedious days to remove the overlying stones, over a thousand rain-soaked cartloads being shifted before the central area was uncovered; and although no stone was too heavy to be lifted by one man the sheer multitude of cobbles and small boulders must have taken a prehistoric group weeks of tedious effort to pile up into the cairn. First they had dragged blocks of sandstone to make a lumpish ring inside which they buried their dead. They filled the interior of this ring with clay on which they lit fires long after the burial, for the clay had been laid over the ground in which a cist had been made. Around it other fires had burned. In the cist were two fine beakers but only the leg bones of a corpse, the rest of which had dissolved in the wet gravel. Elsewhere in the cairn was a later burial, the bones broken and burnt, lying under some heavy stones. With them was a bronze dagger, the gold rim of its pommel intact, a few fibres of its leather sheath still adhering to the blade.

The ring of stones around the Collessie burial, the burning of fires, the tremendous overburden of cairnstones reveal something of the fears that the dead were now generating, quite unlike the neolithic use of ancestral skulls when the dead were companions who were simply no longer in the realm of the living. It was possibly the acceptance of chiefs that engendered these dreads in Bronze Age communities, people believing that men who had been powerful in life could be as potent and dangerous in death. Ceremonies to ensure that spirits could not wander from their graves became lengthier and more emphatic, as Collessie demonstrates. Other burials were less arduous but no less intriguing for the glimpses they give of mysteries that we may never solve.

Only twenty miles from Collessie some people who lived by the sea and who probably sailed and fished the waters of the Firth of Forth raised a barrow over several graves and a cist on a hilltop near Dalgety.[11] Three graves contained wooden coffins, one of them shaped like a boat to sail the ghost to some unseen island, the natural home of the dead to these fishing folk. With the bodies, as well as Bronze Age pottery and implements, there were sinister cremations, one in a sack behind the heels of the corpse in the shiplike coffin, two others in a coffin whose occupant had been buried with his stone battleaxe. One cremation lay in a bag by his hips, the other, of a small creature with a thin skull, rested by his feet.

These graves had been dug around half a dozen scattered cists in which other bodies had been placed, two of them on floors of white pebbles. The head and shoulders of one rested on an animal hide and the burnt bones of another human being were packed into the corner of his cist. Whether these cremations were the sacrifices of followers cannot be known but it is certain that these people, like neolithic groups before them, had used human skulls in their rites. While the hilltop was still open skulls had been temporarily removed from the cists. They had been taken to an unknown ritual centre, perhaps Balfarg only twelve miles away, a circle-henge whose rings of posts had been replaced with a stone circle. There or at some other shrine the skulls had been used. Teeth had dropped from their fleshless jaws and people picked some up from the scatter that had accumulated over the years, returning the skulls to their cists, not realizing that some teeth belonged to people whose bodies had never been buried at Dalgety. Similar activities at Millin Bay, an idiosyncratic stone ring with marvellous carved stones by Strangford Lough in northern Ireland resulted in the loss of several skulls from the skeletons of children whose teeth, in some cases, had been misplaced or even put back upside down in their lower jaws.

Just to the north of the Dalgety graves the people dug pits like those used for storage in their own homes, packing seashells into one as an offering of food. Three other pits near it contained nuts. Yet each of them also held a human skull, testaments to the people's belief that these heads, perhaps of strangers, would guard the barrow when it was raised over the dead.

The boat-shaped coffin at Dalgety allows us the rare privilege of knowing, rather than suspecting, the religious concepts of these prehistoric people. For once we can quite legitimately make an equation: the nearness of the living to the coast + a coffin carved in the shape of a boat = a belief that the dead went on a voyage to a home across the sea. From this, other inferences develop: that exceptionally deep graves imply a belief in a subterranean home of the dead; and that graves consistently aligned towards the east or west and with solar symbols carved on their stone cists reveal a cult of the sun. Neither of these last examples, however, permits an interpretation as unequivocal as the boat-shaped coffin.

There are at least forty tree-trunk coffins known from Bronze Age Britain as far north as Culsalmond in Aberdeenshire, where one was unearthed in a turnip field, down to Stoborough, nearly five hundred miles away by the Dorset coast.[12] Here the dead person had been wrapped in a deerskin shroud embroidered with gold lace. There are several tree coffins in Wales and Yorkshire but not all of them were boat-shaped and it is likely that many were simply timber versions of the stone cist of highland regions. There are, on the other hand, grave-pits which were intentionally dug in the shape of boats. One, under a round barrow near Nympsfield chambered tomb in Gloucestershire, was a rock-cut pit, stone lined, with a flat stern and pointed stem.

71 *Millin Bay, Co. Down, during the excavations of 1953. At least fifteen skeletons were placed in the narrow rectangular cist before a cairn was heaped over it. Round stones or 'baetyls' can be seen on the left. They may have had a sexual-fertility significance*

7 *Goatstones four-poster, Northumberland: cupmarked stone*

8 *Stenness circle-henge, Orkneys*

9 *Newgrange passage-grave, Co. Meath: domed roof*

10 *Mané Lud passage-grave, Carnac, Brittany: megalithic carving*

Like Lligwy in Anglesey this unaptly named Soldier's Grave shows how the custom of communal burial lingered on into the Bronze Age for in it were the bones of nearly thirty people, lying there with joints of food for their long voyage. The situation of their burial place, high up in the Cotswolds, appears to contradict the idea of a journey across water. Yet the prow of their boat faces south towards the headwaters of the River Cam not far away, a stream that tumbles down the escarpment into the Severn and the open sea. In Wales, two boat-shaped graves lay under the Bedd Emlyn cairn near a stream that flowed westwards to join the River Clwyd. A ring of stones surrounded the graves.

These boat-burials precede by more than two thousand years the barge that sailed into the mists carrying the dying Arthur to the Isle of Avalon, a vessel that itself was older than the gold-rich burial of the Saxon king Redewald in his longboat at Sutton Hoo in Norfolk. All these burials, however, may have their origins in the beliefs of Bronze Age seafarers who travelled the waters of the North Sea. Not only are boat-burials known from Scandinavia but there are several others on the Yorkshire Moors where some of these early traders may have settled.

On Glaisdale Moor, having shaped a boat out of an oak tree-trunk, people laid a wide ring of stones around it, separating it from the profane world outside the circular enclosure. In the coffin, on a bedding of reeds and rushes and with a pillow of grass under his head, they put the fully dressed body of a chieftain, his bronze dagger at his side. Alongside the coffin they placed a smaller boat. Over the burial they piled a round barrow of stones and earth. Later, a second rich burial was inserted into this mound at Loose Howe.

The making of such coffins or, indeed, of any burial pit or cist, was almost certainly a religious undertaking that had to be carried out in a series of traditional rituals. When natives of the Trobriand Islands in the Pacific were building their canoes they observed a particular ritual at each stage, and it is likely that the Bronze Age tree-trunk coffins were also prepared according to custom: the tree selected, felled, moved and carved with the shaman watching and dictating every phase of the coffin's construction, a supervision even more rigorously observed if it was his own burial-place that was being created. Tradition may have demanded that stone tools were used.

Near Scarborough, very close to the high cliffs at Gristhorpe, a huge oak coffin under an elaborate mound had been cut down and hollowed out with flint 'chisels and hatchets of stone'. The body of a tall and strongly built man was laid in it, wrapped in a leather shroud. His followers gave him a little bark bowl containing food, and his ornaments and bronze dagger were put down by his side.[13] When his coffin had been covered with the upper part of its split tree-trunk the people lowered it into a deep pit, solemnly placing oak branches across it and sealing everything in the grave under a thick layer of blue clay. On top of this they heaped the round barrow, first a core of stones, then more clay and then a final capping of stones. It rested secure until 1834 when it was clumsily disinterred. The coffin, the finds and the skeleton of the man—having been boiled in gelatine 'through many weary hours'—can now be seen in Scarborough Museum.

Ceremonies such as these, whether of burials in tree-trunks or in cists or ordinary pits reveal something of the complicated nature of religious practices in Bronze Age Britain, and they also tell us a little about the superstitions of the people who used henges and stone circles for their rituals. The actual mound of a round barrow, although it is the most conspicuous feature today, was only the concluding structure of a complex monument of which the first was usually an unbroken ring that ultimately was to be completely hidden beneath the barrow. Circular banks and ditches in Wessex, timber circles in eastern England, rings of stone in the north were the first requirement for the rites that accompanied the burials, physical as well as spiritual barriers that would prevent the ghost from leaving its grave. A low wall of stones surrounded the cist at Parracombe in Devon where people placed a cremation before piling a stack of turves over both the cist and the wall. At Tregulland in Cornwall the rituals were performed inside a ring of slight posts which were removed to make way for a sturdier bank of stones, many of them with cupmarks ground into them as life-giving symbols of the sun. The lighting of fires was followed by the digging of a circular ditch around this bank, providing the earth for the barrow that was heaped over all the structures.

That the ceremonies inside the circles were long drawn out can be deduced from the trampled earth around some of the burials, worn down by dancers who had circled the graves. In Glamorgan, on a slope near the waters of a marsh that dimmed into a far haze of trees, wild birds nesting in the reeds and thickets, some families scraped out a ditch around an oval enclosure.[14] At its centre they quarried a pit into the limestone, shaping it like the canoe that the man they were burying may have used when he hunted for waterfowl. Round the head of his corpse the mourners packed broken pieces of his beaker, and they laid half a dozen arrows beside him, the shafts snapped in half, before pouring basketsful of soil into his grave. While they were heaping a small cairn over it other people moved around them, tramping down the earth as they stamped and danced around the burial-place.

This cairn at Sutton was added to years later by people who put the cremated bones of a young man in it under some heavy slabs. The skeleton of a child close by may have been a sacrifice. Other cremations were brought here, several of children, before the people covered everything under a mound of earth and turves that the families danced around as it was being built. The floor of a ditch of another barrow at Winterborne Whitechurch in Dorset is said to have been worn smooth by human feet as people moved round and round the burial. From the Tumulus cultures on the continent the discovery of agglomerations of fly larvae near the skeletons and of burned frankincense to disguise the stench suggest that the rites there also went on for at least a period of days.

Inside these burial enclosures tokens of magic were provided for the dead. Stones were brought from a distance to enrich the grave. The Rev. J. C. Atkinson of Danby, 't'aud Canon' as his Yorkshire parishioners called him, excavated many cairns on the Moors in the nineteenth century and believed that nearly all of them had been built of stones that had been brought there from some considerable distance.[15] One cist was filled with snow-white sand that must have been determinedly carried seven miles to the cairn. At Freeburgh Hill, at the northern edge of the Moors, there was a cairn within a cairn, the inner one composed of stones, 'many of them as heavy as, putting forth all my strength, I could lift', great lumps of basalt that had been dragged from their source three or more miles away. Another cairn consisted of water-worn pebbles taken from a two-mile-distant stream bed. Mortimer, digging on the Wolds to the south, discovered a barrow with layers of Kimmeridge clay in it, transported to the site from a mile away.

Fragments of oolitic limestone, Coral Rag and Forest Marble from sources thirty miles to the west were remarked on in long chambered mounds around Avebury. If such foreign materials were associated in the people's minds with some desirable property, such as a strangely beautiful colour, or the pure waters of a stream, or rich soil near a stony outcrop, or even something unusual such as the rocky band of whinstone on the Yorkshire Moors from which the basalt was taken, then it is understandable that the builders of these cairns would wish to incorporate the spirits of these odd and beneficent stones in their burial mound. Sometimes corpses were actually laid to rest in these imported materials. Bateman found one embedded in red clay on the Yorkshire Moors in a deep cleft in the rocks. Another at Scamridge was covered with red gravel.

Pebbles strangely shaped or of such attractive hues that they seemed to possess an unworldly vitality were deposited by the sides of other bodies. Two skeletons of infants near Stonehenge had ox skulls laid over them and a polished, banded pebble was placed by the side of them. These little stones, like the fossils laid with other burials, were probably amulets. There was a red pebble with another burial at Collingbourne Kingston and a quartz pebble at Roundway, both in Wiltshire, and one remembers the quartz pebbles above the burials in the Achnacree passage-grave. Black sea-pebbles were left in some cists under a cairn at Cerrig-y-Gof in Wales. Hollow nodules of iron oxide, 'eagle-stones', were found at Upton Lovell, and smoothed pebbles were discovered under another Wiltshire round barrow, alongside a cremation. These, like the large seashells in the neolithic chambers of West Kennet, seem intended to protect the dead, perhaps to be taken with them on their journey as fetishes against the terrors that awaited them. Natives of Ceylon regarded cowrie shells as amulets against the ghosts of the dead, and similar shells have been discovered in several British barrows, perforated to be hung around the neck as safeguards against evil spirits. Even in Christian times some coffins in the Lincolnshire church of Frampton were filled with shells.

Stone discs, like those with neolithic burials, may have had the same purpose, and it is no surprise to find them in stone circles near cremations and in round barrows such as Tregulland where five slate discs had been deposited with the dead. Broken objects were also left with corpses, the spirits released from these killed things, smashed pots at Huish Champflower in Somerset and at the Wick Barrow in the same county, broken axes from Dorset and flint arrowheads with their barbs snapped off from the Somerset Ston Easton. They occur also in Wiltshire and in Yorkshire where Mortimer came across many of these 'murdered' weapons. In a round barrow at Aldro on the Wolds a diamond-shaped arrowhead with the stains of its shaft still visible had its tip broken. It lay near the dismembered bones of a youth. Under another barrow, at Callis Wold, Mortimer found several skeletons lying on a pavement of flat Liassic stones which themselves must have been transported over two miles to their hillside. By one skeleton were the crushed remains of a newly born infant's skull with an arrowhead pointing towards it, and by another skeleton were two arrowheads with their ends snapped.

There is, perhaps, little mystery about these broken articles which serve as reminders of the symbolic, poetical thinking of prehistoric people. More problematic are the bones and skulls of beasts, some of which may have been totems rather than joints of meat. That meals were provided for the dead seems certain, not only from the evidence at Dalgety, but from the legs and trotters of pigs that both Greenwell and Mortimer discovered in Yorkshire barrows, a practice that continued in that part of England down to Iron Age times when Celtic burials often had cuts of pork left with them. Ox bones were commonly left with the dead all over the country. In a more elaborate burial at Ashgrove in Fife a man had been laid down on a bed of moss and fibres, flowers had been scattered over his body and the beaker by his side was filled with a long drink of mead.

It is difficult, however, to believe that food was intended when people put the skulls of two oxen with a burial under Winterbourne Monkton round barrow near Avebury, and the explanation becomes even less likely when applied to the Beaker grave at Hemp Knoll a few miles away. Here in a massive pit the people constructed a subterranean wooden mortuary house and in it they placed a man's body with his green slate wristguard, a beaker by his feet and the corpse of a little child close by. Back into the shaft they tumbled chalk rubble but when the pit was half-filled they stretched out the hide of an ox, skull and hoofs still attached, over the chalk in the same way that earlier people had draped an ox hide over the mortuary house in the Fussell's Lodge long barrow, the spirit of the ox lying above the spirit of the man.

Further south, near Stonehenge, Hoare and Cunnington recovered 'the skeleton of a dog and the head of a deer' from a round barrow. Antlers were even more common in these southern tumuli. Antlers, with their miraculous annual regrowth, must have impressed people as particularly strong symbols of fertility, capable of restoring life to the dead. The discovery of antlers in Wessex barrows reflects this belief in sympathetic magic. Hoare mentions a crouched burial at Winterbourne Stoke, hardly a mile from Stonehenge, with 'an enormous stag's horn' in the rubble above it to pass its generative power to the dead man. Two barrows at the delightfully named Chaldon Herring in Dorset had skeletons propped up in their grave with sets of antlers on their shoulders;[16] another mound at Collingbourne Ducis had a cremation encircled by a ring of antlers inside which were five flint arrowheads and a small red pebble. A dog's skeleton had been laid over the burnt bones.

People frequently put boar's tusks alongside the dead, maybe from a similar belief that the strength and cunning of that ferocious beast would guard the spirit of the corpse. Jaws of this animal were found outside the long mound of Hetty Pegler's Tump in the Cotswolds. Boar's teeth and the teeth of dogs have also been recovered at South Newton in Wiltshire, some of them perforated for a bracelet. Bateman came across a similar charm in the Kenslow Knoll barrow in the Peak District together with a lot of pebbles of quartz and porphyry slate. Other pebbles and teeth were put in another Derbyshire barrow at Ashford-in-the-Water.

The belief in charms and amulets was obviously strong in the Bronze Age and almost any object that was unusual or remarkable for its strength or growth might be used to confer benefits on the living and the dead. It was people with this kind of allusive thinking who built and used the stone circles that still stand on many of our moors, although the evidence for their beliefs comes from the barrows, not the rings. Even their mounds were not casual dumps of earth or chalk thrown over the burial once the rites were concluded but were constructed with ritualistic care. A Dorset barrow at Charlton Marshall was built of alternating layers of flint and chalk, while others in Gloucestershire were of stone and earth. The empty grave of Huish Champflower in Somerset was covered in thick bands of turf and brushwood. Even while these barrows were being put up rites were being performed, people dancing around and on the rising soil and stones, and several cairns in Devon reveal that charcoal was thrown onto the mound while workers were piling up the stones.

On the Yorkshire Moors a barrow at Saintoft was made up of vari-coloured sands in distinctive layers over a bed of stones. The cairn in which Atkinson found the white sand had burning charcoal thrown over it with broken flints and stones scattered across the ground. Frank Elgee, a great archaeological explorer of these Moors, noted that over half the mounds there had sand in them and conjectured that Bronze Age people had hoped that sand would preserve the bodies under their cairns.

The exact nature of the rites that attended these Bronze Age burials can never be known but carvings of scenes on rocks in Sweden do provide us with some fairly clear impressions.[17] It is regrettable that art as representational as this never became fashionable in the British Isles. Along the harsh coasts of the Skaggerak and near Stockholm there are hundreds of rock-surfaces carved in the Bronze Age by the artists of communities of crop-growers and fishermen. As well as depictions of human copulation, presumably representing the times of sowing and harvesting, there are also groups of matchstick men holding axes aloft beneath images of the sun. One cist-slab of the Late Bronze Age from Kivik shows horses and chariots in funeral games, horn-blowing men, helmets, sun-symbols and what has been suggested as processions of robed mourners. They are, however, more likely to have been representations of rows of seals standing upright. Such sea-animals, well known to the people of the fishing community that carved the cist-slabs, may have been regarded as the totemistic spirits of the dead.

The axe is the most common motif in these Scandinavian carvings. Many chiefs in the British Isles were buried with an axe, often in mint condition, a tool and weapon which increasingly signified authority as these chieftains swaggered about in their finery bearing a bright bronze axe at their hip or shoulder. It may be too strong to speak of sun-worship at this time but there is good evidence that the axe became a token not only of the chief but of the sun itself, the beginning of a process which ended with Iron Age people believing that these early leaders had been gods.

Not only axes but miniature axe pendants were buried with the dead. Near Kingswear in Devon a tiny polished axe was placed in a cist with a man's burnt bones. The cremation of a small child lay in a pit nearby. Four shining bronze axes that had never been used were buried with two skeletons at Willerby in Yorkshire under a layer of soft earth, charcoal and flints. Over it a fire had been kept burning long enough for the soil to be deeply reddened. From neolithic times the axe had been a symbol, often found in Europe hidden in bogs or under small cairns as an offering to some male god of the sky. Among other symbols such as the wheel and the concentric circle that represented the power of this god, the axe was the most commonly drawn or carved motif. At the chambered tomb of Manio in Brittany five meandering lines or 'serpents' had been engraved on a standing stone at whose base five polished stone axes were buried, their cutting edges upwards. At Mané er Hroek nearby there were axe carvings on the stones and over a hundred axes of diorite, jadeite and other attractive stones had been left with the dead.

In Britain there is the same picture of the axe being looked on as a specially potent emblem. Henges and earthworks at Llandegai, Cairnpapple, Mount Pleasant and Stonehenge had axes concealed in them. Not only were stone and bronze axes frequently placed in the barrows but quite 'useless' reproductions in chalk were left in pits at Woodhenge and Stonehenge. The famous axe carvings on the sarsens at the latter circle speak just as clearly of rituals in which axes were raised to the skies in honour of the dead and in salutation to their spirits. Nowhere, perhaps, is this more obviously shown than in the cists of cairns in the Kilmartin Valley of Argyll.

Here, very like the linear cemeteries of barrows in Wessex, a long line of mounds extended north-north-east and south-south-west from a neolithic chambered tomb.[18] Just to its west the little stone circle of Temple Wood, with a double spiral on its north stone, had an entrance at the south-east through which the dead may have been carried for the rituals which preceded their cremation. The ring was later despoiled by people who built a low stone wall around its pillars, burying several cisted cremations in its interior. These people who made pots known as food vessels and who may have built and used the Ballymeanoch henge on the other side of the river near a row of cup-and-ring marked stones, wrecked or transformed many other stone circles, as will be seen, and their desecration of Temple Wood reveals something of the antagonisms and schisms that wracked prehistoric societies during this period of change.

One of the Kilmartin cairns, Nether Largie North, had a large cist in it, the underside of whose capstone was covered with cupmarks and carvings of flat bronze axes that only the dead would have seen. Other axes in a style dated to about 2200–2100 BC were carved on the end-slab at the head of the cist. Nether Largie is open to the public and a mile away to the south at Ri Cruin another cist may be seen, bearing not only very clear axe carvings but a possible depiction of a boat, sometimes interpreted as a vessel to carry the dead to the Other-World.

72   *The megalithic chamber of Nether Largie South in the Kilmartin valley, Argyll*

The Kilmartin Valley is so close to an important sea route between Ireland, south-west Scotland and the Outer Isles of the Hebrides that it is not at all surprising to discover symbols of boats carved in its tombs. With the growth of specialist crafts—bronzesmiths, herders, workers in jet and faience, seafarers and others—a myriad of minor cults was developing in the Bronze Age, each with its own symbolism. Some people buried the dead with their axes, some held their ceremonies in moonlight, some used antlers, sun-motifs or water associations as the dominant theme in their rituals. Many of them intermingled in a flurry of local sects.

73   *Baluacraig, Argyll. This highly decorated outcrop in the Kilmartin valley, Argyll, has over 130 cupmarks and 23 cup-and-ring marks carved on it. The stone has now been grassed over*

The carvings on many cist-slabs in the British Isles show just how much variation there was, and perhaps no other single facet of prehistoric life shows how important symbolism was to those people.[19] Cupmarkings are very common and can even be found in some rings of stones, especially the recumbent stone circles of northeast Scotland. These carvings, hollowed out by grinding with a harder stone or pebble, may have been intended as lunar symbols and may be of considerable antiquity in these islands. Indeed, so potent did such ancient art seem to newcomers that occasionally a cupmarked pillar was pulled down and smashed into a size and shape that permitted it to be reused as a slab for a cist. One stone from Walltown in Angus, its sides shortened, had a swirl of cupmarks with surrounding circles, the cup-and-ring marks which also are a feature of this early native art. This pillar, which may once have stood alongside a trackway, was probably transferred to a cist.

Cupmarks were not only for the dead. Single standing stones were decorated with them, near trade routes, by the coast or on hillsides where they were visible even to distant passers-by. Many still stand—the Caihy Stane in Midlothian, nine feet high with half a dozen cupmarks on its eastern face; a small slab at Newbigging in Perthshire; the Irish stones at Rahee near Dublin; the abundantly carved pillar at Burgatia in Co. Cork near Ross Carbery Bay, an inlet to which many copper prospectors voyaged. At least forty cupmarks can be seen on this stone but in no discernible pattern and the same is true of the ponderous block at Ardmore near the wide bay of Lough Foyle in Co. Donegal. Cupmarks and cup-and-ring marks festoon the south-east side of this seven-foot high pillar, a groove or gutter leading from the centre of one of them. In contrast there is just one cupmark on the opposite face. One might speculate that the art was somehow related to the midwinter sunrise but quite what the purpose of stones such as these was is unclear. It is possible that it was the stone that was important as a territorial marker and that the cupmarks were added to it to endow it with even more significance.

These carvings in northern Britain, often found on natural rock-surfaces, were quite different from the passage-grave art of the Irish megalithic tombs. Such art is also found on some Bronze Age cists and on standing stones. The artists used only a limited repertoire of concentric circles, spirals and semi-circles, and outside Ireland their influence was largely restricted to the region of the Cheviots and Pennines. Their symbols may have been solar in origin, as in the earlier passage-graves, although the eyebrow patterns on the mysterious chalk drums at Folkton have been thought to stand for the watchful gaze of some female deity, traces of whose cult have almost vanished from the enigmatic debris of our past. As with cupmarks there were instances where this art was added to an older monument, and anyone visiting

74 *Cup-and-ring marks on an outcrop at Achnabreck, Argyll, in the Kilmartin valley.*
Grooves can be seen radiating from some of the central cups

the awesome stone circle of Long Meg and Her Daughters in Cumberland will find half-circles and spirals on the sandstone outlier, carved not on the side that faces south-west towards the midwinter sunset but on the adjacent surface, as though the carver was unaware or indifferent to the stone's solar situation.

Other cist-slabs have geometrical designs on them, often of inset lozenges or diamonds like the gold plaques that adorned the clothing of the man buried under Bush Barrow near Stonehenge. Perhaps the most intriguing of all this megalithic art are the representational carvings of axes, daggers and of human feet. The axe carvings in the Kilmartin Valley and, of course, at Stonehenge were presumably reflections of the same solar-axe cult already mentioned, and the dagger carvings can also be explained as part of the similar association between the regalia of a chieftain and the power of the spirit-world, an integration of beliefs which ultimately resulted in the emergence of gods and their worldly ministers, priests.

Footprints are rather different.[20] Several stones in cists have carvings of feet upon them, a lovely slab from West Harptree in the Mendips having four alongside a group of cupmarks. One wonders at the symbolism of these. Impressions of hands may have represented gestures of prayer and salutation. Many Scandinavian rock-carvings show men with arms raised and fingers outstretched, as though acknowledging a god; but other carvings on rocks at Bohüslan and Ostergotland bear footprints, often associated with ships carrying the dead to their new life. Here the footprint seems to signify the dead man going away, the last signs of him being his tracks, still to be seen long after he had disappeared. At Scania one composition showed a footprint being transformed into the disc of the sun, the change from life to death, and even in the Iron Age a Swedish jug was decorated around its belly with two stamps, a series of footprints with sun-discs impressed in the clay above them.

Imagery such as this helps to uncover a little of the beliefs of people in prehistoric Britain. We can also see how creeds could sometimes merge without conflict. Hardly a day's sail from Anglesey, where the passage-graves of Bryn Celli Ddu and Barclodiad y Gawres stood, there was a chambered tomb at the mouth of the Mersey close to the mudflats and marshes, a lonely place but well situated for the riverways that led inland towards the Peak District and Yorkshire.[21] This Calderstones tomb had a large and impressive mound with tall stones in its passage and chamber, some of them carved with concentric circles, lozenges and spirals. Cupmarks had also been ground into these slabs. All this was passage-grave art, well executed but not extraordinary in a tomb so close to Ireland. On three of the stones, however, footprints had been carved, probably later than the other art which they overlapped. Traders from the east, even from across the North Sea, may have passed this way during the Early Bronze Age, visited the tomb in its last years, and piously added their own symbols to a home of the dead. The mound was destroyed in the early nineteenth century and the decorated stones now stand in the conservatory of Calderstones Park in Liverpool.

None of this art would have surprised a Bronze Age traveller, wherever he went in the British Isles. He would expect the land marks of standing stones and would look for the signs that told him he was entering a new territory with its chief, shaman,

75 *One of the Calderstones, Liverpool, before its re-erection. Carvings of footprints are rare in British megalithic art*

warriors and peasants; he would behave cautiously until he discovered what the customs were in each new place he came to, perhaps hoping that he would find the sanctuary of a henge or a stone circle while he bartered with the natives. He would not be perplexed at local superstitions for he too had his amulets and charms. Rituals of celebration at the times of sowing and harvest, the painted people dancing and chanting, the days of mourning when the pyre was lit and the ashes carried to their grave, these he would have observed on a hundred occasions. Yet each district was different and from north to south the differences were extreme. Few people were buried inside stone circles and henges in lowland Britain but in Scotland and Ireland few stone circles did not have burnt bone in them.

Sometimes these cremations were dedications, placed there when the ring was constructed. Sometimes they were added later. Knowing something of the beliefs of these Bronze Age societies it is easier to conjecture what happened inside the circles. At Tillicoultry near the Firth of Forth people put up a large oval of stones on a sandy ridge overlooking the River Devon.[22] How long they used it is not known but at some time another group came who buried their dead inside the ring, placing one cremation in an urn by a stone, another in a cist at the centre of the ring, packing the cist's corners with clay and heaving a four-ton stone over the grave. Inside the cist they had spread sifted sand, placing white quartz pebbles on it. When the corpse was laid down they put a roll of red felt, made from dog or fox hair, under his head. His cist-slab was carved with magical circles and loops with grooves running from them to the edge of the stone.

None of this was the work of the stone circle builders. The ways in which the cult of the circle flourished, or was sometimes confronted by hostility, and how it finally died away are questions whose answers, faint and fragile, are contained in other facets of Bronze Age ritual, magic and fanaticism in the British Isles.

Mother and Child.
Cemetery or Sacrifice?

'We may from hence infer that this Circle of Stones was ... a place of
Idolatrous worship ... as well as other such Circular Monuments in
Britain and Ireland (wheoref I presume that there are not less than 100
yet remaining)'.

John Aubrey, 'Monumenta Britannica'

Had Aubrey guessed at a thousand rather than a hundred stone circles in the British
Isles his observations about these places of 'Idolatrous worship' would have been
even more perceptive. The slow construction of a few huge rings in the last centuries
of the Late Neolithic was followed by a scurry of building in the Early Bronze Age
when the climate was at its most benevolent, warm, dry and equable, permitting
people to farm the stone-littered uplands of Britain for the first time. Scores of circles
were erected on these previously unoccupied wildernesses, each standing in its own
clearing.

While the large enclosures such as Arminghall, Stonehenge and Arbor Low continued to be the ceremonial centres of whole regions, individual groups of families
raised smaller rings in their own territories. There were several of these minor circles
within a few miles of Avebury, all of them smashed unrecognizably today, and in
some cases the ring took over the role of an older long barrow. The architecture
of these new shrines and temples varied from locality to locality in Britain, centre
stones appearing in some, avenues in others, concentric circles in parts of Ireland
and Scotland, plain rings without burials or extra stones being preferred in the greater
part of southern England. And it must always be remembered that rings of posts,
now long vanished, or of earth were just as popular in that period even though,
to our eyes, they do not possess the same dramatic romance as the weathered circles
of stone.

That these rings were ritual centres seems clear not only from their contents
but from the fact that they were often built a long way from the burial-places and
settlements of their users, set apart from the ordinary world in their own sacred
area. Although there were at the very least a hundred and fifty barrows in the Stonehenge area, there is hardly a mound within half a mile of the circle itself, apart from
one little group just to its west. Similar voids exist elsewhere. The Arran circles
on Machrie Moor were built well away from the settlements. In the Peak District
the seventy cairns on Stanton Moor are well to the south of the Nine Ladies ring
there. At Danby Rigg, a plateau on the Yorkshire Moors settled in the Bronze Age,
walled fields and remains of huts mingle together but the circle in which Canon
Atkinson found two burial urns stood well away from them with only overgrown piles
of cleared stones near it. As with the chambered tombs on Rousay the stone circle
builders obviously did not consider it necessary to erect these rings close to their

76 *Torhousekie stone circle, Wigtownshire, from the north-east. The three stones and the slight mound at the centre suggest that this might be a form of recumbent stone circle. The circle-stones rise in height towards the south-east*

77 *The ruins of Circle IV on Machrie Moor, Arran. On the left is the one remaining stone of Circle III*

78 *Machrie Moor XI, Arran, a stone circle discovered in 1978 buried under peat that accumulated because of climatic deterioration since the Bronze Age*

homes and, indeed, may have actually considered it dangerous to have such temples near them. Five rings, three of lumpish granite boulders, two of delicate columns of sandstone that glow goldenly in the evening sunlight, were grouped together on Machrie Moor, a fertile triangle on the Isle of Arran. They had been put up over the generations on land already sanctified by the presence of chambered tombs, and in 1978 we discovered a further stone circle close to them, hidden when peat had formed over the moor. This area was holy ground and it is noticeable that the dozens of huts whose ruins litter the moor were built well away to the west, none of them near these powerful and lonely stones.

Erected by natives of these islands with their superstitions, cults and barbaric burial rites, the Bronze Age rings remain mysterious if only because so little has been recovered from them by excavation. Some hints of their purpose are provided by their design yet even that treasure-house of architecture, Callanish in the Outer Hebrides, near to the sea, with its avenue and rows of stones leading to the circle, with its central pillar, its burial chamber and its astronomical alignments, has hallucinated scholar and visionary alike with the evanescence of the clues they seek. Its stones stand sharply against the western skyline as bleakly as a winter coppice of trees, pencils and pillars of sandstone that have thwarted explanation ever since John Morison around 1680 reported that 'it is left by traditione that these were a sort of men converted into stones by ane Inchanter'.[1]

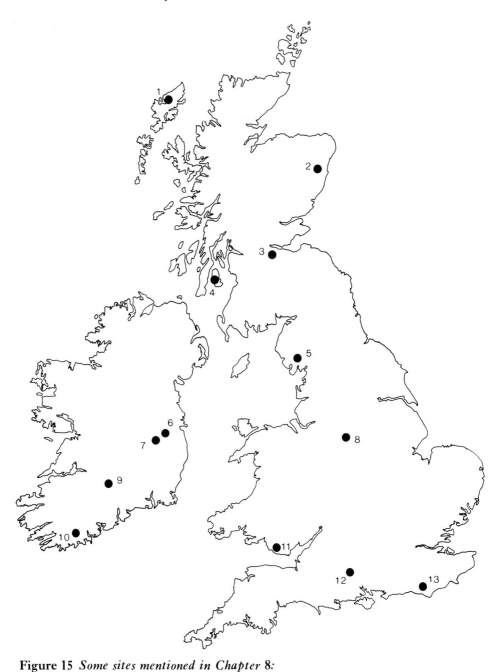

Figure 15 *Some sites mentioned in Chapter 8:*
1 Callanish, NB 213330; 2 Broomend of Crichie, NJ 779196; 3 Cairnpapple Hill,
NS 987717; 4 Machrie Moor stone circle complex, NR 911324; 5 Banniside Moor,
SD 285967; 6 Longstone Rath, N 936206; 7 The Curragh henge, N 780130;
8 Parcelly (Parsley) Hay round cairn, SK 144631; 9 Cullen Bog,
R 807393; 10 Reanascreena recumbent stone circle, W 265410; 11 Pond Cairn,
Coity, SS 297819; 12 Wilsford Shaft, SU 108414; 13 Itford Hill settlement,
TQ 447053

11 *Stanton Drew, Avon: the Cove*

12 *Crow Stone, Wigtownshire*

In the eighteenth century Callanish was always a 'Temple of the Druids' and John Toland thought it was a ring devoted to their worship of the sun. William Borlase believed it was a megalithic calendar with the stones recording the numbers of weeks and months in the year, an idea developed by James Kerr in 1873 who referred to the tall central pillar as the 'great stone gnomon', a pointer that acted as the rod of a sundial to indicate the time of day. Rather differently, John Palmer called the same stone the 'Callernish phallus', placed thrustfully erect in the middle of a ring dedicated to rituals of sex.

More recently several astronomers, Somerville, Hawkins and Thom among them, have calculated that the rows may have been aligned on the risings of various stars—Capella, Altair or the Pleiades—or on the setting of the moon. Dates around 1800–1760 BC have been suggested by them for the construction of the ring. By 1857, when the chambered tomb inside the circle was rather casually excavated, peat had accumulated to a depth of five feet all over the site, making it very difficult to distinguish between it and the prehistoric soils beneath. All the diggers found were 'some minute fragments of what we suppose to be bones found in the chamber, and a specimen of a black unctuous material ...'[2] The bones were human but why there was a passage-grave inside a stone circle, why there were rows and an avenue leading to—or from—the ring, why there was a centre stone or two other stones placed oddly just outside the circle, no one could explain. It was also puzzling that there were at least three more megalithic rings within two miles of Callanish. Legends spoke of processions, strangers and sun-ceremonies but quite how death, the sun and the stars combined at Callanish forty centuries ago no one knew.

> *Many the burials, many the days and nights, passing away,*
> *Something that shall endure longer even than lustrous Jupiter,*
> *Longer than sun or any revolving satellite*
> *Or the radiant sisters the Pleiades.*

> Walt Whitman, 'On the Beach at Night'

It is likely that Callanish was added to over the years with some sections never completed and that it was finally taken over by people to whom a stone circle was little more than a conveniently powerful place to bury their dead. It is the thinness of the evidence that makes such famous rings frustrating to anyone seeking their answers. They are famous because many of their stones remain but, on occasion, an almost completely ruined site is more helpful. Almost every feature at Callanish was matched two hundred miles to the east at Broomend of Crichie near Inverurie in Aberdeenshire. Here there was a little henge with a stone circle and a possible central pillar inside it, two avenues, one of them leading from water, and several burials inside and outside the ring. Although today the monument has been almost entirely destroyed by the combination of road and railway construction and the quarrying of sand enough is known about it and its people to permit an imaginative reconstruction of its history and purpose.

Nearly four thousand years ago some families turned inland from the coastal plain near modern Aberdeen, travelling upriver along the valley of the Don until

79   *Callanish stone circle in the Outer Hebrides. The ring is small but three lines of stones and an avenue make it a complex unmatched in the British Isles. Between the central pillar and the circle-stones to its left is a tiny passage-grave*

they came to the place where the Urie swirled into it, flowing eastwards from the foothills of the Grampians. It was an attractive area, the soil sandy and rich with dark stands of trees by the meadows fringing the watersides, but in the surrounding hills the country was already settled by people of different beliefs, the builders of circles with a massive block laid flat between the two tallest pillars of the ring. Some of these recumbent stone circles were already generations old when the new group entered the valley below them. Easter Aquorthies to the west, Kirkton of Bourtie and Balquhain to the north were all less than four miles away, hardly an hour's walk from the henge, and it must be assumed that the hillpeople who used these rings were prepared to let the newcomers put up their earthwork by the river.

We should be mistaken if we thought that this open-air structure was the counterpart of a modern church. In prehistoric times the secular and the ritual were not kept as separate as today's supermarkets, chapels and factories, and it is quite possible that Broomend of Crichie was both a trading depot and a temple. Although

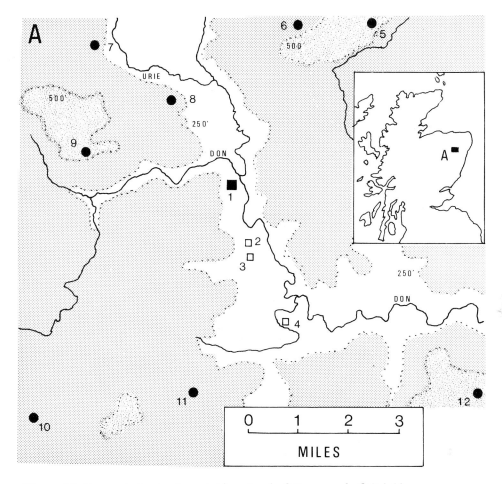

Figure 16 *Stone circles in the neighbourhood of Broomend of Crichie, Aberdeenshire:*

1 Broomend of Crichie, NJ 779196; 2 Fullerton embanked circle, NJ 783179; 3 Cairnhall embanked circle, NJ 785175; 4 Tuack embanked circle, NJ 795154

Recumbent stone circles:
5 Sheldon, NJ 823249; 6 Kirkton of Bourtie, NJ 801250; 7 Balquhain, NJ735241; 8 Brandsbutt, NJ 760223; 9 Easter Aquorthies, NJ732208; 10 Castle Fraser, NJ715125; 11 South Ley Lodge, NJ767132; 12 Dyce, NJ860133

it was small, with a central plateau less than twenty paces across, its bank was several feet high, the earth coming from an inner ditch deep enough for its diggers to be hidden from sight and too wide for most people to jump. Two gaps for entrances were left at north and south, one for people approaching from the river, the other perhaps for native families. The earthwork offered some protection from attack and yet a score of workers could have dug it out of the sandy soil in less than a fortnight. There were other little henges almost identical to this in Scotland where the communities seem to have been smaller than in parts of England: one at Ballymeanoch across the river from the Kilmartin cairns, another at the Muir of Ord near the Beauly Firth in a region of chambered tombs, even one ten miles east of Broomend at East Whitestripes Farm near the River Don. A really diminutive earth ring, barely a quarter the size of Broomend, was erected twenty miles to the west where the Ealaiche Burn joined the Kirkney Water at the very edge of the mountains.

Such places may have been sanctuaries. With the expanding demand for bronzes and exotic materials, trading networks were reaching into all parts of the British Isles, extending along the ridgeways and the rivers that offered easier transportation for the heavy bundles of trade-goods. But safeguards were needed for the people carrying these luxuries. Custom and good sense required that the pedlars should be assured of protection, and as barter itself was almost a ritual activity that followed prescribed patterns of etiquette and formality, it is likely that special places were assigned for the occasions when native and stranger met. Even in the Neolithic the links between henges and the stone axe trade have been noticed[3] and stone axes from the Lake District and northern Ireland have been discovered as far north as Aberdeenshire. Broomend of Crichie's little henge may have been a centre for trade as well as a temple, people coming in from the neighbouring hillsides to meet with the river-people, to celebrate and to barter for the bronzes and the ornaments that have been found in their graves.

In many parts of Britain pairs and groups of stone circles and henges stand

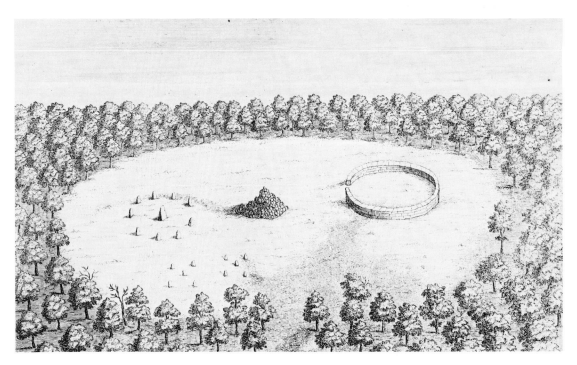

80   *An imaginary 'Druidical grove' on Anglesey drawn by William Stukeley from a sketch by Henry Rowlands. Only the stones of the circle are known to have existed*

close together as though for different communities that were to meet warily at the borders of their homelands. At Broomend a late version of a recumbent stone circle may have been built close to the henge so that the natives could perform their own ceremonies there.[4] Although the monument was demolished during nineteenth-century sand-quarrying William Maitland in 1757 described it as a large ring of three concentric circles of stones with a small cairn at their centre. Many recumbent stone circles in Scotland consisted of a circle of stones with a ring-cairn inside it, a structure which had an outer kerb of big stones with another ring of stones lining the open central space. It may have been three circles like these that Maitland saw. There is a recumbent stone circle, the Blue Cairn of Balronald, miles to the west of Broomend, that had a cairn on which the huge recumbent actually rested. These huge blocks, nearly always in the south-west quarter of the ring, sometimes had cupmarks on them and Maitland mentioned an 'altar of one stone, with a cavity in the upper part, wherein some of the blood of the sacrifice was put'. Although cupmarks were never intended as receptacles for gouts of blood the existence of one on this 'large flat stone' suggests that the families inhabiting the uplands around Broomend had constructed something like a traditional recumbent stone circle near the henge, and for years the traders and the local people assembled here by the river, performing their own ceremonies before mingling together.

It did not last. The dynamic of prehistory in the Bronze Age is a story of change, sometimes peaceful, sometimes turbulent. Other people came into the valley, perhaps from Perthshire where rings of stone were already standing on the hillsides, and they put up a circle of six granite stones inside the henge. What opposition, even conflict, there was we cannot tell, but at the centre of the ring these intruders raised a pyre and on it they burnt a human body about which we know nothing except that it was cremated. Its later treatment suggests that it was needed for the rites that followed.

When the ashes were cold the people scraped up the bones and then dug a wide, tapering grave into the area where the fire had burned, digging down until the pit was too deep for them to lift their basketloads of sand over its rim.[5] Then, at the bottom of this hole, the men set up coarse granite slabs for a cist into which they placed the dedicatory burial of a man. His corpse had been buried elsewhere some years before and only parts of his skeleton were brought to the circle having perhaps been carried for miles along the rivers and tree-scattered coastlands of eastern Scotland. His skull was set down at the west of the cist, his leg bones arranged crosswise at the other end. Then the burnt bones, gathered into a bundle, were handed down and laid between his bones in the middle of the cist. Slowly the workers lowered a capstone into the pit, the sand collapsing behind them as they levered and heaved two other gross slabs on top of this lid to seal the man in his burial-place. The grave was filled in. The people carried hundreds of cobbles and stones to the shaft, dropping them in, kicking and shovelling back the heaps of sand at the edges of the hole, stamping the stones and sand down. Finally the charcoal and ash from the pyre were tipped onto the trampled mass, forming a thick black patch on which a pillar may have been erected at the centre of the ring.

Whether this stone ever stood in the circle is unclear but it is certain that a long avenue of stones was raised for this new ring inside the henge, leading a quarter of a mile from the river, widely spaced at first but narrowing and with taller stones as it neared the ring. It can hardly be doubted that this was for processions but at Broomend these did not end at the little six-stone circle. Instead, a further stretch of avenue, slightly out of line, led fifty yards more to the bigger circle with its cup-marked stone.

It is natural to ask what this complex was used for, what the purpose of the avenues, the ring of stones, the deep grave and the central stone was, and why the avenue should continue to a low cairn having passed through the henge. Avenues and single rows of stones leading to henges and megalithic rings had two recurring associations, water and death, something to be expected if the idea of these avenues developed from the use of cursuses and mortuary enclosures. On the Yorkshire Wolds neolithic people had erected avenues of posts at Kilham and the nearby Kemp Howe, timber-lined ways along which the dead were carried to a stockade where their decaying corpses would be safe from scavenging animals. Avenues of stones linked a meandering line of cairns at Moor Divock in Westmorland, rows of stones climbed uphill towards Bronze Age cairns on Dartmoor and in northern Scotland, and down in Dorset a small barrow at Poole that was spectacularly ringed with posts had an avenue approaching it from the south-east. Another, also on Canford Heath, its mound scattered with flints and flakes, had a similar avenue.

These avenues were often close to a river or stream, and perhaps when the flesh had gone the human bones were taken in a procession of wailing, face-painted mourners to be washed clean before their final burial or cremation. Both of the avenues at Avebury were near streams, the Kennet Avenue leading from the Sanctuary on Overton Hill, a wooden hut which may have been a mortuary house, downhill past the springs that bubbled around Silbury Hill, and then northwards towards the great stone circles inside Avebury's earthwork. At Stanton Drew the avenues led from the River Chew towards the rings of coarse, pebble-rough blocks. A stone row near Exmoor was so close to water that today it is submerged whenever there is a high spring tide in the Taw estuary. Stonehenge's avenue of earthen banks ran down to the Christchurch Avon and it may have marked the course along which the bluestones were dragged by Beaker people, if they were responsible for bringing them from Wales. One of their leaders had been buried near the River Wye under a cairn at Clap-yr-arian, his superb dolerite battleaxe laid by his side.

Fieldworkers have found it difficult to make plans of these avenues. John Aubrey was prevented by rain from plotting the stones at Avebury and two hundred years later Lukis had the same problem. William Stukeley, looking at the hilly avenues at Shap in Westmorland, grumbled that 'the raining weather, which in this country is almost perpetual, hindered me from making at this time a thorough disquisition into it'.[6] There may have been three avenues here, almost linked together like the Dorset cursus or the Stallmoor row, over two miles long on Dartmoor. One of the Shap avenues had a stone circle at one end and a small barrow at the other. They are now almost completely wrecked. In the seventeenth century William Camden described them as 'large stones in the form of Pyramids (some of them 9 foot high and 14 thick) set almost in a direct line, and at equal distances, for a mile together' but even in his time they were so damaged that he refused to speculate on their purpose because 'the injury of Time has put it beyond all possibility ...' We can, however, notice the barrow, the circle and the course of the avenue over a brook that flows into the River Lowther just as another avenue may have led from the loch to the ring of Stenness although now only one or two stones remain of it.

Avenues and death go together and Broomend of Crichie is no exception. Near its southern end cists have been discovered in a sandy ridge, one empty, another with the skeletons of two men in it covered in an ox hide with their beakers behind their heads and a mixture of twigs, flints and charcoal over them.[7] A third cist paved with small pebbles held the crouched skeleton of a man, an ox hide or felt cloth over him, a beaker with a ladle made out of well-tanned hide standing in it placed behind his back. Propped in the corner of the cist was the skeleton of a little girl no more than a year or two old from the evidence of her teeth, some of which had no roots while others had hardly erupted. Close by was a fourth cist, tiny and having only a beaker, some fragments of a child's skull and a few half-formed teeth in it. These burials of Beaker people, probably placed there within a century of 2100 BC, are little different from the burials along Avebury's Kennet Avenue. Unlike the deep burial at the centre of Broomend's circle, however, their corpses had been buried

81 *A reconstructed stretch of the Kennet Avenue, Avebury, Wiltshire, leading northwards to Avebury. More stones may be buried in the field to the south*

soon after death, carried down the avenue to the waiting cists, perhaps with the comfort of a servant to wait on their departing spirits. They were buried about the same time that warriors and peasants under the command of some great chieftain were pulling down the concentric circle of bluestones on Salisbury Plain before those rings were completed, replacing them, sarsen by heavy sarsen, with the immense structure that the world recognizes as Stonehenge today.

There are hints that the people who built the henge at Broomend of Crichie intended to include astronomical lines in it. The entrances were aligned almost perfectly north–south. There are so many of these cardinal point orientations in stone circles and henges that they are unlikely to be coincidental. One might add that corpses taken along the avenue towards the henge would be moving towards the north, where the sun and moon never appeared in the sky, whereas when they were taken back towards their cists they would be going to the south, where both sun and moon were at their highest in the heavens. Whether this symbolism was intended we cannot tell but with the deliberate orientation of cists and bodies to face the sunrise or sunset it is an explanation that may contain some truth.

The stone circle to which the bodies had first been taken was the focus of the people's lives and religious existence. Like many others it was a simple ring, here composed of six rough blocks. It is a number so often repeated in the circles of central Scotland where there were also eight-stone rings and rectangles known as 'Four-Posters' that it has to be assumed that the stones had been counted by people who possessed at least elementary systems of numbering. Many recumbent stone circles consisted of ten stones, whatever the length of their circumference, and it seems that a circle was not a casual construction but was erected following strict traditions about the number of stones, the shape of the ring and the architectural features to be included in it. The stones marked its limits, forming a spiritual barrier around the sacred ring whose potency was heightened by the stone and the burial at its middle.

Sometimes an outer bank or ditch emphasized this boundary between the worlds of men and spirits. There is, rather intriguingly, a second cluster of recumbent stone circles a full five hundred miles from the Aberdeenshire hills in south-west Ireland. A group of them around Ross Carbery were also built of ten to twelve stones but the connections between these Irish rings and those in Scotland are obscure because their features are distorted. In Cork and Kerry not only were the rings smaller but the tallest stones were erected opposite the recumbent stone rather than alongside it. At Reanascreena on the easy slope of a hillside a few miles from the coast a family of a few people dug a circular ditch and bank before putting up the stones, placing the recumbent stone at the west towards sunset or moonset in Spring and Autumn.[8] Nearby a body had been burnt. In 1960 the excavators noticed how the mourners must have walked or danced among the ashes of the pyre, treading the charcoal on their feet into the earth around the portal-stones when they carried a few bits of cremated bone to the circle. People had returned to this holy place so often that they had worn down the soil around the entrance and the area had to be repaired. Well-trodden patches where people had passed into the circles were observed during two other recent investigations at Bohonagh and Drombeg nearby. At Reanascreena the people had buried the burnt bone inside the ring. They may also have put up a centre stone but, if so, later people removed it and only its earth-filled hole survived.

Only about thirty rings in the British Isles had standing stones inside them,[9] but often these pillars stood against a central burial explaining why 'centre' stones are rarely found at the precise centre of any ring. It was the burial that was important, a dedication or an offering that the stone commemorated and whose spirit it embodied. There is a concentration of these rings in Cornwall and south-west Ireland, especially among the largest circles which may have been the most important. Some have marvellous central pillars, such as the leaning stone at Boscawen-Un in Land's End, or the Irish recumbent stone circles at Maulatanvally and Templebryan

82   *Boscawen-Un, Cornwall. The fine central pillar is believed to tilt because treasure-seekers have dug at its base*

with low pillars of quartz in their interiors, a mineral chosen for its magical properties although it is unlikely that the people who built these rings were aware of the electrical propensities of quartz. Like the central 'hearth' at Stenness or the stone in the forecourt of Cairnholy chambered tomb a 'centre' stone was the pivot of the ceremonies with offerings laid around it as the people performed their rites.

The excavation of a henge near Naas in Co. Kildare, a region of circles and amazingly tall standing stones, discloses some of the rituals that accompanied these dedicatory rites.[10] At the crown of a gentle hill that was visible for miles around people hacked a stonehole into the slatey bedrock and then burned off the tangle of scrub and brushwood that littered the ground. When the soot and charcoal had

83   *The Long Stone at Punchestown, Naas, Co. Kildare. It is 19 ft 6 in. high. An empty cist was found at its base when it was re-erected in 1934. There are many other tall standing stones in this part of Ireland including that at Longstone Rath three miles north-north-east*

settled they battered out a long pit against the stonehole, packed its floor with stones and put the bodies of a well-built man and of a woman into it. A thick pyre of oak and hazel branches was heaped over them and set alight. Hours later the still-glowing ashes and bones were raked and scooped into the centre of the pit which was then lined with massive slabs. An urn was pushed onto this confusion of bone and ash over which earth was tipped, filling the cist to ground-level. The people hauled a splendidly high limestone pillar upright in the stonehole and from it scribed out a circle with a long rope, digging a ditch and piling up a bank to mark this enclosure off from the ordinary world. Even this was not sufficient. Before the ring could be used its contents had to be sealed in and the men and women carried basketloads of earth and stones into the interior, spreading them all over the ring until only the pillar and the surrounding bank could be seen.

Folk stories help us understand the significance of this henge, known as Long-stone Rath or Fort. Until modern times legends of fertility were attached to it and girls hoping to get married hammered pins into a hawthorn tree that had grown inside the ancient ring, a diluted memory of the rites that once were held there to ensure the well-being of the people. More revealingly still, the centre stone was called *Fear breagach*, 'the false man', not because it was thought to be a statue but, as the excavator R. A. S. Macalister pointed out, because it was a 'receptacle for the life and the soul of a person buried beneath it', the embodiment of the guardian spirit of the ring.[11] If there ever had been a central stone at Broomend it probably had the same meaning, the symbol and the essence of the man imprisoned in his stone-piled cist deep beneath the ground.

Deep, massively blocked graves like this, showing the fear people had of wandering ghosts, were not uncommon in the Bronze Age. Bateman excavated one at Shuttlestone in the Peak District where a man wrapped in animal hide and lying on a bed of fern leaves had been buried in a pit hacked eight feet down into the solid limestone. Another man was buried sitting upright in a rock fissure at Parcelly Hay, trapped in his grave by several immense slabs above his head. Both these men had cairns of thousands of stones over their graves.[12]

Not all deep shafts imply fear. Only the piling of stone over the burial suggests that. At Garton Slack in Yorkshire there were other pits, one of them thirty feet wide and seven deep, another near it over twelve feet deep.[13] Alongside it was a pit with a dome of earth at its centre. Antlers had been laid around its base, covered over with gravel, and people had trampled round this below-ground barrow in funeral rites before the dead were buried in their deep graves. The digging of these pits may indicate the beginnings of a return to earlier neolithic beliefs in the spirits of the earth. The ritual pits of the Goodland sites, the Aubrey Holes, the shafts at the henge of Maumbury Rings, perhaps mark the gradual re-emergence of native customs that the cult of the circles and the introduction of Beaker creeds never eradicated. Ultimately these half-forgotten traditions would become widespread once again.

Signs of this strength of custom can be seen at Broomend itself. The most potent part of the complex was the aberrant recumbent stone circle at the head of the

84 *Thomas Bateman's extremely imaginative sketch of the Parcelly Hay cairn in the Peak District which he opened in 1848. In it he found a Beaker burial with a broken pot and some animal bones. Five vast limestone blocks had been dragged over the rock-fissure in which the corpse was propped*

avenues. In the hills around were dozens of these strange rings, the stones rising in height towards the recumbent block where pieces of white quartz were scattered and where cupmarks were sometimes carved. The mountains at the edge of the Grampians could be seen from many of the circles, dominated by the crouching granite bulk of Mither Tap, the Mother of the Top, a mountain traditionally sacred and belonging to the range known as the Paps of Bennachie. These, like the Paps of Anu of Ireland, may have been thought of as the living body of a goddess of nature but today we can do no more than guess.

The recumbent stone circles around the Bennachies are so close, within two or three miles of each other, that they were probably family shrines. They are wonderful rings, the recumbent often colossal like the stone at Old Keig, fifty tons or more in weight and yet exactly horizontal, balanced nicely upon its tapering base. As at Longstone Rath fires had burned inside the rings consuming the bodies of men, women and, particularly, of children, but in each circle so few cremations have been found that they must have been offerings rather than the ordinary burials of a family group living in the vicinity of the ring for generations. At Sunhoney, a reconstructed ring near Echt, fires had burned at the centre, bones and charcoal had been left there and stones and earth had been spread over these deposits, hiding them from view. The outer face of the fallen recumbent stone has over thirty cupmarks on it, some grouped, some in lines, some isolated, all of them as inscrutable as those on rocks and stone elsewhere.

They can, however, be linked to another feature of these rings, the position of the recumbent stone itself, which was always placed between the south-west and the south-south-east of the circumference. The one exception was thought to be at Strichen, where the recumbent stone lay at the north of the ring which was destroyed in 1965, but our excavations in 1979 showed that this was because the ring had been rearranged in the early nineteenth century. The recumbent stone had, as usual, originally been near the south of the circle.

85 *Loanhead of Daviot, Aberdeenshire, from the north-west. In this photograph of the recumbent stone circle the internal ring-cairn, the broad recumbent stone and the graded heights of the circle-stones can all be seen*

86   *The gigantic recumbent stone at Old Keig, Aberdeenshire. It weighs about fifty tons.*
This view, from outside the ring, shows how level the tops of these massive stones can be

The reason why these recumbents occupied such a restricted arc of the ring baffled scholars for a long time until it was realized that the builders had aligned these stones on the midsummer full moon, not at those moments when it rose or set but when it was shining high in the sky. At its maximum the moon would have been a spectacular object, perhaps visualized as the home of the dead by the natives who raised these stones. If the symbolism is correct then the cupmarks are lunar motifs and the quartz, pieces of white rock that epitomized the distant land of death, would have been entirely appropriate placed close to the recumbent stone in family rings at whose hearts human offerings lay.

These were mystical lunar alignments. A recumbent stone was too long for it to be used as a precise foresight for any scientific observation of the heavens. In these circles the ceremonies were for the benefit of the living, even though dead bodies may have been brought here before burial. It is likely that the same applied at Broomend, the people gathering around their own imitation of a recumbent stone with its cupmark, supplicating the spirits of the Other-World for a good harvest and for the safety of their own lives.

This may also have been true at Callanish, whose features were so similar to those at Broomend, not because the people who built those rings were in any way related but because, fundamentally, their needs were alike. At Callanish the avenue climbs from the direction of the bay towards the little ring with its centre stone where once human bone may have been buried. Beyond the ring another row of stones leads precisely southwards towards a rocky knoll from which the full moon could have been seen skimming the horizon at midsummer. People from the outlying rings may have assembled at Callanish on special occasions for their shaman to lead them in communal ceremonies. Legends speak of a Great Priest wearing a cloak of coloured feathers, of Callanish being the annual meeting-place of giants, of fertility rites and of a 'Shining One' who walked along the avenue when the cuckoo's Spring song was first heard. It is interesting that the flattened arc of the circle does face exactly east towards the Spring sunrise at the vernal equinox and that the row of stones there runs towards the east-north-east where the sun would rise in April when the cuckoo was announcing the coming of Summer

> *Breaking the silence of the seas*
> *Among the farthest Hebrides.*
>
>   William Wordsworth, 'The Solitary Reaper'

A problem is that Callanish appears never to have been finished. Although there is a complete avenue to the north there are only single rows to east, west and south as though the project had been begun but had been interrupted. It is possible to see what had happened. Other people had come to the circle and inside it they had built a passage-grave, the smallest in the British Isles because it had to be fitted in between the 'centre' stone and the circumference of the ring. It changed Callanish utterly, transforming its open interior into a pointless clutter in which the chambered tomb was the most obvious feature. Such destruction was almost a commonplace at this time. Cists and a ring-cairn were added to a circle at Dun Ruadh in Co. Tyrone. The bluestone circle at Stonehenge was torn down and the ring of sarsens was put up in its place. A stone circle was begun at Cultoon on the island of Islay but was never finished and some stones were left lying by their stoneholes, slowly covered with peat. The little rings at Temple Wood in the Kilmartin Valley and at Balbirnie in Fife had drystone walls put up between their pillars just as the recumbent stone circle we excavated at Berrybrae in Aberdeenshire did, the tops of its stones smashed, its ring-cairn demolished to provide material for the wall, all done by Food Vessel people who did not believe in the traditional rites of the circle builders but who did like to bury their dead inside these hallowed places.

Cairnpapple near Edinburgh is a dramatic example of the restlessness that brought alteration and damage to so many of these rings.[14] Here newcomers had already built a henge with north–south entrances, a stone circle and a Cove over an arc of neolithic ritual pits, but their circle-henge was itself changed when Beaker people buried a body in its interior, standing a stone at his head and raising a small cairn over the grave. Years later Food Vessel people came, knocking down the stones of the circle and using them as kerbstones when they enlarged the Beaker cairn after

87   *Balbirnie, Fife. The drystone walling between the stones was added by later Food Vessel people who transformed the circle into an enclosure with a continuous bank around it*

they had buried cists with both corpses and cremations in them and with a cupmarked stone nearby. Some decades after this, another group clumsily added stones around the sides of this cairn, so increasing its size that it overlapped part of the henge ditch. These families had parcelled the burnt bones of their dead into urns which they buried in shallow pits before they heaped the stones untidily over them. One of the hollows was filled with earth and charcoal scooped from the floor of a hut in which the dead man may have lived. Finally, perhaps two thousand years after the first neolithic family had settled here, Iron Age people dug four graves into the bedrock of what was left of the henge's open space.

Food Vessel and Urn communities were fascinated by the great megalithic rings, even though they did not wish to use them for anything but cemeteries. Several burials in urns were found by the stones of the ring inside Broomend of Crichie, one of them containing the burnt bits of a woman's jaw and some bird's bones. To the

88 *Cairnpapple, West Lothian. Inside the circle-henge with its Cove later Beaker incomers buried one of their dead in this cist and heaped a mound over it*

south, down the valley of the Don, were small embanked rings at Fullerton, Cairnhall and Tuack with urns and cremations in them. A huge round barrow circled by standing stones stood on a hill between these rings but it was removed around 1850 when railway navvies used it for ballast.

These monuments, spread out over nearly three miles, were almost but not exactly in a straight line and inspection of their remains makes one wonder how anyone could believe in the modern day cult of ley-lines which are claimed to extend for many miles across uneven country, undeviatingly straight, their course defined by structures of widely different periods and purpose. The Broomend group of rings, all roughly of the same age, type and purpose, were misaligned by over two hundred yards, obviously an imperfect attempt by people in the Don Valley to lay out a straight line over a relatively short distance. Similar errors can be observed in the Dorset cursus, in the Yorkshire henges at Thornborough, on Stanton Moor in the Peak

89   *A food vessel from Yorkshire. Native people who made such pots often damaged stone circles and henges in the Early Bronze Age. This heavy, hand-coiled pot from Garton Slack has a series of lugs around its neck. It is about 6 in. tall*

90   *An urn and an 'accessory' or miniature cup from Yorkshire. Cremated bones were placed in such urns, sometimes accompanied by a tiny pot. The urn is 9 in. high*

District and in all the linear Wessex barrow cemeteries. It must be concluded that absolute straightness in these alignments was not of obsessive importance to the people who set them out.

What prehistoric people did erect during the centuries that saw the waning of the megalithic tradition were standing stones—single, in pairs or in rows—that were sometimes aligned on the sun or the moon. One stone by itself can tell us little of its original purpose. Many of them, standing by tracks that were old but rarely straight, were probably intended to mark out indefinite sections of these routes. Others, however, were set up in lines like late and emaciated versions of the great avenues that had been pathways for the dead.

These stones retain their associations with death and fertility in legends that have endured, diluted and misunderstood, long after the generations of families who used the pillars have been forgotten. Here and there, isolated stones are whitewashed, at Carnalridge in Co. Londonderry and at Edenmore in Co. Down, for reasons that no one can remember. Enormous pillars, weighing many tons and standing alone and stark, still rise, teasingly silent, around the Wicklow mountains in Ireland.

Such stones were not only the places to which the newly dead were brought but were also the foci of fertility rites so strong and vital that they still whisper in our memories. Until a few years ago local people would meet for an August festival at a row of stones on a hilltop near Shantemon in Co. Cavan, and other assemblies on New Year's Eve were held at the Stan Stane, a holed stone on North Ronaldsay, one of the few islands in the Orkneys to lack a chambered tomb.

The pillar at Coolineagh in Co. Cork with a quartzite stone balanced on top of it was supposed to possess the power to heal and to make women fecund. Curative properties were linked to many stones with holes in them. The prehistoric people who raised them must often have had traditions reaching back to the times when skeletal bones were handed out through the entrances of neolithic tombs to be used in rites for the well-being of the community and, centuries later, these rituals persisted, now performed by shamans, often connected with the sun. The Men-an-Tol ('the stone with a hole') in Cornwall was believed to cure their illnesses if children were passed through it, boys pushed through by a woman to a man, girls by a man to a woman, always passed towards the sun. Even as far away as Tobernaveen in Co. Sligo similar beliefs were held.[15]

Other standing stones were directly joined to death. Pillars at Try, Gulval, in Cornwall and at Drumnahare in Co. Down were set up on top of cremations, and a small stone circle, now gone, near Applecross in Scotland had a central stone with a hole into which local people would put their heads, 'which if they could doe ... they expect thair returning to that place, and faileing they conceaved it ominous!' Yet such stones were as strongly associated with fertility. Like the outlying Stone of Odin by Stenness, girls could be betrothed by holding their lover's hand through the hole. At Doagh in Co. Antrim and at Aghade in Co. Carlow it was a custom that lasted for almost four thousand years and in Co. Meath a 'Teltown Marriage' was one contracted by a man and a girl joining hands through a hole in a wooden gate. It seems significant that Teltown is a legendary cemetery and assembly place

91 *The Men-an-Tol, or the Holed Stone, Cornwall. Fertility legends attached to such perforated stones are widespread in the British Isles. The Men-an-Tol stones have probably been rearranged*

of the Iron Age Celts with earthworks resembling henges and cursuses close to the banks of the River Blackwater.

Sometimes pairs of stones were put up, a tall thin pillar and a squat, lozenge-shaped slab that have been interpreted as representations of male and female sexual organs, a visual symbolism that would be quite in keeping with the imagery of life, death and magic in prehistoric times. It was not only the Kennet Avenue at Avebury that had such fertility stones. There were others, in pairs, at Sandville and at Crew Lower in Co. Tyrone, and in central Scotland there were several set up near late stone circles such as the rectangular settings of four stones known as Four-Posters, set at an angle to the ring just as the final miserable avenues in Wales and on Dartmoor were built at a tangent to their circles. In the bottom of the east stone-hole of one pair at Orwell in Perthshire people placed the cremations of men and women mixed with the bones of dog and pig before raising the stone over them. Other cremations near the stones, and the presence of cists and pockets of burnt

92 *A pair of stones at Penrhos-feilw, Anglesey. The purpose of such settings of stones is still debatable*

bone in the ground around them, show that these two stones remained the centre of ritual activity for a long time.

Without doubt the most spectacular of all the stones are those that people arranged in short alignments, rows of ponderous slabs, some as early as the beginning of the Bronze Age, and with quaint names—the Three Fingers, the Eleven Shearers, the Nine Maidens. In Pembrokeshire near the village of Llan Llawer eight stones led towards the megalithic tomb of Coetan Arthur. The name of the row, Parc y Meirw, 'the field of the dead', shows how probable it is that funeral processions once passed by these stones. Professor Alexander Thom, in an analysis of many stone monuments in Britain, concluded that this row had been aligned on the moon at its minimum setting. He also suggested, rather less convincingly, that the Five Kings in Northumberland pointed towards the setting of the star Vega around 1820 BC, the exact position on the horizon being marked by a distant standing stone. The row itself, on a bracken-covered hillside, had two of its stones set at right-angles like the

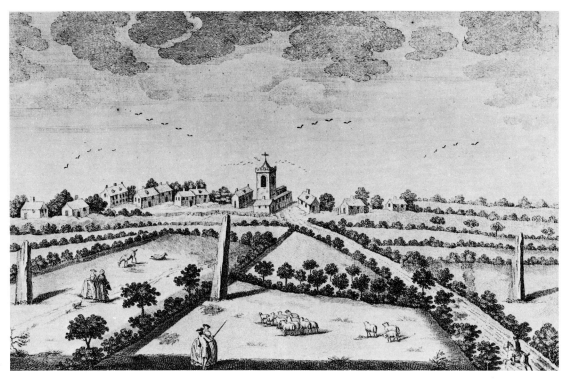

93   *The Devil's Arrows, Yorkshire, drawn by William Stukeley. There were at least four stones in the row in the seventeenth century when William Camden mentioned two close together in the middle with two farther apart at the ends*

sides of a Cove suggesting that funerary rites took place here. Emphasizing the funereal associations of some of these rows, other people put up a row at Eightercua by the shores of Ballinskelligs Bay in Co. Kerry, the pillars rising in height towards what is left of a prehistoric cairn.

The Devil's Arrows near Boroughbridge in Yorkshire had associations with water and Summer gatherings. Today only three enormous pillars of millstone grit remain, each twenty tons or more in weight and hauled several miles from a source near Knaresborough, standing on a slope that rises from the River Ure to the north, the tallest stone, twenty-three feet high, at the far crest. The monstrous size of these rain-runnelled giants compels a realization of the effort that went into their erection, put up by people in a region where megaliths were almost unknown. Huge man-deep stoneholes were dug for them. Once there were four or five stones in this line but one was pulled down in the hope of finding treasure beneath it and it was later dragged away to make a footbridge over a stream. Two acquaintances of William Stukeley, Roger Gale and a local clergyman, dug down to the foundations of another stone and, as a record of their excavation, they 'put four half pence in a leaden box underneath'. Stukeley did not approve. 'I could not commend them for it, as it could only tend to mislead the curious of future times.' Although nothing is known of the purpose of the Devil's Arrows, this stone row is as likely as the others to have been an assembly place for fertility rituals and well into the eighteenth century the fair of St Barnabas was held near the stones on midsummer's day.

Knowing the associations that existed in the prehistoric mind between death, the sun and the moon, it would be surprising if some of these rows did not have astronomical alignments built into them. Although some of the earliest rows may have been directed towards the sun increasingly many of them were aligned upon the moon. It may be that the solar cult of the passage-graves never became firmly rooted in Britain and although it was practised by the chieftains and the shamans in the henges and great stone circles it was the ritual pit and lunar creeds that native families preferred in their own small shrines. Thom's researches have apparently revealed so many of these moon 'temples' that he has entitled one of his books *Mega-lithic Lunar Observatories*.

Country people, living in the open and knowing every aspect of their skyline, would have had little difficulty in deciding where the sun or moon could best be seen and the architecture of the rows reflects this familiarity. One setting of three stones at Drumtroddan in Wigtownshire, very close to a rock face covered in cup-marks, concentric circles and channels, was aligned towards midsummer sunrise.[16] The Eleven Shearers, a row of low stones near the ruins of a Roman fort far out in the Cheviots, may have been directed towards the equinoctial sunrise, and the sites of some late circles, their stones usually no more than knee-high, may have been chosen because there was an astronomically suitable notch or gap on the horizon from that spot.

Yet the lines, as in the past, were for the dead. One of the most convincing of what have been claimed to be prehistoric observatories is a line of three stones at Ballochroy on the lovely Kintyre peninsula. This spoiled row stands on a hill ter-race that overlooks the Sound of Jura and the islands that rise against the waters of the Atlantic and it was aligned upon the sun. Today one has an almost uninter-rupted view of Cara island, over which the sun sets at midwinter, but what cannot be seen are the cairns that once loomed in the middle of the row, blocking the island from sight. Edward Lhuyd, the antiquarian, drew them in 1699 before farmers carted the cobbles away to make field-walls, and it is clear that, as always, Bronze Age peasants at Ballochroy had integrated a symbol of life and death, the sun at the chil-ling set of Winter, into the place they had built for their dead.

More and more people in those years were abandoning the custom of building rings of stones and, instead, were scraping up low circular banks of rubble, leaving a gap through which they could enter these unimpressive circles that are known as enclosed cremation cemeteries. Some of them may have been simple burial-grounds but a rather horrifying number have the cremated remains of a woman and an infant at their centres. Whether we interpret this as evidence of the dangers of childbirth or of the sacrifice of human beings to sanctify the new ring with their imprisoned spirits we are reminded of the differences between our way of life and that of the people who laid out these late, last circles. Weird Law, a ring so low that it can hardly be seen in the wind-bent grasses of the Cheviots, held the remains of a woman and child buried alongside their pyre. An enclosure on Penmaenmawr in North

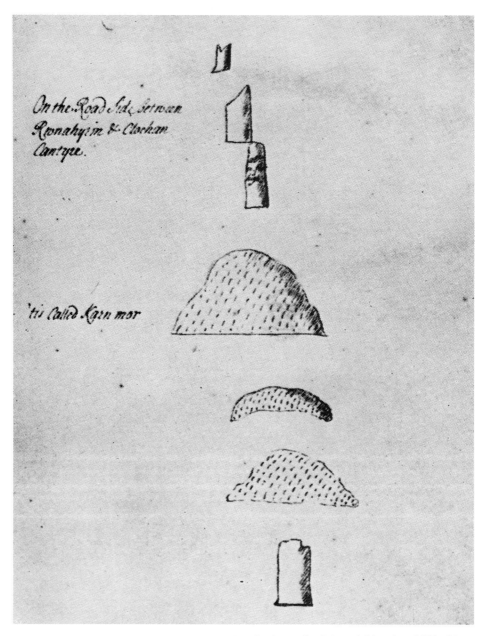

On the Road Side between
Rwnahysin & Clachan
Cantyre.

'tis Called Kairn mor

94 *The cairns and stones at Ballochroy, Argyll, drawn by Edward Lhuyd in 1699. Since then the cairns have been removed*

Wales, built about the same time as Weird Law around 1800 BC, had the burnt bones of a woman concealed in a niche in its surrounding wall. Another ring at Brenig in a great cemetery of cairns and barrows, now submerged beneath a reservoir in Denbighshire, had been built on an area from which the turf had been stripped and charcoal strewn about before the cremations of an adult and child were buried there.

Beneath the mountainous sides of the Old Man of Coniston in the Lake District a family had gone to just as much trouble to make a proper enclosure for their rituals, levelling the ground and constructing a thick and well-built wall of stones that incorporated a natural boulder at its south-west, perhaps in line with the midwinter sunset. This ring on Banniside Moor contained a central cremation in an urn that had been set upright on a slate slab with quartz scattered around it. Nearby was a blackened patch where the pyre had burned. More urns and food vessels were buried nearby, one with a lump of red ochre near it, and to the north, just inside the ring in a hole in the bedrock, was a finely decorated urn with a heavy collar that was stamped around its rim and shoulder with tiny circles. Inside was a little pot, some threads of soft and loosely woven woollen cloth and the burnt bones of what the excavators surmised were the bodies of a mother and a two- or three-year-old child.[17]

Ear bones of children have been recognized from Bronze Age cairns in Wales, and at Port Dafarch near Holyhead one of the barrows in a long-used cemetery had equally grim contents. The ashes of a young woman and a dog lay under an upturned urn around which pebbles had been arranged. Inside it people had put a diminutive pot which they had lined with bracken. Only a few of the bones of an infant were found in the vessel suggesting that this might not have been a normal death. In the same way other women and babies were buried under a cairn at Cefn Golau to the west of Mold in Flintshire. The name of the mountainside on which they lay, Moel Famau, means The Mothers' Mountain and later became the legendary home of a Celtic goddess of fertility.

These were strange times, years of change when the climate was worsening, becoming colder and wetter, when people were being driven off the uplands because the increasing rain kept their fields waterlogged, and when peat was accumulating on sodden moors whose protecting trees had long since been cut down. The old sacred circles seemed to be losing their powers. The spirits had become more demanding, no longer appeased by ordinary rites, and it was perhaps for that reason that children were sometimes desperately sacrificed in futile efforts to halt the decline of the land.

Some people held stubbornly to tradition. Others adopted new customs. Still others combined the old with the new, producing novel patterns of ritual in monuments that were both circles and cairns. One of these sites was only a few miles north of Sutton where the Beaker man lay buried in his boat-shaped pit, his broken arrows beside him. Pond Cairn near Coity in Glamorgan was excavated in 1937 by Sir Cyril Fox, an archaeologist who was able brilliantly to reconstruct the events that had taken place there late in the Bronze Age, performed by a group of crop-growers who undertook such an involved sequence of rites that it seems very unlikely that cairns like this were ever simple places of burial. To the contrary, some, like neolithic barrows before them, must have been monuments that covered bodies whose bones had been placed there for the benefit of the living.

The builders of Pond Cairn lived in a landscape of heath and marsh with forests spreading inland up to the mountains, a countryside of small communities occupying patches of good soil that would support families as long as the climate was kind.[18] Early one Spring, maybe in March before the first leaves appeared on the hazels and hawthorns at the edge of the woodlands, a man's body was cremated and the people, two or three families, no more, packed his bones into an urn. They had already killed a child, burnt the corpse, washed the splintered bones clean and carried them to a hummock that they had chosen for their rites. A long pit had been dug here and into it the child's bones were thrown, mixed with sandstone pebbles and a flint flake before the hole was sealed with a layer of clay. Over it a paving of stones was laid and just to the north a second pit was dug with a trench shaped like a phallus leading into it. A shaman set the cremation urn on the paving, putting a little pink slab on top of it. From the cold ashes of the pyre people carried charcoal with bits of bone and a sheep's tooth among it, dropping handfuls into the new pit. Then, facing the sunset through the smoke as he lined the hole with sticks of burning charcoal, the shaman invoked the spirits of the earth to bring the people a good harvest. Some heavy sandstone blocks were heaped around the urn and then turves were cut from the muddy shores of the marsh and stacked up in a great drum that covered the little cairn, the trench, everything. All this can be deduced from the excavation. What cannot be recovered are the incantations, the dances and the orgies that may have accompanied this Spring ceremony when the seeds were to be planted in the fields.

The weeks passed and Summer winds blew earth from the turf drum onto the ground beside it. Day after day the ten or so men and women laboured, building a ring-cairn around the area, a high and wide wall of stones that encircled the turf-stack on whose top the shaman threw wood ash when the ring was completed. Then they danced round it, trampling the earth hard around the drum in a ritual designed to bring strength to the growing crops.

For a while the place was left in peace. On the heaths the gorse lost its yellow flowers and children hid and played in the bright green bracken that crowded the borders of the fields where the wheat and barley flourished. On the trees the hazel nuts ripened, acorns appeared, the first buds of the hawthorn berries could be seen and, at last, the crops were harvested. Then the people tore down part of the ring-cairn's wall at the east, just leaving a ramp that sloped down to the central space and the dome of turves. Here they dug a pit. After lighting a dedicatory fire by it the shaman, as he looked towards the setting Autumn sun, put burning sticks of gorse and twigs into the pit. Then he laid down sheaves of wheat and barley as thanksgiving to the forces of Nature that had given the people food, placing a grey Liassic stone among the cereals before setting fire to the offering.

We cannot tell for how many years the people returned to this shrine but, recognizing the meaning of their rites of fertility we ask, as Cyril Fox did, who was the man whose bones were buried at the centre of the ring? His may not have been an ordinary death. 'Was he a corn king—an embodiment of the corn spirit?' We can speculate about the sacrifice of the child, the meaning of the phallic trench and the potent fire that had burned at the end of it, but even if the details elude us the overall significance is apparent, that Pond Cairn was built and used by people as anxious to ensure their sustenance as neolithic families had been and whose rituals, although more elaborate, were fundamentally the same.

In southern England peasant societies were burying their cremated dead in pots so poorly fired that they caused Jacquetta Hawkes to exclaim that 'of all the dreary sights to be seen in our museums, none is more inevitably dreary than the contents of an average large Deverel–Rimbury cemetery, rows upon rows of urns ...' It is true that the vessels are rarely more than utilitarian. Yet these skilful farmers with their neat fields and droveways were no less aware of the need to propitiate Nature than their predecessors had been. Near the settlement of Itford Hill in Sussex, dated to about 1250 BC, a family had put up a ring of twelve posts and inside it, over the years, they had buried the bones of their relatives, many of them children, with a few wretched possessions, often merely a pebble from the estuary nearby. 'They represent the remains of humbler folk, to whom death was no stranger. Not for them the trappings of rank or fortune, but the cast-off pots as used in daily life.'[19] The last thing the survivors did before they moved away to another home was to heap a low barrow over this pathetic cemetery. The first thing the people had done when they had been building their houses a generation earlier had been to deposit a chalk-carved phallus in the doorway posthole of the largest hut, its top level with the floor to bring safety and luck to the occupants.

These were Deverel–Rimbury people, a name derived from two separate groups, one of whom had inserted some burials into the sides of a barrow at Deverel and another that had buried their dead in a more customary flat urnfield at Rimbury. The excavation of one of these cemeteries at Kallis Corner, Kimpton, near Andover in Hampshire, showed that dead bodies had been laid in a circular mortuary hut, taken from there to the pyre and when their bones had been burned and buried in the urnfield to the north the remaining ashes were brushed into baskets and carried to a ring whose sarsen blocks had been dragged from a considerable distance. Some of the urns had been intentionally broken, sherds from four being laid out like a mosaic floor on which an upturned urn had been set. Elsewhere there was a cist with just one large sherd, a lot of black soot and a perfect and unburned flint arrow-head.[20] Finds such as these seem as eccentric as the cremation under a barrow at Winterslow in Wiltshire, the bones wrapped in cloth and accompanied by a collection of eyebrows, shaved from the foreheads of the dead person's family as a sign of mourning.

The phallus at Itford was not only part of a fertility cult whose origins extended a long way back into antiquity but it also anticipated many votive offerings that would be made to the spirits of the earth and of water in the last centuries of British prehistory. Deep pits were dug, reaching far down into the ground, and into them gifts were dropped. On occasion they took excavators by surprise. Digging a little 'pond' barrow near Stonehenge in which they expected to find cremations and urns the archaeologists instead discovered a pit so deep that air- and water-pumps and closed-circuit television had to be obtained before the bottom could be reached. This Wilsford Shaft, dug out with antler picks around 1700 BC by Deverel–Rimbury people, was six feet wide and had been quarried a hundred feet down into the chalk before the workers finally reached water-level having shifted and dragged over a hundred tons of rubble out of this incredible black and airless pit.[21] It was not a well. The sides were too nicely smoothed and finished and, in any case, water could more easily have been obtained nearby. Other pond-barrows, circular banks with saucerlike interiors, contained cremated burials but some of them also had pits, perhaps to receive offerings just as the deep shafts of the neolithic henge at Maumbury Rings had potsherds, animal bones and chalk carvings concealed in them.

At Wilsford there were also pots in the shaft, an ox skull, wooden tubs and bits of rope made from wild bryony fibres that must have been used to haul the chalk to the distant surface. At the bottom there were bone pins and amber beads that had been dropped there as offerings to the spirits of earth and water. Propped against the side was a short, stout timber. This oak post, like the branches found on the Gristhorpe tree-trunk coffin, may be an indication that a tree cult was developing. The association of Iron Age druids with sacred groves and with the oak are well known and Bronze Age rock-carvings in Scandinavia showing men dancing around trees suggest that the tree may have become a symbol of fertility well before 1250 BC.

Hazel branches were found inside the Loose Howe tree-trunk burial on the Yorkshire Moors and John Mortimer, in his excavations of barrows on the Wolds to the south, recorded several instances of hazel bark or nuts in the graves. One at Riggs had hazel and a branch of heather lying near the skeleton of a robust man who had also been given two discs of black flint to take with him, all these things being expected, presumably, to give him life and strength. The upright post at the bottom of the Wilsford Shaft, placed there by the last of the workers before he scrambled out of the terrifying pit, probably had the same purpose.

New elements of savagery were entering ritual practices as society itself became more disturbed with the shifting of population in the later Bronze Age. A shaft at Swanwick in Hampshire had a post in it around which were traces of dried flesh or blood just as an Iron Age shaft at Holzhausen near Coblenz in Germany had blood, flesh and fat congealed around its timber upright. In this period, when swords and shields were being manufactured for the first time in the British Isles and when defensive banks and ditches were being thrown up around hilltop settlements, some changes in religion expressed the impact that killing and warfare were having on the minds of the people. 'Blood is a beggar' wrote Thomas Kyd, the Elizabethan playwright, and when life was cheapening the spirits and the gods demanded more and more for their acquiescence and protection. There were even hints that head-hunting, prevalent in the Iron Age, was known centuries before then. A cult of the head seems certain. In 1960, at the western rim of the Lake District mountains, in a Bronze Age cairn on Irton Fell, excavators found a water-worn stone of Borrowdale lava. Not much bigger than a boxing glove it had been carved crudely into a human face with thin lines for the beard and holes for the eyes pecked out in the coarse surface. It seems that spirits were being personified and given human identities, becoming gods.

Traders no longer travelled freely with their wares but hid the bulk of them before entering settlements, taking only a few articles with them to each village. Many of these hoards were never recovered, an unpleasant indication of how troubled the times were. There were other, different hoards, deposits of votive offerings in streams, lakes and bogs made by people who were turning to the fertile spirits of water for help as the climate deteriorated and grey, cold pools formed on the empty moors. Bronze swords were thrown into a swamp on Shuna Island in Argyll and shields into a bog at Luggtonbridge in Ayrshire. Even more spectacular were the bronze drinking horns and pony cap flung into a marsh by Iron Age people at Torrs near Castle Douglas. These were offerings to water deities and occasionally they tell us something of the people who gave them. Unlike the gifts of swords there was a huge area of eastern England from the Yorkshire Wolds down to the Thames Valley in which the hoards consisted mainly of spears, as though the region was ruled by warriors to whom the sword was an unacceptable weapon.

Models of boats inlaid with gold tell the same story of a revival of water cults whose origins reached back to the offerings of stags by the mesolithic hunters of Meiendorf and Stellmoor. In the east of Ireland scores of magnificent gold articles were dug out of Cullen Bog in the eighteenth century.[22] This had once been a great cult centre, just as Stonehenge must have been, dominated by kings and warriors whose powers were strong and widespread in the centuries when people were desperate for their protection. The discovery of over a hundred precious objects, made by craftsmen who lived in the safekeeping of the kings, from this one bog alone reveals the astonishing wealth these men had acquired. It also shows the compulsions of religion that such riches should be given freely to the greedy spirits.

Overlooking the bog, on a low hill to the west, there was a henge with a wide bank and ditch, a barrow at its centre where a tall rectangular pillar stood, the place where the people assembled for the seasonal gatherings of their clans. Here the king would have paraded, a golden gorget around his neck, twisted gold bracelets at his wrists, his chequered cloak fastened with gold lockets, an ornate crown of thin gold like the helmet of a Spanish conquistador upon his head, a heavy bronze sword in its decorated leather scabbard high on his side. Surrounded by jostling warriors and peasants the priests at the centre of the henge blew their long curved horns and shook their rattles of bronze in a cacophony of discords and janglings that aroused the gods at the times of sowing and harvest and when the cattle were to be driven from their stalls onto the pastures of Spring grass, farming occasions that developed into the four great Celtic festivals of Beltane, Lughnasa, Imbolc and Samhuin.

There were other times of propitiation when the gods had been offended and when jewellery and valuable household things were taken out to the middle of the lake and thrust into the waters where reeds and peat were already gathering. From this 'Golden Bog of Cullen' bronze cauldrons, spears, swords, axes and horns were recovered by amazed peat-diggers three thousand years later. Bars of gold, dress-fasteners, chains, golden discs with sun-motifs incised upon them and ear-rings were unearthed by peasants between 1731 and 1845, although sadly they often failed to benefit from their fortune (J. N. A. Wallace, 'The Golden Bog of Cullen', *North Munster Antiquarian Journal*):

> A fool, cutting turf, found three rings like ring-dials; one of which he put on the end of a walking staff, whereon it remained until his father found it was gold,

and took it from him. He hid the other two, cannot recollect where; and now they cannot be found. He says, he also at the same time found a lump in the form of a large egg, with a chain hanging from one end of it; which he either lost, or had it stolen out of his pocket by one of the labourers.

The bronze horns found in the bog, ornamented with tiny spikes, were for religious ceremonies. Some had a hole for a now-rotted mouthpiece, not at the end but in their sides, and were almost impossible to blow. Dr Robert Ball of Dublin did succeed in producing the one note these instruments were capable of, a deep bass sound very like the bellowing of a bull, but attempting to repeat it he burst a blood-vessel and died shortly afterwards. The 'end' horns were rather better and provided a range of up to four notes not one of which could felicitously be described as musical. Their shape, obviously imitating genuine bull's horns, and their sounds have led to suggestions that they were used in the rites of a bull cult, a suggestion which is strengthened by the discovery in Ireland of bronze crotals, globular or pear-shaped rattles that produced ear-aching clatters but which may have been regarded as likenesses of a bull's testicles. Such imagery is not improbable when one remembers the pairs of chalk balls from some Irish neolithic tombs and from Windmill Hill where carved phalli were also found.

A masculine bull cult, moreover, practised alongside a lake would fit well with other known associations of horned fertility gods with water. For the first time in the prehistory of these islands the associations were recorded in myths and folk-stories which were written down almost a thousand years after the end of the Iron Age and maybe twice as long after they were first recited. There were instances when the bull and the water were joined into one supernatural being. The name of Boand, the goddess of the River Boyne, means 'She Who Has White Cows', and Verbeia, a goddess of the River Wharfe, means 'She Of The Cattle'. Sometimes carvings of a goddess show her with horns on her head. One from Ribchester in Lancashire may represent Modron, the mother of Maponus, a god of hunting. In Co. Tipperary other stories which could have been familiar to the people around Cullen speak of a lazy wife whose spinning was done by ghostly horned women.

At Cullen the strength of the bull, epitomized by the king, was fused with the fertile and life-giving power of the watery body of a goddess to whom rich offerings were given. But, like the later Iron Age bog-burials in Denmark where sacrifices were drowned in lakes, there were more dreadful gifts. Among the bronzes and the gold from Cullen were human remains, skulls 'surprisingly thick and round'.

In another henge, on the eastern side of Ireland in Co. Kildare, a region of many standing stones, there was another cult-centre of immense antiquity. Even today fairs are held there, tinkers assemble and the public race-course is a living relic of the gatherings that have been known at the Curragh for well over two thousand years.[23] Several circular earthworks were raised here, one of them with entrances at both west and east where two great posts may have been aligned on the Spring and Autumn sunrises. In the middle of this henge was an oval grave, also aligned east–west, nearly four feet deep and packed tight with gravel.

At the bottom, head to the west, was a skeleton lying on its back, its arms pushed hard against the sides of the pit, legs wide apart and its skull, lower jaw thrust out, pressed tightly down onto its chest. It was a young woman who had been buried but in so strange a posture that the excavators at first thought her position was the result of the setting in of ordinary rigor mortis. This, however, was unlikely. The contortions of the head and limbs were excessive and quite unlike those of a normal corpse. An alternative explanation, that the grotesque arrangement of the bones had been caused by instantaneous rigor, the body being buried immediately after the woman had been violently killed, was just as improbable because of the difficulty people would have had in forcing her rigid limbs into the narrow grave. Nor had any attempt been made to dispose them decently.

The facts were better accounted for by Dr McGrath, State Pathologist and Professor of Medical Jurisprudence. The most feasible though dreadful solution to the mystery was that this had been the body of a woman who had offered herself to be buried alive. She had lain down in the deep grave, unbound, involuntarily tensing herself as the clay and gravel was shovelled onto her, holding her head forward to avoid the grit and dust getting into her eyes, choking and writhing as the pit was filled. The dead and burnt bones of sacrifices were no longer sufficient for the dark gods. Now only the living would satisfy them.

9
The Severed Head

'At the present day, Britannia is still fascinated by magic, and performs its rites with so much ceremony, that it seems as though it was she who had imparted the cult of the Persians.'

Pliny the Elder, *Natural History*, *c.* AD 75

In 1857 a superb shield, as long as a man's trunk, was dredged from the Thames at Battersea. It was made of thin sheets of bronze to which three curvilinear discs inlaid with red glass had been attached, and at its centre a huge swelling boss, protecting the hand-grip, stared out like the great eyes of an owl.

Although this magnificent work of art could have been dropped as its owner fled in panic during one of the Roman invasions, equally ornate objects have been found in other rivers and the Battersea shield was more ornamental than practical, a parade-ground article rather than a piece of military equipment. It is more likely that it was intentionally flung into the water as an offering to one of the Celtic goddesses of the Iron Age. The Black Lake at Dowloch in Dumfriesshire, renowned for its healing powers, was still having shreds of clothing and parcels of food thrown into it in our own century.

The Battersea shield was not only an astonishing demonstration of Celtic craftsmanship but, like many Iron Age shields, scabbards, pots and brooches, it also had obscure animal symbolism in its design. When the wearer of the shield looked down as he held it on his arm he saw, glaring back at him, a human face with bulbous nose, eyes formed of two rivets and, above them, the two long and curling horns that signified a creature from the Other-World. Turned upside down the design became the face of an open-mouthed man with a long, twisted moustache. These patterns gave spiritual strength to the shield. The double meanings and abstract images concealed in this apparently uncomplicated shield characterize the elusive, mystical thinking of Iron Age people in the British Isles, almost incapable of being understood today. Much of it must have derived from the earlier communities of the Neolithic and Bronze Ages but it is only in the final centuries of prehistory that, because of some written records, we are able to perceive how full of poetry and metaphor even the most ordinary object may have been to its owner.

* This book has been concerned with religious practices in the early prehistoric period of the British Isles but it would be wrong to end it without a sketch of ritual and belief in the Iron Age when, for the first time, the archaeological evidence is enriched by the introduction of Celtic mythology, a combination so complex that only a long survey could do it justice. Excellent books already exist about this period, Anne Ross's *Pagan Celtic Britain*, Stuart Piggott's *The Druids*, and Vincent Megaw's *Art of the European Iron Age*. Readers interested in learning more about this turbulent time are recommended to these works.

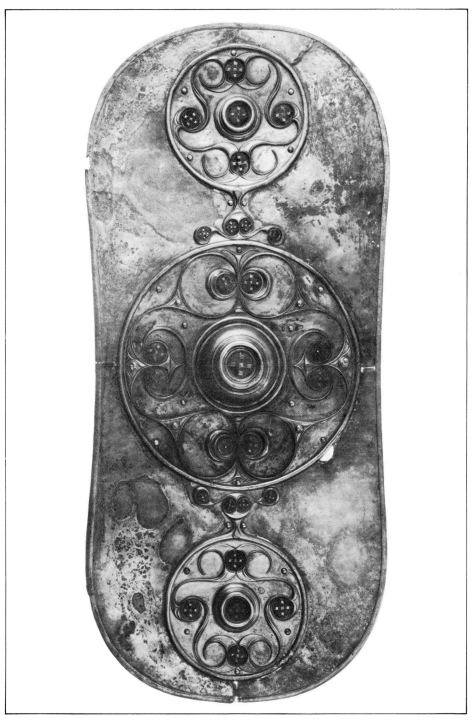

95   *The Battersea shield. This superb object made of four thin bronze sheets attached to a wooden or leather backing is 2 ft 6 in. long. It was manufactured quite late in the Iron Age*

Celtic artists often expressed their beliefs through animal art, whose waddling ducks and bristling boars are quaint and attractive to our modern eyes but which represented supernatural powers to their makers. The boar, much respected for its ferocity and cunning, typified the spirit and joy of the hunt as did the stag and the horse. In parts of Britain there may have been a bull cult based upon older fertility rites. Among the birds, often charmingly arrayed around the rims of cauldrons and bowls, the swan was a symbol of purity and good luck but the crane and the raven were considered evil creatures, deceitful, dangerous and associated with death. Flights of birds were carefully watched and their calls noted before any serious enterprise for they were purveyors of omens that no one would sensibly ignore after they had been interpreted by the priest or shaman.

By the beginning of the Iron Age in Britain there were many tribes, living in territories defined by hills and rivers, by forests and swamps. These were fiercely independent, aristocratic societies of warriors ornamented with amulets and talismen, torcs worn around the neck affirming allegiance to a particular goddess. Even the horses were decked out with charms to fend off ill-fortune. Not comprehending the magical protection that body-painting was expected to give, Julius Caesar in his *Gallic Wars* wrote that the 'Britons dye their bodies with woad, which gives them a blue colour and this produces a terrifying effect when they go into battle'. This misunderstanding by a cultured and sceptical Roman about the beliefs of his 'primitive' opponents exactly mirrors the reaction of white settlers to the 'war-paint' of American Indians. It also reveals how very difficult it is for us, over two thousand years later, to enter the world of the Iron Age.

It was a world well described as 'tribal, rural, hierarchical and familiar', each tribe having a king with his warlike noblemen, with a class of craftsmen, poets and priests below them and, lowest of all, the hundreds of peasant freemen who worked the land from their scattered farmsteads. Although these Iron Age people are called Celts, somehow implying that the population of the British Isles had suddenly become composed of continental invaders, by far the majority of the British were of native descent and their beliefs were still the traditional ones, now sharpened and made more severe by the nature of those unsettled centuries. Cults of water, fertility, skulls and sacrifice continued among noble and peasant alike, and although the burial of ordinary folk reveals less about their beliefs than those of previous ages, their myths and legends tell us a great deal about the fears and superstitions of these Celts. They were a people who loved hunting, fowling and feasting, and one of the high rewards for warriors was the king's feast with pork seething in the cauldron and strong mead poured freely as the garishly dressed nobles shouted and bragged in the great hall.

By now the great tribal assemblies were led by druids, the honoured class of priests who probably had their origins centuries before in the shamans and witch-doctors and who gradually became the leaders of more organized rituals. Attempts have been made to transform these druids into wise and dispassionate scholars more interested in philosophy than sacrifice but this seems to be a distortion of the few facts known about them. It is true that these priests and law-givers had a long training, twenty years it is said, but this time would have been spent in learning by rote the thousands of bardic verses concerning ritual, the interpretation of omens, the myths of creation and the ancestor-lists that are normal among many primitive societies. Roman stories of druids believing that the particular ways in which disembowelled prisoners writhed could be used to foretell the future, of men and women being burnt alive, and of sunless glades in which people were sacrificed to the gods cannot all be discounted as prejudice.

It was a sombre time and even the great pastoral festivals of Beltane and Samhuin were held at night, ending when daylight came. Beltane in May was an occasion of cattle and fires. More solemn and fearsome was Samhuin at the end of October, often held by the shores of lakes to which offerings were given. This dying of the year was the beginning of the Celtic year, when the malignant dead in the shape of birds had to be placated and when the raven-god had to be destroyed by fire and sacrifice if the land were not to be devastated by the evil spirits. Frazer in *Balder the Beautiful* assembled many records of Hallowe'en Fires in Britain and Ireland, even into the nineteenth century when fiends and birds were thought to rush out of a limestone cave at Cruachan in Co. Roscommon, 'the Hell-Gate of Ireland', blighting the crops and killing animals. A small henge and standing stone nearby are signs that people gathered at this sacred place, the mythical home of the goddess Mebd or Maeve, whose connection with drunkenness suggests something of the orgiastic revelling that took place at such times of fear and celebration.

Hallowe'en Fires were also lit in Wales, as protection against winds that had blown over corpses and brought death to anyone they touched, and in Scotland where highlanders feared Hallowe'en Night when goblins would try to steal their babies. Death and darkness went together as winter came on. Water, birds and fire were the elements of one side of Celtic religion, held in control by the power of the druids. Imbolc and Lughnasa, the ceremonies of food and fertility, completed the cycle of sowing and harvest upon which the people depended.

It was a society of contrasts between the boasting that often led to quick-tempered brawls and the courteous hospitality offered to strangers; between the flamboyant art and the melancholy awareness of death that pervaded the poems of the bards; between the crude sexuality of some of the people's idols and the complete morality expected of the women. One armless figurine from Ralaghan in Co. Cavan, cut out of bog oak, had an unsmiling face and above its carved legs there was a clearly defined vulva and a hole, probably for a detachable penis, like others from Essex and Devon. This hermaphroditic statuette was very similar in concept to the 'god-dolly' discovered under the neolithic trackway in Somerset. Another Iron Age idol from Broddenbjerg in Denmark had a hugely extended penis, and its discovery in a bog with some Bronze Age objects suggests that the lake there continued to receive ritual offerings for as long as a thousand years.

Ultimately the fertility cults of which these idols were manifestations seem to have developed into the bawdy yet fearsome *sheelagh-na-gig*—carvings of naked women mainly to be found in Christian churches and castles in Ireland, lewd figures whose sexuality is so blatant that even today they are rarely illustrated in books.

96   *Over 4 ft long this idol carved from bog-oak was found at Ralaghan in Co. Cavan. It has a hole either for a detachable penis (see Plate 101) or a vulva. This equivocally sexed figure was probably set up in an open-air sanctuary during the Iron Age*

They have been compared with other Indo-European effigies, particularly those of the Hindu goddess, Kali, who was usually shown garlanded with skulls and brandishing a blood-stained sword in one of her many arms, and yet she was also regarded as the goddess of love and fertility. This duality of roles is characteristic of Celtic thinking. The devouring and disgusting *sheelagh-na-gig* seem strangely in contrast with the draconian social code against immorality that the Celts observed.

The execution of the shaven-headed Windeby girl in Denmark has been described much earlier in this book but far less well known is the burial of a thirty-year-old woman and a youth in a deep grave at Garton Slack on the Yorkshire Wolds.[1] They lay side by side with a wooden stake driven through their arms, pinning them together to the ground. They had been buried alive and below the woman's pelvis were the almost undetectable remains of a premature baby, expelled from the womb when the mother was unconscious in her death agonies. This couple, surely put to death for adultery, reveal the insistence among Iron Age people of fierce and unbreakable standards of conduct.

It was an insistence that applied not only to everyday behaviour but also to religion and warfare. Every warrior was expected to act honourably towards his opponent but, once again, contradictions and ambiguities in their thinking appeared when the winner of a fight might quite normally cut off the head of a man he had defeated and carry it home to embalm it for display or to use the skull as a drinking vessel. Skulls of enemies were stuck on poles above the entrance of the Bredon hillfort in Worcestershire, a fortification with magnificent views across the Vale of Evesham to the Malverns and the Forest of Dean. These heads might not have been simply bleak warnings to other enemies but, as in the past, they could have been expected to guard the hillfort with their spirits. Skulls complete with lower jaws and part of the spinal column still attached have been found in the pits and ditches of the neolithic causewayed enclosure of Hambledon Hill in Dorset, causing the excavators to conclude that they might have been placed there 'to reinforce or enhance' the boundary to the enclosure. In the hills north of Marseilles a temple at Roquepertuse had an entrance whose pillars were brightly painted in bands of red, white and yellow, and on the lintel above them was the heavy carving of a bird of prey, the supernatural being that watched over this holy place. Each of the five niches carved in the pillars of this gateway—through which any visitor had to pass—held a fleshless human skull. Other skulls came from the defences of Stanwick in north Yorkshire and from Hunsbury hillfort in Northamptonshire, one with three holes bored in it perhaps, as Diodorus Siculus the Roman historian described, so that it could be suspended from the horse's neck when the victor went on his travels.

One of the most remote places where skulls were left was discovered in 1926 when the ground gave way under the weight of a steam-thresher leaving a farm at Rennibister near Kirkwall in the Orkneys. The machine had fallen partly into an earth-house of which others are known in the islands, an underground structure with a curved passage leading to a subterranean chamber whose roof was supported by four pillars. The passage was blocked with earth and whelks, cockles and cowrie-shells, suggesting that people had lived in the gloomy cell, much as the animal bones

Figure 17 *Some sites mentioned in Chapter 9:*
1 Rennibister earth-house, HY 397127; 2 Newstead Roman fort, NT 571344; 3 find-spot of the Broighter hoard, C63.25.; 4 Garton Slack cemetery, centred on SE 953600; 5 Tara enclosure, N 920595; 6 South Cadbury hillfort, ST 628251; 7 Harlyn Bay cemetery, SW 877754

on top of the Grain earth-house nearby intimated that a family had squatted on the roof of their home in the warm summer days. A dozen miles to the west neolithic people had done the same on the middens of Skara Brae.

The contents of the Rennibister chamber were not what would be expected from an ordinary dwelling-place. There was no occupation rubbish there but, instead, around one pillar, were four skulls, not always on the correct jaw. Elsewhere there were other skulls, only one of which was of a person who had lived beyond the age of forty and the majority were of children between five and seventeen years of age. Perhaps two or three families had lived here but before they moved away they left the skulls of their ancestors behind, exactly as the users of the stalled cairns and the chambered tombs had done over two thousand years before.

To the Celts the head was the seat of the soul, much as neolithic families had venerated the skulls of their ancestors, and many carved stone heads dating from the Iron Age have been discovered, especially in the north of Britain, bearded and moustached faces with staring eyes. Some of them have hollows in their crowns for

97   *The subterranean chamber at the end of the curved passage at Rennibister, Orkney*
Mainland

98   *A stone head from Bradford, now in the Manor House Museum, Ilkley, Yorkshire, carved from a glacial sandstone boulder. It has the typical upcurved moustache of many Celtic carved heads but its date is unknown*

offerings of drink or food showing that these were probably the local personifications of family spirits whose protection and help was needed. One such head was found at the stone circle of Beltany in Co. Donegal, a dilapidated ring with burials in it and with a high triangular stone covered in cupmarks that had been set up in line with the sunrise at the beginning of May. An outlier may have been aligned on mid-winter sunrise. The very name of the circle implies that this sanctuary was used well into the Iron Age for the May Day festival of Beltane, once again affirming the continuity of tradition that existed between the early and the later prehistoric periods in these islands.

Much of the information we possess about Iron Age religion comes from literary sources, first and most directly from classical writers such as Caesar and Tacitus, who were contemporaries of the events they described. They are sometimes unreliable, however, first because they did not always understand the customs they had seen, and, second, because they were not invariably objective when they deplored the barbaric ways of the Iron Age savages. Then there are the poems, myths and folk-stories, some from Wales, many from Ireland, which echo the actual words and beliefs of the Celts themselves but which were written down so late, with additions by later bards and with deletions by monkish scribes, that it is very difficult to distil the original tales from them. Indeed, as Anne Ross has remarked, without a deep knowledge of Celtic languages it is almost impossible for anyone to appreciate the 'oblique, indirect, circular approach of these peoples to art, religion, literature and social transactions' so that 'certain aspects of Celtic religion are likely to remain permanently beyond our comprehension'.[2]

It can be seen that we shall delude ourselves if we believe that written records, however old, will explain clearly how the Celts regarded their world. To the contrary, if we peer through the opacity with which Time has blurred the words we become aware of a swirling richness of imagery in the minds of Iron Age people, a poetic vision of the world that Neolithic and Bronze Age men and women quite probably possessed also. Of their poems and stories, however, not a word survives that we can identify, and this loss should warn us against the dangers of oversimplifying the archaeological evidence which is our only guide for periods earlier than the Iron Age.

For these centuries of Celtic Britain archaeology is, in one sense, less helpful than before. There are very few megalithic structures from this time, as though the custom of building in big stones had been abandoned. Some standing stones in the south-east of Ireland around Co. Carlow, tall pillars with artificial grooves in them, may belong to this period. Another at Mullamast, not far away in Co. Kildare, its top notched and with three grooves in its west face, had been dragged from its granite source five miles away by people who had not given up the old beliefs in these ancestor stones; but this is a rare example. More usual were much lower stones, carved in curling patterns of tendrils and leaves, squat pillars such as the Turoe Stone in Co. Galway that once stood protectively outside Feerwore ring-fort, a domed cylinder of granite which is phallic in shape and which is yet another facet of the fertility cults which were so widespread in the British Isles. There is a rather similar stone at Castlestrange in Co. Roscommon and another at Killycluggin in Co. Cavan, a pillar which may have stood outside the entrance to an ancient passage-grave. It was not far from here that St Patrick is said to have thrown down 'Crom Cruaich', the pagan stone at the centre of a circle which was still being used as late as the fifth century AD.

By the Iron Age there was a whole pantheon of gods and goddesses and, behind them, a chaos of shapes and phantoms that animated every part of the Celtic world, most of them menacing and unconquerable except by gift and sacrifice. From the remote past in which these spirits had inhabited springs, rocks, trees and clouds there had come the belief in another world, the counterpart of man's own, populated with forces that were the mainsprings of Nature. At first these unearthly beings had been communicated with through man's ancestors but gradually shamans took over this role, speaking only through the medium of the most powerful of all the people's ancestors, the forefathers of the rich, bronze-decked chieftains, and it was these mighty and dimly remembered ghosts who came to be regarded as gods, endowed with the attributes of the old nature-spirits, a god of thunder, of rain or of war.

The places where these distant chieftains rested were thought to be the entrances to the Other-World, and tombs such as Newgrange were looked on as the homes of fearsome deities just as some round barrows were avoided as mounds in which lesser spirits lay. Even in the Middle Ages many of these barrows were called 'fairy houses', places in which there was everlasting revelry, not to be visited by ordinary mortals. To the Celts, myths of life and death and the turning of the seasons, all born from the ancient rituals of sowing and harvest, became commonplace, symbolized by the marriage of a young man to an old woman, the Hag who would never die and the young man who would die and be reborn.

There was no ranking or order of gods for these dreaming, superstitious Celts and it is probable that each tribe had its own deity. Dagda, 'the good god', is one that is known to us, a divinity that was supposed to have mated with an earth-goddess who was the fertility of the land. These symbols were not intellectual. Such goddesses were not symbols of the soil, they were the soil itself, and in Co. Kerry two rounded hills are still called the Paps or Breasts of Anu, with people walking reverently across the countryside that was her living body. This undying crone was also believed to live in Knockmany chambered tomb, known sometimes as Annia's Cove. Not far away, in Co. Meath, the great passage-grave cemetery of Loughcrew had the name of *Sliabh na Caillighe*, the Hag's Mountain.

In the Scandinavian Bronze Age it was the male gods that first appeared, and in the earliest stages masculine articles predominate in the votive offerings. Rock-carvings show unearthly men holding up axes and wearing horned helmets, the regalia of these powers of life and rebirth. Slowly female figures supplant them and by the latest periods, around 1000 BC, statuettes of naked goddesses wearing twisted neck-rings, hands held under their breasts, far outnumber the men.[3] Ancient Scandinavian sagas associated the goddesses Freya and Nerthus with cults of fertility and the same was probably true in the British Isles with life-giving but life-demanding deities such as Anu gaining more and more power in people's minds. Other goddesses reflect the darkness and savagery of the time: Brigid, the 'High One', with her sacred fire, sometimes portrayed as the magical three-persons-in-one; Coventina, goddess of water who also was carved as a triple being; Flidais, goddess of forests and hunting; and Morrigna, the raven goddess who was war and doom and who could foretell the future for those brave enough to wish it.

Goddesses and gods with triple aspects were common in Celtic art and mythology just as the triad, a group of three statements or verses, was the normal means of recording oral lore and bardic poetry. The significance of the number three to Iron Age people has not been clarified although many attempts at interpretation have been made, but it is clear that the carvings of triple goddesses and of stone heads with three faces must have had an intense symbolism for their owners. It is arguable that the group of three chalk drums from Folkton with eyes and eyebrows carved on them was an early representation of a triple-natured goddess whose origins lay not in the Iron Age but in the much older tradition of a deity who watched over the dead. Death, fertility and the cycle of warmth and cold are familiar features of the Celtic goddesses but every one of these themes had ancient roots. It was only in the Iron Age, however, that we can be certain that these forces became personified as mystical and yet semi-human goddesses.

With them were the Iron Age gods, often localized and possibly gradually becoming of less importance: Lugud the warrior; Maponus, god of hunting; Mogons; Belatucadros; Nodons; horned gods; warrior gods; serpent gods. There were deities everywhere in the Celtic world, all of them dreaded, all of them demanding death in return for their favours, but none of them having temples aligned upon the sun or the moon, none of them demanding that their devotees make careful observations of the heavens.

It is sometimes asked why there is so little evidence of astronomical practices in the Iron Age if the Neolithic and Bronze Age people who erected the precisely aligned megalithic rows and circles had been so skilfully obsessed with astronomy. It may be that Celtic observers were frustrated by the cloudy decline in the climate but this seems a trite explanation when one considers the many astronomical observations that have been claimed in recent years when the weather has been no better. The answer is probably twofold. In the first place, the earlier alignments that did exist were almost certainly symbolical rather than scientific, incorporating the sun and moon into rituals concerned with death and fertility. If this is correct then, with the Iron Age deification of the old spirits, the sun and moon would have become Celtic gods or goddesses with widespread powers. This does seem to have happened with gods such as Belatucadros and Belenus, the Shining One, who was also god of water, healing and hunting.

There is much solar symbolism in Celtic religion as the feast of Beltane shows, but there is no good evidence for a cult of the sun, nor is there anything to suggest that the druids, the descendants of Bronze Age shamans, were knowledgeable astronomers rather than barbaric priests to whom the moon and the night were representations of death and sacrifice. It may be that one would more nearly approach the truth if instead of projecting hypothetical Bronze Age astronomers into the Iron

Age we used our knowledge of Iron Age metaphor more objectively to understand how people had really regarded the sun and moon in earlier times.

Even the graves of the Celts show little more awareness of the skies than the time-heavy custom of arranging the corpse's head towards some celestial event such as sunset, facing the land of death. Quite unlike previous centuries burials of even the richest nobles do not provide a great deal of information about the beliefs of these Iron Age people. In part, this is because of a comparative dearth of cemeteries from this time. Indeed, because of the archaeological imbalance in our knowledge about settlements and graves there is an epigram that Beaker people died but never lived whereas Iron Age people lived but never died. Although, quite obviously, it must be an exaggeration to speak of an absence of burials it is true that those that are known tell us remarkably little about ritual and religion in late prehistory.

There was a special group of 'chariot' burials in Yorkshire where the natives, under the direction of pork-eating Frenchmen from Champagne and Burgundy, dug out great square pits into which they lowered dismantled two-wheeled carts with the body of their owner and sometimes of his charioteer who, presumably, had been killed to accompany his master on his deathly ride. These graves show that mortal women as well as goddesses could enjoy high status in the Iron Age, as the examples of Boudica and Cartimandua demonstrate, women who were accepted as queens by their high-spirited and quarrelsome Celtic warriors. At Arras, overlooking the dreary Vale of York near Market Weighton, one of the three cart-graves contained the body

99   *Excavation of an Iron Age cemetery at Burton Fleming, Humberside. Each grave is surrounded by a square ditch. Similar cemeteries in Yorkshire sometimes had chariots buried in them*

of a middle-aged woman, lying there with her iron mirror and the carcases of two sucking-pigs. Joints of pork were common in these richer graves. Nearer Driffield the overgrown cemetery of Danes Graves—now almost unapproachable because of an abattoir—had about five hundred little barrows heaped up in it over the years, mostly covering the bodies of peasants with only a miserable pot to take with them, but in the one cart-grave the dead man had been given half a pig. At Burton Fleming a few miles away, a linear cemetery of square-ditched graves held the crouched skeletons of ordinary men and women, their bodies laid out north–south, accompanied by a few pots, poor personal ornaments and joints of pork.

Garton Slack, that remarkable valley of the dead on the other side of Driffield from Danes Graves, with its Neolithic, Bronze and Iron Age graves offers a little insight into the funerary practices of this part of England. A cart-burial was recently discovered here, the nobleman and his whip placed by the vehicle whose poleshaft had been broken to fit it into the pit. A pig's head, cut in half, had been put on top of the corpse, a youngish man, one leg shorter than the other, who may have died of a brain tumour. Near his grave was a circular mortuary house in which his body may have rested while his grave was dug. Similar enclosures in this valley had ritual pits alongside them containing the bones or the skulls of pigs, a creature that had been a cult animal on the Wolds for over two thousand years as the pig bones from Hanging Grimston long barrow remind us.

At Garton Slack there was also a rectangular stockade with ox burials by it but even more interesting than these animal cults were the chalk plaques found in the ditches of the stockade, finger-length representations of warriors with swords. Every one of the heads had been snapped off. Like stone heads from other parts of Yorkshire the decapitation of these thin chalk carvings must have been part of the country-wide cult of the severed head and the ancient veneration of skulls.

On the continent some Celtic burials contained swords that had been bent to 'kill' them, an interesting relic of the breaking of axes and pots and, in Britain, a rare cemetery of Iron Age graves also contained evidence of this lingering on of traditions. In 1900, during the digging of house foundations at Harlyn Bay near Padstow in Cornwall over a hundred cists of local slate were discovered, many of them buried under tons of deep, wind-blown sand.[4] The appalling and ill-recorded excavation did little to advance our understanding of these graves but it is known that the cists had been arranged in lines and that one of them had been a kind of ossuary into which discarded bones had been casually dropped. In the decades around 300 BC the few families in this sheltered settlement with its growing rubbish dump of shells and bones had buried their dead in these cists, the corpses fully clothed and wearing their trinkets. *Purpurea lapillis* shells, for making purple dye, show that the clothes were coloured, and the discovery of quartz and feldspar fragments in the graves is a vivid link with earlier customs.

On 1 March 1902, a grave was unearthed whose contents were very similar to the defleshed bones of older times. 'Today's a wonderful cist' exclaimed the excavator who went on to describe a circular cist, divided into two compartments, the eastern of which held the bones of a child and two adults whose skulls had been separated

100 *A hand-sized chalk figurine of an Iron Age warrior from Fimber, Yorkshire. Like others from Garton Slack and elsewhere it has been 'beheaded'*

from their bodies. The west partition contained the smashed skull of another adult lying upon a large piece of quartz.

The breaking of skulls to prevent the ghost from straying out of its grave has been noticed elsewhere and so have foundation sacrifices. To the west of the Harlyn Bay cemetery were the ruins of a drystone wall and beneath it, under some cumbrous slabs, were the skeletons of an adult and a child, both of them crushed almost flat by the weight of the stones on top of them. Remembering the old women under the neolithic house at Skara Brae it is likely that these burials were intended to keep the wall strong. In the Iron Age, with its sacrifices and ferocity, such burials would not be unlikely but it is something of a surprise to learn that foundation-deposits of human beings survived at least until the sixth century AD, in one instance being buried by Christian missionaries. According to an Irish account when St Columba was preparing to build his monastery on Iona he said to the people, 'It is permitted to you that some of you go under the earth of this island to consecrate it', whereupon his companion, Odhran, volunteered to be buried alive under the new church. Little could be more alien to modern thought but neither Odhran nor the woman at the Curragh was exceptional because similar ritual deaths are recorded in the British Isles, one under the walls of a native Romano-British settlement at Lowbury Hill in Berkshire.

Yet the most frightening of all the places of death were the tribal sanctuaries, the groves and the temples of the druid priests where everyone assembled for the great festivals of the year. Lucan, a historian who committed suicide during Nero's reign, described one of these forest clearings that had been discovered by Caesar when he ordered his legionaries to cut down trees for the siege of Marseilles in 49 BC, only five years after his attempted conquest of Britain:

> The axe-men came on an ancient and sacred grove. Its interlacing branches enclosed a cool central space into which the sun never shone, but where an abundance of water spouted from dark springs. ... The barbaric gods who worshipped here had their altars heaped with hideous offerings, and every tree was sprinkled with human blood. According to the local tradition, no birds ventured to perch upon these trees, and no wild beast made his lair beneath them; they were proof also against gales and lightning, and would shudder to themselves though no wind stirred. The images were stark, gloomy blocks of unworked timber, rotten with age, whose ghastly pallor terrified their devotees...[5]

Archaeology is unlikely to discover any traces of these long-decayed groves but there is other evidence that they existed in Britain. The Latin word 'nemus', meaning 'a clearing in a wood', has survived in some place-names given because of the proximity of a sacred wood to a Roman settlement. There was *Vernemeton* near modern Lincoln; *Nemetostatio* by North Tawton in Devon; *Medionemeton*, perhaps the circle-henge of Cairnpapple near Edinburgh; and *Aquae Arnemetiae*, the Roman name for Buxton in the Peak District. Just as convincing is the description by Tacitus of druids performing their rites in the forests of Anglesey before the Roman attack in AD 60. Even more horrifying is the account by Dio Cassius of Boudica's sacrifices in a grove sacred to the goddess Andraste, 'the Invincible', where women captured in London had their bodies skewered to the ground and other atrocities inflicted upon them before death.

Here and there in Britain more formal Iron Age shrines have been found, almost by accident, the postholes of a village of round houses and a colonnaded rectangular temple being uncovered when the ground was being bulldozed for a runway at Heathrow. At Frilford in Berkshire excavations located a circular enclosure like a small henge in which wooden figurines of a goddess may have stood. Near them a ploughshare in one pit and models of native swords and shields in another were offerings of sympathetic magic little different from the deposits of rich earth and flint at Goodland three thousand years before. Sometimes the gifts were sacrificial. At the most awesome of hillforts, Maiden Castle in Dorset, which was clearly more than just a defensive work and which had been built on the site of a neolithic ritual centre, there was a tiny circular temple with the dedicatory burial of an infant just inside its doorway. At the summit of another hill, around which ran the fortified banks and ditches of South Cadbury in Somerset, there was a cramped and rectangular timber-built shrine with a verandah and gloomy inner sanctum. In front of this temple a fully grown cow had been buried and on either side of the processional way that led to the holy place there were ritual pits, those to the south containing peasant-offerings of young animals—piglets, lambs and many calves—those to the north having the richer gifts of the nobles—iron daggers, sheaths and swords.

Rock-cut pits in the same hillfort are reminders that the deep shafts of the Bronze Age had not gone out of fashion. The custom survives to this day in our wishing-wells and the coins that we throw into fountains. At South Cadbury these pits often had carefully buried skulls of horses and cattle in them, and animal bones have been found in many other pits in Britain.[6] In a cement works at Northfleet in Kent neat collections of bones were recovered from a pit, offerings dropped there by Iron Age peasants as gifts to the spirits. In Roman times at the fort of Brocolitia near Carrawburgh in Northumberland a well dedicated to Coventina was cluttered with bronze figurines, stone altars, a human skull and an astounding accumulation of thirteen thousand coins offered by legionaries and civilians to this Celtic goddess. Another Roman frontier fort at Newstead in Roxburgh had a great number of these shafts and from one of them excavators retrieved, in order: some antlers and Roman pottery; below them, a birch branch standing upright like those from Wilsford and Swanwick; then two human skulls and some bits of oak; another human skull and two wooden wheels which may have been sun-symbols, just as burning wheels were rolled down hillsides at midsummer in some parts of Britain; below them, the skull of a horse; and at the bottom of this choked, thirty-foot-deep shaft, some red deer antlers and the skulls of five dogs.

Many of these offerings must have been dropped into wells, pits which satisfyingly combined the spirits of the earth with the fecundity of water, and wooden idols whose fertility was made explicit by the emphatic carving of their sexual organs have been discovered near lakesides and rivers. In the Lower Teign valley in Devon a goddess, shaped out of oak, was dug out of twenty-five feet of alluvial gravel. Other idols came from Dagenham in Essex, Ralaghan in Co. Cavan and from near the ferry at Ballaculish in Argyll. This last female figurine, carved out of oak and lying in the peat with wickerwork and wooden poles around it, may have been protected from the weather in a cramped wattle hut. Its agate eyes are reminiscent of the group of naked warriors, cut out of pinewood, that were discovered by labourers in 1836 while they were digging a ditch at Roos Carr in Yorkshire. These miniature swordsmen had eyes of quartz and neatly drilled into their bodies was a hole for a penis, perhaps also of quartz, but the significance of these figures remains uncertain. Other votive deposits in lakes such as Llyn Cerrig Bach on Anglesey can be seen as the offerings to the gods that had piled up over the years of the Iron Age, but the

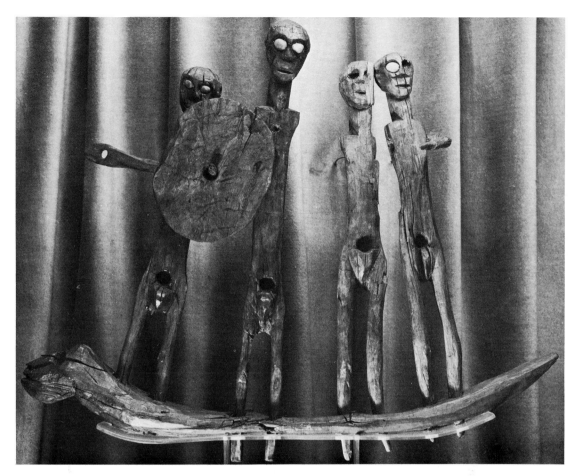

101 *The Roos Carr boat-group, Humberside. Carved from pinewood these warriors stand on a snake-headed boat and carry round shields of the Late Bronze Age. The men seem to have had detachable penises (see Plate 96), perhaps of quartzite like their eyes. They are very like the sexually explicit rock-carvings of the Scandinavian Bronze Age*

delightful, enigmatic Roos Carr men are more puzzling.

One is reminded of the magnificent 'hoard' of gold objects reputedly discovered in 1895, in truly Celtic circumstances, by the shore of Lough Foyle at Broighter in Co. Londonderry. After much wrangling over the reward the case was taken to court but even legal minds failed to clear up the mysterious discovery of this treasure which included a superb torc—supposedly hidden in an old umbrella—a beautiful model of a ship with mast, oars and benches, a bowl, pins, two necklets and two chains, all of pure Irish gold. Archaeologists instantly asserted that this assemblage must have been a votive hoard, buried at the waterside by a rich Celtic chieftain hoping for the protection of the gods before he crossed the stormy waters of the Irish Sea. The judge was sardonically unimpressed by the argument.

The defendants' suggestion is that the articles were thrown into the sea, which they suggest covered the spot in question, as a votive offering by some Irish sea king or chief to some Irish sea god at some period between 300 BC and AD 100, and for this purpose they ask the court to infer the existence of the sea on the spot in question, the existence of an Irish sea god, the existence of a custom to make votive offerings in Ireland during the period suggested, and the existence of kings or chiefs who would be likely to make such votive offerings. The whole of their evidence—if I may so describe it—on these points is of the vaguest description.[7]

Never satisfactorily explained, the gorgeous Broighter hoard, a treasure without a beginning, is in harmony with the other mysteries of prehistoric ritual and religion in which death, fertility and the powers of ancestors have been constantly linked from the earliest times down to the end of the Iron Age. There was a continuity of belief that remained steadfast despite the changes in society, the coming of the Beaker people, the discovery of metalworking, the rise of chieftains, the destruction of monuments, the worsening weather, the fighting and rivalry of late prehistory. Shadows of the old ways can still be seen in places today, notably in the great Irish horse-fairs, and it seems fitting that a book about ancient religion in the British Isles should conclude with the description of an Irish sanctuary because nowhere in this country has tradition survived so long as in Ireland, that misting and lovely land of the Celts.

Nor is there a sanctuary that more strikingly demonstrates how the past conditioned the future, an Iron Age tribe worshipping and assembling at a monument

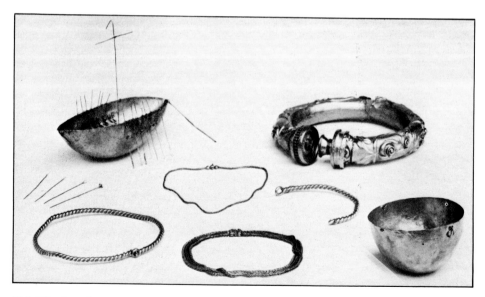

102 *The Broighter hoard. These lovely gold pieces include necklets, a bowl, a diminutive boat and, in the background, a torc with a rotating terminal to allow it to be placed around the neck*

that Bronze Age people had built on top of a neolithic burial-mound. Twenty miles north-west of Dublin, in Co. Meath, a limestone ridge overlooks the fertile plain and here, on the low hill of Tara, are earthworks so traditionally sacred that late in the nineteenth century some enthusiasts actually dug into one of them in the hope of finding the Ark of the Covenant. They failed because the sanctity of Tara, like so many other prehistoric shrines, was born of its long association with death, reaching back thousands of years to the time when a neolithic family built a passage-grave there above the lush grasslands, choosing a prominence from which the dead could see the herds of cattle grazing, a green landscape edged with forests and flickering with the brightness of tiny loughs.[8]

Around 2700 BC, late in the New Stone Age, people constructed their megalithic tomb with its stone-lined passage and chamber, not very large but with magical circles, zigzags and arcs carved into the stones by which the cremations lay with their pots, beads, pins and pendants. It was a place of death but it was also a place of fertility and among the ornaments there were over thirty balls of chalk and stone, symbols of growth and sexuality that would bring life to the dead and good fortune to the living. A granite pillar, like a guardian phallus embodying the ancestral spirits, stood near the mound.

As much as five hundred years later, when the tomb was overgrown and abandoned, Food Vessel people came to the hill, shoving the burnt bones to one side, clearing the chamber, bringing in their own dead, placing their own finely decorated vessels beside them. Later still, other groups found this ancient shrine and, just as people had done at Cairnpapple, they heaped layers of stones and clay over the mound, covering the passage-grave under a wide, high barrow that in Christian times became known as the Mound of the Hostages. Nearly forty cisted cremations were packed into the sides of this cemetery that was used well into the Middle Bronze Age.

It was a conspicious land mark, known to everyone on the plain, and by the Iron Age it was thought to be the home of the gods, the place where tribal kings would be chosen by signs given from these long-dead ancestors. Around it an enormous and irregularly oval earthwork was thrown up, like a henge with its internal ditch but palisaded for defence, the barrow just inside the northern limits of this spacious enclosure that was over a minute's walk from side to side.

Outside it, leading towards the enclosure from the north, was a thin avenue of parallel banks very like a cursus along which the dead may have been carried. It is called the 'Banquet Hall' but without excavation its purpose can only be surmised, although there is a somewhat similar U-shaped 'avenue' alongside the passage-grave of Newgrange. There are legends that once a great timber building stood here, divided into compartments where the king and nobles feasted. The 'Banquet Hall', however, is similar to other rectangular enclosures known on the continent, one at Libenice in Czechoslovakia having two posts at its south-eastern end aligned on the midwinter sunrise. Both were probably carved in the shape of a goddess whose torcs lay on the ground where they had fallen from the rotting figures. Pits nearby contained the bones of animals and children that had been sacrificed to this deity, and near the centre of this open-air sanctuary there was the burial of an elderly woman whom the excavators suggested had been the temple's priestess. Tara's rectangular enclosure, leading uphill to the crest where the passage-grave stood, may have combined the functions of a cursus and a temple, a processional way along which the royal dead were borne and where the druids performed the barbaric rites that accompanied the death of a king.

Tara, it seems, was never a settlement. It was a sacred place of assembly for the great and joyful harvest festival of Lughnasa when the dead were honoured and when the first fruits were offered to them, partly from respect, partly to ensure their continued blessing and guardianship of the soil. Until quite recently horse-fairs were held both here and at other pagan sites in Ireland on 1 August, the date of Lughnasa. The races at Teltown, Wexford and the Curragh were direct and unbroken links

103 *Tara, Co. Meath, from the south-east. In the centre of the large earthwork enclosure are two raths with defensive banks and to their right is the low round barrow of the neolithic passage-grave*

with the boisterous horseraces and games of the Iron Age there.[9] As long ago as AD 1169 it was said that the queue of horses and chariots waiting to enter Tara on Lammas Day, at the beginning of August, was six miles long, and this vast earthwork, the Royal Enclosure, must have seen festivities, fairs and sports held inside it for many centuries before then.

There is little doubt that the merrymaking at the Lughnasa festival included rituals of fertility whose details are now lost to us. Just outside the enclosure where a Christian church has been built there are two standing stones, one of them a domed phallic block of limestone, the other a rectangular sandstone pillar with a carving of the horned god of fertility on it. Licentious rites would not be unexpected at this celebration of the fertility of the land, when the last sheaf to be cut was tied and carried to the feast where it was hailed as the 'Hag', and often given to a young maiden who was the spirit of next year's crop. This annual cycle of decay and rebirth may have survived in the custom recorded up to the nineteenth century at Tara's yearly August fair of women being bought as wives for a year.

Tara was a cult centre in which many religious activities merged. An old Irish poem mentions a stone circle, long since destroyed, that stood nearby and which in its last days was used by Celtic warriors before they went into battle, 'a sward with luck before going to death, where men used to turn right-hand wise', following the sun in their dances inside the ring, swords and shields raised, seeking the promise of safety in a circle constructed by farming people two thousand years before them.

All these things—the races, the dances, the fertility ceremonies—attest to the antiquity of the traditions that surrounded Tara, and yet it was the manner in which the great kings of Ireland were chosen here that reveals most powerfully the mysticism and poetry of prehistoric religion in which a chieftain was not only a temporal ruler but also the essence of the spirits and gods who guarded the crops and the herds. To the herdsmen who gathered at Tara it was fitting that the identity of their new king should be divined through the Bull-Dream.

On such occasions a white bull was slaughtered and a druid was gorged on its flesh and broth until he fell into a deep, troubled sleep. Four other druids chanted incantations over him and in his slumber, so like the trance of shamans, he had a vision of where the king-to-be was to be found and what he looked like. When these revelations were announced the man was searched for and brought to Tara where he had one, vital test to undergo. Like the British Arthur, who had to withdraw a sword from a stone, so this future king had to touch the stone that stood outside the barrow where the gods rested. If he were the true king, so the legends say, the stone screamed when it felt his hands upon it. The pillar is called *Lia Fail*, 'the stone penis', the stone of fertility that was the essential symbol of prehistoric religion, and it is easy to imagine the wild scene at this inauguration—the king by the magical phallic stone, the druids, the whirring and rattling of the wooden bull-roarers that sounded like the bellowing of bulls as they were swung on their long thongs by the priests, the blare of the harsh horns, the warriors beating their shields with their swords and stamping their feet, and the pushing, shouting, unorganized rush and pandemonium of people everywhere as the king was proclaimed.

104 *A prehistoric standing stone at St Duzec, Brittany, which has been 'christianized' by having a cross carved out of its top*

Even then it was not over. Before he had any power the king had to have a queen and he undertook a ritual wedding with a goddess. Tara has associations with at least two of these deities, Mebd and Edain, who, as well as having other attributes, were goddesses of sovereignty without which no king could reign. Otherwise his would have been the true Celtic paradox, a ruler who could not rule. How the marriage was solemnized we are not told but there followed a great mead-feast, a tradition that ended only in the sixth century AD when a king of Tara was baptized, the first of a hundred generations to become a Christian. The old ways were not forgotten even a thousand years after that time.

Even as Tara mouldered, neglected and weather-torn, its spirit flowered into the romance and poetry of the Celts, like so many other prehistoric temples. Giants had fought in these halls, lovely girls had danced here and behind everything, dim in this twilight of the gods, there were the wraiths of men and women who had tilled the ground, cut down the trees, raised the stones and carried the skulls of their dead to them, the ancestors of our islands.

> *Shining was your wall, spacious and splendid,*
> *and your fortress encircled with green-leaved oaks.*

> *Rarely comes any that would be better;*
> *every fame shall be laid low.*
> *You shall be a hall for tearful, austere nuns,*
> *though now you are grass-grown and bare.*

> Irish Elegy, eleventh century AD

Gazetteer of Sites and Objects to See

Some readers will wish to visit the places described in the previous chapters and they may also like to know the whereabouts of some of the articles and ornaments used by prehistoric people in their rituals. To avoid a waste of time going to monuments that are either destroyed or badly ruined only the sites worth seeing are included. For those who want more information about other chambered tombs, barrows, stones and circles the following guidebooks are recommended: J. Dyer, *Southern England: An Archaeological Guide*, Faber, London (1973); E. Evans, *Prehistoric and Early Christian Ireland: A Guide*, Batsford, London (1966); R. Feachem, *A Guide to Prehistoric Scotland*, Batsford, London (1963); C. Houlder, *Wales: An Archaeological Guide*, Faber, London (1974); E. W. MacKie, *Scotland: An Archaeological Guide*, Faber, London (1975); N. Thomas, *A Guide to Prehistoric England*, Batsford, London (1976). Shire Publications, Princes Risborough, have produced some good and inexpensive paperbacks, their Regional Archaeology series, which include: I. Anthony, *Wales*; J. Dyer, *The Cotswolds and Upper Thames* and *Eastern England*; L. Grinsell, *South Western England*; L. Grinsell and J. Dyer, *Wessex*; B. Marsden, *Central England*, *North Eastern England* and *North Western England*; and E. Sammes, *South Eastern England*.

For objects discovered by excavations and now in museums the location of the most interesting is also given here. It should be added that some pieces may be in store although most of them, because of their uniqueness, will be on display. Most museums have collections of archaeological material although the quality of the assemblage is very dependent on what has been found in the region so that the Midlands and the north-west tend to have less to show than the museums of the south and north-east. The annual publication, *Museums and Galleries in Great Britain and Ireland*, lists the places with archaeological material. Particularly rewarding are the great National Museums in Belfast, Cardiff, Dublin, Edinburgh and London, and to this list I would add as a personal choice the museums of Armagh, Avebury, the Cambridge Museum of Archaeology and Ethnology, Dundee, Hull, Inverurie, Salisbury and Sheffield. No one at all interested in prehistory should miss that treasure house of prehistoric riches, the magnificently arranged Devizes Museum in Wiltshire.

In the list that follows, in order to help the reader distinguish between them, the names of sites to visit appear in bold type followed by their county and OS grid references, whereas museum objects are printed in italics. Where available,

radio-carbon 'dates' and their corrected equivalents are quoted to provide a chronological background to the sites.

Annaghmare, Co. Armagh (H 905178). A neolithic court-cairn with a pronounced forecourt. 1½ miles north of Crosmaglen. The cairn was blocked up about 2445±55 bc (c. 3170 BC). It was excavated in 1963–4.

antler frontlets, Mesolithic. In the Cambridge Museum of Archaeology and Ethnology.

arrowheads, broken. In Hull and Sheffield Museums. Neolithic and Bronze Age.

Ballaculish wooden idol. In the National Museum of Antiquities, Edinburgh. Iron Age.

balls, stone. In Dublin, Edinburgh and Inverurie Museums. Neolithic and Bronze Age.

Ballybriest, Co. Londonderry (H 762885). A court-cairn with two galleries and with a little portal-dolmen to the south. 4 miles south of Draperstown. It was excavated in 1937. Neolithic.

Barclodiad-y-Gawres, Anglesey (SH 328708). A neolithic passage-grave with magnificent carved stones in the chamber. 2 miles north-west of Aberffraw. It was excavated in 1953. The site is usually locked but a key may be obtained, on prior application, from 22 The Square, Caernarvon.

Battersea shield. In the British Museum. Iron Age.

Broighter hoard. Perhaps the most splendid hoard of goldwork in the British Isles. In the National Museum of Ireland, Dublin. Iron Age.

Bush Barrow, Wiltshire. A round barrow in the Normanton barrow cemetery, centred on SU 118413. Stonehenge is visible to the north. Copies of the finds from this barrow are in Devizes Museum. Bronze Age.

Cairnholy, Kirkcudbright (NX 517538). A neolithic long chambered cairn with imposing forecourt. 4 miles south-east of Creetown. It was excavated in 1949.

Cairnpapple, West Lothian (NS 987717). On this low hill a neolithic ritual site was followed by a late neolithic circle-henge, a Beaker burial, a food vessel and an urn round barrow. Finally there were Iron Age burials here. Admission charge. Pamphlet available on site. 1½ miles east-south-east of Torphichen.

Calderstones, Liverpool. These tall, rearranged stones from a neolithic passage-grave have carvings of spirals and footprints on them. They are protected in a conservatory in Calderstones Park, Menlove Gardens, Liverpool.

Callanish, Isle of Lewis (NB 213330). A stone circle with centre stone, avenue and rows, and with a small passage-grave inside it. 13 miles west of Stornoway. Probably Bronze Age.

Camster Round, Caithness (ND 260442). A neolithic passage-grave with a stalled chamber. Reconstructed. 6¼ miles south of Watten.

Carles, Castlerigg, Cumbria (NY 292236). A fine stone circle, probably
neolithic, with pronounced entrance at the north. 1½ miles east of Keswick.

chalk carvings: balls. In Avebury, Dublin and Salisbury Museums.

phalli. In Avebury and Dorchester Museums.

Celtic warriors, beheaded. In Hull Museum and in the private museum
behind Grantham's butchers' shop, Driffield.

goddess from Grime's Graves. In the British Museum.

Collessie cairn grave-goods. In the National Museum of Antiquities,
Edinburgh. Early Bronze Age.

Coventina's Well, Northumberland (NY 859711). Just outside *Brocolitia*,
Carrawburgh, the seventh fort on Hadrian's Wall, close to the temple of
Mithras. There is very little to see of the well today.

Creswell Crags, Derbyshire (SK 535742). The caves are not open to the
public but there is a car park and information centre nearby with leaflets
and an exhibition. Finds from Pin Hole Cavern are in Sheffield Museum.
The caves were occupied in the Late Old Stone Age, around 12,000 BC. 3
miles east of Clowne.

crotals and rattles. Iron Age musical instruments of bronze. In the British
Museum and in Dublin.

Cruden cairn grave-goods. In the National Museum of Antiquities,
Edinburgh. Bronze Age.

cupmarked stones. As well as many in Yorkshire, Northumberland and in
south-west Scotland there are others in the museums of Bradford, Carlisle
and Scarborough.

discs, stone. In the museums at Avebury, Cardiff, Devizes and Edinburgh.

Fochabers, Moray. Nothing remains of the barrow, but an Iron Age skeleton
and some neolithic pottery are on display in Elgin Museum.

Folkton Drums. In the British Museum. There are copies in Hull Museum.
Bronze Age.

Garton Slack chariot burial. Finds from this splendid grave are on display in
Hull Museum. Iron Age.

god-dolly, Somerset trackways. In the Cambridge Museum of Archaeology
and Ethnology. Neolithic.

Gough's Cave, Cheddar Gorge, Somerset (ST 466538). This cave, occupied
late in the Old Stone Age, around 12,000–8000 BC, can be visited. There is
an admission charge. Finds such as the carved bones can be seen in the
museum at the entrance to the cave.

Grime's Graves, Norfolk (TL 817898). These Late Neolithic and Bronze Age
flint mines can be visited. Clean clothing and high heels are not
recommended. There is an admission charge. 5¼ miles north-west of
Thetford. The chalk 'goddess' is in the British Museum.

Gristhorpe tree-trunk burial. There is nothing to see of the barrow but the
coffin and the reconstituted skeleton are well displayed in Scarborough
Museum. Early Bronze Age.

Harlyn Bay, Cornwall. Some of the cists used to be displayed at SW 877754 but they have now been covered over. The little museum has also been closed. Iron Age.

heads, stone. These 'Celtic' carved heads may date from anywhere between the Iron Age and the nineteenth century AD. There is an interesting collection of them in Bradford Museum.

horns, 'Druidical'. In the British Museum and in the National Museums at Cardiff, Dublin and Edinburgh.

Kilmartin Valley, Argyll (NR 828979). In this valley there is the neolithic chambered tomb of Nether Largie South, Bronze Age cairns such as Nether Largie North with its carved cist stones, Temple Wood stone circle, standing stones, carved rock-surfaces and Ri Cruin cairn, all of which can be visited without charge. $6\frac{1}{2}$ miles north-north-west of Lochgilphead.

Knockast, Co. Westmeath (N 245435). This very low cairn contained many cists and pottery of the Early Bronze Age. 4 miles east-south-east of Ballymore.

Liff's Low grave-goods. The Early Bronze Age cairn is virtually destroyed but the finds from it are displayed in Sheffield Museum.

Lligwy, Anglesey (SH 501860). Although this tomb cannot be entered today because of surrounding railings it is well worth seeing because of its huge capstone. $\frac{1}{2}$ mile north of Llanallgo. Probably Late Neolithic.

Longstone Rath, Co. Kildare (N 932206). An elegant granite pillar, 17 feet high, stands at the centre of a low circular enclosure with an external ditch. 3 miles east-north-east of Naas. Late Neolithic to Early Bronze Age. To the south-east, at N 918165, is the tallest standing stone in Ireland, the Long Stone at Punchestown.

lunulae, gold. These Early Bronze Age neck ornaments, possibly imitations of the crescent moon, can be seen in the National Museum of Ireland, Dublin. There are other splendid examples in Truro Museum.

Machrie Moor, Isle of Arran (NR 911325). Following the path from the country road the visitor will see several fine examples of stone circles and cairns including the rings from which Bryce recovered food vessels in 1861. Further excavations in 1978–9 uncovered another circle at NR 921325. 3 miles north of Blackwaterfoot.

Maes Howe, Orkney Mainland (HY 317127). This is one of the most magnificent chambered tombs in the whole of Europe. It is a passage-grave built around 2020 ± 70 bc, 2185 ± 65 bc (*c.* 2670 BC). A rock-cut ditch surrounds the barrow with its long passage and corbelled chamber. Other neolithic tombs and stone circles are in the immediate vicinity. Admission charge. $4\frac{1}{2}$ miles north-east of Stromness.

Maumbury Rings, Dorset (SY 690899). This Late Neolithic henge with its deep shafts, now filled in, was converted into an amphitheatre by the Romans. A Civil War gun emplacement was dug in the bank opposite the entrance. Excavated 1908–13. Finds in Dorchester Museum. On southern outskirts of Dorchester.

Mid Howe, Rousay, Orkneys (HY 371306). An immensely long stalled cairn. Excavated 1932–3. 4½ miles west-north-west of Brinyan pier. Late Neolithic.

Nether Largie North cairn (see Kilmartin Valley).

Newgrange, Co. Meath (O 007727). A superbly decorated passage-grave built around 3250 BC (2465±40 bc; 2475±45 bc; 2585±105 bc) in the Middle Neolithic period. It had fallen into disuse by about 2560 BC (2100±40 bc; 2040±40 bc; 1935±35 bc). Following excavations between 1962 and 1975 it has been reconstructed. Admission charge. Excellent booklet available on it and the neighbouring tombs. 2¾ miles east of Slane.

Newstead Roman fort, Roxburgh. Nothing is now visible of this great fortification but the finds are in the National Museum of Antiquities, Edinburgh.

paint and paint-pots. Neolithic. Some are on display in the National Museum of Antiquities, Edinburgh, and there are others to be seen in the little museum at Skara Brae, Orkney Mainland.

Palaeolithic carved bones. In the museums at Cheddar and Sheffield.

passage-grave ornaments and pendants. In the National Museum of Ireland, Dublin.

Pin Hole Cavern, Derbyshire (see Creswell Crags).

Pool Farm slab with carved footprints. In Bristol Museum. Bronze Age.

Ralaghan wooden idol. In the National Museum of Ireland, Dublin. Iron Age.

Reanascreena, Co. Cork (W 265410). A fine recumbent stone circle, excavated in 1960. 3 miles north-north-west of Ross Carbery. Probably Early–Middle Bronze Age.

Rennibister, Orkney Mainland (HY 397127). This reconstructed earth-house probably dates to the Iron Age. 3½ miles west-north-west of Kirkwall.

Rillaton, Cornwall (SX 260719). Although this round barrow is now badly neglected it commands a fine view across the lowlands to the north and stands only a little way from the Hurlers stone circles on Bodmin Moor. 6½ miles west of Callington. The gold cup is in the British Museum. Early Bronze Age.

Rollright Stones, Oxfordshire (SP 296308). This famous stone circle has an outlier, the King Stone, and there are the remains of a portal-dolmen, the Whispering Knights, in the field to the east. Postcards available on site. 2½ miles north of Chipping Norton. Probably Early Bronze Age.

Roos Carr figurines. These Late Bronze Age–Iron Age wooden carvings are on display in Hull Museum.

Rudston, Yorkshire (TA 097677). This pillar of millstone grit is the tallest standing stone in the British Isles. It may date to the Late Neolithic period. It stands by the church in the graveyard and there are the slabs of a cist by the churchyard wall.

Sanctuary, Wiltshire (SU 118679). Concrete slabs and pillars mark the positions of former posts and stones of circles on Overton Hill near Avebury. It was excavated in 1929. Finds are in Devizes Museum. Middle

Neolithic to Early Bronze Age. Round barrows stand along the Ridgeway immediately to the east of the Sanctuary. 5 miles west of Marlborough.

sheelagh-na-gig. For Irish locations see E. Evans, *Prehistoric and Early Christian Ireland: A Guide.* There is a sheelagh-na-gig in the church of St Mary and David, Kilpeck, Herefordshire.

Skara Brae, Orkney Mainland (HY 230187). This is the best-preserved neolithic village in Europe. Five C-14 dates, averaging 2436 bc, suggest it was built around 3155 BC and continued in use until about 2435 BC. Admission charge. Excavations in 1927–30 and from 1972–3 recovered much evidence of the economy of the inhabitants. There is a museum with literature for sale on the site. $6\frac{1}{2}$ miles north of Stromness. Most of the finds are in the National Museum of Antiquities, Edinburgh.

Slieve Gullion, Co. Armagh (J 025202). A good example of a passage-grave, reached after a two-mile uphill walk from the mountain road. A radio-carbon date of 2005 ± 75 bc suggests the tomb was built around 2525 BC. 5 miles south-west of Newry.

South Cadbury, Somerset (ST 628251). This hillfort, the legendary home of King Arthur, was extensively excavated in 1966–70. Neolithic occupation around 4125 BC (3350 ± 800 bc; 3300 ± 800 bc) was followed by the building of the hillfort around 1180 BC (985 ± 90 bc; 925 ± 90 bc). The site was later remodelled during the Dark Ages. Finds in Taunton Museum. $5\frac{1}{2}$ miles west-south-west of Wincanton.

Stenness, Orkney Mainland (HY 306125). Excavated in 1973–4, this stone circle was surrounded by a rock-cut ditch and was proved to have an intriguing complex of features inside it. Two C-14 dates of 2356 ± 65 bc and 2238 ± 70 bc suggest it was built late in the Neolithic period around 2970 BC. The Ring of Brodgar circle-henge stands just to its north. 4 miles east-north-east of Stromness. Finds in the National Museum of Antiquities, Edinburgh.

Stonehenge, Wiltshire (SU 123422). Although it is no longer possible for the visitor to walk inside the circle one can still walk around outside the ditch of this henge and megalithic ring. Informative models are displayed on site and there is a little bookstall. Admission charge. Three corrected C-14 dates suggest the earthwork was begun around 3055 BC and that some of the Aubrey Holes may have been redug around 1848 ± 275 bc (*c.* 2300 BC). Three other dates (1620 ± 110 bc; 1728 ± 68 bc; 1770 ± 70 bc) indicate that the bluestone ring and the avenue were being constructed around 2100 BC but that the project was abandoned and the sarsen structure commenced. A further date of 1240 ± 105 bc (*c.* 1550 BC) suggests that the monument was still being modified in the Middle Bronze Age. There have been many excavations this century. Finds in Salisbury Museum. 2 miles west of Amesbury.

Tara, Co. Meath (N 920595). A passage-grave built around 2700 BC (2310 ± 160 bc; 2130 ± 160 bc; 1930 ± 150 bc) was enclosed in a great earthwork during the Iron Age. Excavations between 1955 and 1959 recovered much information about the modifications made to the site over the centuries. 6 miles south-east of Cavan.

Torrs chamfrain. In the National Museum of Antiquities, Edinburgh.

Trethevy Quoit, Cornwall (SX 259688). A neolithic portal-dolmen with a massive capstone. The oval mound that covered it has been removed. $2\frac{3}{4}$ miles north-east of Liskeard.

Waylands Smithy, Oxfordshire (SU 281854). A long megalithic tomb built on top of a small earthen long barrow. A C-14 date of 2820 ± 130 bc suggests the transition occurred around 3600 BC. Excavations in 1919–20 and 1962–3 recovered much neolithic material which is now in Reading Museum. $7\frac{1}{2}$ miles west of Wantage.

West Kennet, Wiltshire (SU 104677). A half-mile walk up a hillside will bring the visitor to one of the finest long megalithic tombs in the British Isles. It was reconstructed following the excavations of 1955–6. Finds in Devizes Museum. $5\frac{1}{2}$ miles west of Marlborough.

Windmill Hill, Wiltshire (SU 087714). Although there is virtually nothing to see on this gentle hill except some later Bronze Age barrows this causewayed enclosure is considered one of the most important sites in prehistoric Britain. Excavations by the late Alexander Keiller showed that there had been a neolithic house here around 3740 BC (2960 ± 150 bc), succeeded by a ditched enclosure for trade, ritual and defence around 3345 BC (2580 ± 150 bc) which was still being used as late as 1900 BC (1550 ± 150 bc). Finds in Avebury and Devizes Museums. $1\frac{1}{2}$ miles north-west of Avebury.

Woodhenge, Wiltshire (SU 150434). Concrete pillars mark the positions of the ovals of great posts that once stood here. A concretion of flints indicates the grave of the little girl. The ditch of this Late Neolithic ritual site was dug around 2285 BC (1867 ± 74 bc; 1805 ± 54 bc). Finds in Devizes Museum. 1 mile north of Amesbury on a side road off the A345.

Booklist and Notes

Although there is no single book devoted to a study of religious customs in the prehistoric British Isles, a comprehensive list of works dealing partly with this subject would itself fill a volume. Here only the titles of the most accessible and generally useful are given. First there are the books that provide accounts of various aspects of ritual and magic in these islands before writing was introduced. Then, divided into chapters, come the Notes that quote the sources of information for the most important sites mentioned in the text. There is one important, pioneering series of articles that does deserve special mention. Entitled 'Ritual Practices in British Prehistory', it was written by the late John Corcoran and appeared in the *Archaeological News Letter* 6, 1958, in issues nos 8, 9 and 10.

Books

General

G. Clark. *Aspects of Prehistory*. University of California Press, Berkeley & London, 1974.

J. G. Frazer. *The Golden Bough*, I–XI (3rd edition). Macmillan, London, 1911.

L. V. Grinsell. *Barrow, Pyramid and Tomb*. Thames & Hudson, London, 1975.

W. Johnson. *Byways in British Prehistory*. Cambridge University Press, Cambridge, 1912.

J. Maringer. *The Gods of Prehistoric Man*. Weidenfeld & Nicolson, London, 1960.

M. Mead & N. Calas (eds). *Primitive Heritage*. Gollancz, London, 1954.

J. V. S. Megaw & D. D. A. Simpson. *Introduction to British Prehistory*. Leicester University Press, Leicester, 1979.

T. G. E. Powell. *Prehistoric Art*. Thames & Hudson, London, 1966.

E. E. Evans-Pritchard. *Theories of Primitive Religion*. Oxford University Press, Oxford, 1966.

I. Simmons & M. Tooley (eds). *The Environment in British Prehistory*. Duckworth, London, 1981.

G. E. Swanson. *The Birth of the Gods*. Michigan University Press, Michigan, 1964.

W. Torbrügge. *Prehistoric European Art*. Abrams, New York, 1968.

Palaeolithic and Mesolithic

F. Bordes. *The Old Stone Age*. World University Library, London, 1968.

J. G. D. Clark. *The Stone Age Hunters*. Thames & Hudson, London, 1967.

E. Hadingham. *Secrets of the Ice Age*. Heinemann, London, 1979.

I. Lissner. *Man, God and Magic*. Jonathan Cape, London, 1961.

A. Morrison. *Early Man in Britain and Ireland*. Croom Helm, London, 1980.

J. E. Pfeiffer. *The Emergence of Man*. Nelson, London, 1970.

P. J. Ucko & A. Rosenfeld. *Palaeolithic Cave Art*. World University Library, London, 1967.

Neolithic

P. Ashbee. *The Earthen Long Barrow in Britain*. Dent, London, 1970.

A. Burl. *The Stone Circles of the British Isles*. Yale University Press, New Haven & London, 1976.

A. S. Henshall. *The Chambered Tombs of Scotland*, I & II. Edinburgh University Press, Edinburgh, 1963, 1972.

M. Herity. *Irish Passage Graves*. Irish University Press, Dublin, 1974.

S. Piggott. *Neolithic Cultures of the British Isles*. Cambridge University Press, Cambridge, 1954.

T. G. E. Powell, J. X. W. P. Corcoran, F. Lynch & J. G. Scott. *Megalithic Enquiries in the West of Britain*. Liverpool University Press, Liverpool, 1969.

Bronze Age

P. Ashbee. *The Round Barrow in Britain*. Phoenix House, London, 1960.

C. Burgess. *The Age of Stonehenge*. Dent, London, 1980.

C. Fox. *Life and Death in the Bronze Age*. Routledge & Kegan Paul, London, 1959.

W. Greenwell. *British Barrows*. Oxford University Press, London, 1877.

J. Mortimer. *Forty Years' Researches in British and Saxon Burial Mounds of East Yorkshire*. A Brown & Sons, London, 1905.

Iron Age

B. Cunliffe. *Iron Age Communities in Britain*. Routledge & Kegan Paul, London, 1974.

P. MacCana. *Celtic Mythology*. Hamlyn, London, 1970.

S. Piggott. *The Druids*. Thames & Hudson, London, 1968.

T. G. E. Powell. *The Celts*. Thames & Hudson, London, 1963.

A. Ross. *Pagan Celtic Britain*. Sphere, London, 1974.

Notes

In the Notes authors already cited in the Book List are quoted by name and date only, e.g. W. Greenwell (1877), and not, W. Greenwell, *British Barrows*, London, 1877. All other authors and titles of books and papers are given in full.

Chapter 1

1   W. Greenwell (1877), 205–8. Barrow XLIX.
2   B. Marsden. *The Early Barrow Diggers*. Shire Publications, Princes Risborough, 1974. 100–1.
3   W. Greenwell. *Archaeologia* 52, 1890. 14–16, 25–7. Barrow CCXLV.
4   I. F. Smith. *Windmill Hill & Avebury*. Oxford University Press, Oxford, 1965. 136–40.
5   J. G. D. Clark (1967), 117–19; M. Boule & H. V. Vallois. *Fossil Men*. Thames & Hudson, London, 1957. 349–51.
6   V. G. Childe. *Skara Brae. A Pictish Village in Orkney*. Kegan Paul, London, 1931; D. V. Clarke. *The Neolithic Village at Skara Brae, Orkney, 1972–3 Excavations*. HMSO, Edinburgh, 1976.
7   J. Mellaart. 'Excavations at Catal Huyuk'. *Anatolian Studies* 12–14, 1962–4; ibid, *Earliest Civilisations of the Near East*. Thames & Hudson, London, 1965. 89–101.
8   K. Schlabow, W. Hage & H. Jankühn. *Praehistorische Zeitschrift* 36, 1958; P. V. Glob. *The Bog People*. Paladin, London, 1971. 81–4.
9   Cornelius Tacitus. *Germania*. Book 19, 116–17 in (ed. H. Mattingly) *On Britain and Germany*. Penguin, Harmondsworth, 1948.
10   P. V. Glob (note 8), 21–32.
11   Tacitus (note 9), Book 40, 133–4.
12   K. Cameron. *English Place Names*. Methuen, London, 1969; E. Ekwall, *The Concise Oxford Dictionary of Place-Names*. Oxford University Press, Oxford, 1959; F. T. Wainwright. *Archaeology, Place-Names & History*. Routledge & Kegan Paul, London, 1962.
13   L. V. Grinsell. *Folklore of Prehistoric Sites in Britain*. David & Charles, Newton Abbot, 1976. 32, 91; *Archaeological Journal* 24, 1867, 189.
14   J. G. Frazer (1911), II, 103–4.
15   R. C. Hoare. *The Ancient History of South Wiltshire*. W. Miller, London, 1812. 202–5.

Chapter 2

Because most of the original sources for this chapter are in untranslated foreign journals I have quoted secondary English sources which are available to the reader.

1   J. E. Pfeiffer (1970), 162–4; M. Day. *Guide to Fossil Man*. Cassell, London, 1967. 37–42.

2   J. E. Pfeiffer (1970), 169–71; A. H. Brodrick. *Man & His Ancestors*. Hutchinson, London, 1971. 175–6.

3   G. Constable. *The Neanderthals*. Time-Life Books, Chicago, 1974. 98–100; J. E. Pfeiffer (1970), 167–8.

4   I. Lissner (1961), 183–96.

5   P. J. Ucko & A. Rosenfeld (1967).

6   D. A. Garrod. *The Upper Palaeolithic Age in Britain*. Clarendon Press (OUP), London, 1926. 49–64; K. P. Oakley. 'The Date of the "Red Lady" of Paviland'. *Antiquity* 42, 1968, 306–7.

7   *Proceedings of Bristol University Spelaeological Society* 7, 1954, 23.

8   J. W. Kitching. *Bone, Tooth and Horn Tools of Palaeolithic Man*. Manchester University Press, Manchester, 1963.

9   I. Lissner (1961), 291–7; G. Bibby. *The Testimony of the Spade*. Collins, London, 1959, 168–79.

10   G. Grigson. *The Painted Caves*. Phoenix House, London, 1957, 209–13; J. G. D. Clark (1967), 100, 117.

11   S. Palmer. *Mesolithic Cultures of Britain*. Dolphin Press, Poole, 1977.

12   J. G. D. Clark. *Excavations at Star Carr*. Cambridge University Press, Cambridge, 1954; ibid, *Star Carr: a Case Study in Bioarchaeology*. Addison-Wesley, Reading, Massachusetts, 1972.

13   K. Jazdzewski. *Poland*. Thames & Hudson, London, 1965. 52–4.

14   P. R. Giot. *Brittany*. Thames & Hudson, London, 1960. 24–6.

Chapter 3

1   S. Milisauskas. *European Prehistory*. Academic Press, New York & London, 1978. 173–6.

2   S. O'Nuallain. 'A Neolithic House at Ballyglass near Ballycastle, Co. Mayo'. *Journal of the Royal Society of Antiquaries of Ireland* 102, 1972, 1–11.

3   S. Piggott (1954), 42, 46, 61, 86, 88.

4   S. Piggott (1954), 42.

5   *Larousse Encyclopaedia of Prehistoric and Ancient Art*. Hamlyn, London, 1962. 79.

6   J. M. Coles & F. A. Hibbert. 'Prehistoric Roads and Tracks in Somerset, England'. *Proceedings of the Prehistoric Society* 34, 1968, 238–58.

7   P. Ashbee (1970), 28–9.

8   P. Ashbee. 'The Fussell's Lodge Long Barrow Excavations, 1957'. *Archaeologia* 100, 1966, 1–80.

9   P. Phillips. *Early Farmers of West Mediterranean Europe*. Hutchinson, London, 1975. 116.

10   T. C. M. Brewster. 'Garton Slack'. *Current Archaeology* 51, 1976, 106–7.

11   J. Mortimer. *Forty Years' Researches in British and Saxon Burial Mounds of East Yorkshire*. London, 1905. 102–5.

12   H. Case. 'A Ritual Site in North-East Ireland' in: *Megalithic Graves and Ritual.* Jutland Archaeological Society, Moesgard, 1969. 173–96.

Chapter 4

1   S. Piggott (1954), 122–276; J. V. S. Megaw & D. D. A. Simpson (1979), 112–41, 191, 284.
2   T. G. E. Powell, J. X. W. P. Corcoran, F. Lynch & J. G. Scott (1969), 5–6, 20–1, 96–7, 124–43.
3   W. Borlase. *Antiquities Historical and Monumental of the County of Cornwall.* W. Bowyer and J. Nichols, London, 1769. 226–7.
4   A. Keiller & S. Piggott. 'Excavation of an Untouched Chamber in the Lanhill Long Barrow'. *Proc. Prehistoric Soc.* 4, 1938, 124–31.
5   S. Piggott. *The West Kennet Long Barrow Excavations, 1955–6.* HMSO, London, 1962. 81.
6   A. S. Henshall (1963). Isbister, 205–6; Knowe of Yarso, 215–18; Round Camster, 263–6.
7   A. Burl. *Prehistoric Avebury.* Yale University Press, New Haven & London, 1979, 98; H. O'Neil & L. V. Grinsell. 'Gloucestershire Barrows'. *Transactions of the Bristol and Gloucestershire Archaeological Society* 79, 1960, 3–148.
8   S. Piggott & T. G. E. Powell. 'The Excavation of Three Neolithic Chambered Tombs in Galloway, 1949'. *Proceedings of the Society of Antiquaries of Scotland* 83, 1948–9, 103–61.
9   H. Case. 'Settlement-Patterns in the North Irish Neolithic'. *Ulster Journal of Archaeology* 32, 1969, 3–27.
10   M. Herity (1974).
11   C. O'Kelly, *Illustrated Guide to Newgrange and the Other Boyne Monuments.* C. O'Kelly, Wexford, 1978; G. Coffey. *New Grange and Other Incised Tumuli in Ireland* (1912). Dolphin Press, Poole, 1977; S. P. O'Riordain & G. Daniel. *New Grange and the Bend of the Boyne.* Thames & Hudson, London, 1964.
12   T. G. E. Powell & G. E. Daniel. *Barclodiad y Gawres. The Excavation of a Megalithic Chamber Tomb in Anglesey, 1952–3.* Liverpool University Press, Liverpool, 1956.
13   R. J. C. Atkinson. 'The Dorset Cursus'. *Antiquity* 29, 1955, 4–9.
14   A. S. Henshall (1963), 12–39, 358–91.
15   A. S. Henshall (1972), 355–6; J. G. Scott. *South-West Scotland.* Cory, Adams & Mackay, London, 1966. 28–9, 79; *Proc. Soc. Ants. Scotland* 9, 1870–2, 409–15; *Proc. Soc. Ants. Scotland* 7, 1866–8, 286.
16   T. G. Manby. 'The Excavation of Green Low Chambered Tomb'. *Derbyshire Archaeological Journal* 85, 1965, 1–24; B. M. Marsden. *The Burial Mounds of Derbyshire.* Bingley, 1977. 1–7.

Chapter 5

1 R. J. C. Atkinson. *Stonehenge.* (Revised reprint.) Penguin, Harmondsworth, 1979.

2 J. G. D. Clark. 'The Timber Monument at Arminghall and its Affinities'. *Proc. Prehistoric Soc.* 2, 1936, 1–51.

3 C. A. Newham. *The Astronomical Significance of Stonehenge.* J. Blackburn Ltd, Leeds, 1972.

4 A., A. S., & A. S. Thom. 'Stonehenge'. *Journal for the History of Astronomy* 5, 1974, 71–90; ibid. 'Stonehenge as a Possible Lunar Observatory'. *J. Hist. Astron.* 6, 1975, 19–30.

5 P. Ashbee (1970), 165–7. These pages list the long barrows on Salisbury Plain East and West.

6 R. Bradley. 'Maumbury Rings, Dorchester. The Excavations of 1908–13'. *Archaeologia* 105, 1975, 1–98.

7 A. Burl (1976). 64–9; ibid. *Prehistoric Stone Circles.* Shire Publications, Princes Risborough, 1979, 13–18.

8 A. McL. May. 'Burial Mound, Circles and Cairn, Gortcorbies, Co. Londonderry'. *Journal of the Royal Society of Antiquaries of Ireland* 77, 1947, 5–22.

9 A. S. Henshall (1963), 45–120, 183–256.

10 A. C. Renfrew, D. D. Harkness & R. Switsur. 'Quanterness, radiocarbon and the Orkney cairns'. *Antiquity* 50, 1976, 194–204.

11 D. A. Davidson, R. L. Jones & C. Renfrew. 'Palaeoenvironmental reconstruction and evaluation: a case study from Orkney'. *Transactions of the Institute of British Geographers* 1, 1976, 346–61.

12 J. N. G. Ritchie. 'The Stones of Stenness, Orkney'. *Proc. Soc. Ants. Scotland* 107, 1975–6, 1–60.

13 A. Burl (1976), 105–6; ibid *Prehistoric Avebury.* Yale University Press, New Haven & London, 1979. 158, 163, 218–20.

14 A. S. Henshall (1963), 219–22.

15 M. Spence. *Standing Stones and Maeshowe of Stenness* (1894). Rilko, Paisley, 1974; N. Lockyer. *Stonehenge and Other British Stone Monuments Astronomically Considered.* Macmillan, London, 1909, 123–32.

16 G. M. Brown. 'Winter at Maeshowe'. *The Orcadian,* 1974, 95–7.

Chapter 6

1 W. K. Dover. *Transactions of the Cumberland & Westmorland Antiquarian & Archaeological Society* 6, 1883, 505.

2 W. Greenwell (1877), 510–13. Barrow CCXXVIII.

3 A. W. R. Whittle. *The Earlier Neolithic of Southern Britain and its Continental Background.* British Archaeological Reports, Oxford, 1977. A. Burl. *Prehistoric Avebury.* New Haven & London, 1979. 113–16.

4   P. Ashbee. *The Ancient British*. Geo-Abstracts Ltd, Norwich, 1978. 133–59;
       J. V. S. Megaw & D. D. A. Simpson (1979), 178–207.

5   R. C. Hoare. *The Ancient History of South Wiltshire*. London, 1812. 163.

6   R. C. Hoare (note 5), 44. The barrow is Mere Down 6a, ST 802353.

7   E. N. Baynes. 'The Excavation of Lligwy Cromlech, in the County of
       Anglesey'. *Archaeologia Cambrensis* 1909, 217–31.

8   H. O'N. Hencken & H. L. Movius. 'The Cemetery Cairn of Knockast'.
       Proceedings of the Royal Irish Academy 41C, 1934, 232–84.

9   R. J. C. Atkinson, C. M. Piggott & N. K. Sandars. *Excavations at
       Dorchester, Oxon*. Ashmolean Museum, Oxford, 1951.

10   J. Mortimer (1905), 23–42.

11   M. E. Cunnington. *Woodhenge*. G. Simpson, Devizes, 1929, 13, 52.

Chapter 7

1   M. E. Cunnington. 'The "Sanctuary" on Overton Hill near Avebury'.
       Wiltshire Archaeological Magazine 45, 1931, 300–35; A. Burl.
       Prehistoric Avebury. New Haven & London, 1979. 196–8.

2   V. G. Childe. *Prehistoric Communities of the British Isles*. Chambers,
       London, 1940. 180–1.

3   P. V. Glob. *The Mound People*. Faber, London, 1973. 114–16, 162; J. M.
       Coles & A. F. Harding. *The Bronze Age in Europe*. Methuen, London,
       1979. 308, 520–1.

4   T. Bateman. *Ten Years' Digging in Celtic and Saxon Grave Hills in the
       Counties of Derby, Stafford and York. From 1848 to 1858*. G. Allen,
       London, 1861. 20–1. For Upton Lovell, see: S. Piggott. 'From
       Salisbury Plain to South Siberia'. *Wilts. Arch. Mag.* 58, 1962, 93–7.

5   A. Burl (note 1), 217–18.

6   T. Bateman. *Vestiges of the Antiquities of Derbyshire*. G. Allen, London,
       1848. 41–3. The cairn was at SK 15315866.

7   A. J. Evans. 'The Rollright Stones and their Folklore'. *Folklore* 6, 1895, 5–51.

8   A. Burl (1976).

9   L. V. Grinsell. *The Stonehenge Barrow Groups*. Salisbury & South Wiltshire
       Museum, Salisbury, 1978; Royal Commission for Ancient & Historical
       Monuments, England. *Stonehenge and its Environs*. Edinburgh
       University Press, Edinburgh, 1979.

10   J. Anderson. 'Notes on the Character and Contents of a Large Sepulchral
       Cairn of the Bronze Age at Collessie, Fife...'. *Proc. Soc. Ants.
       Scotland* 12, 1876–7, 439–47.

11   T. Watkins. 'Dalgety'. *Current Archaeology* 40, 1973, 133–5.

12   J. Rowley. 'Prehistoric Tree-trunk Coffins of North-West Europe'.
       Unpublished dissertation, Hull College of Higher Education, 1979.

13   W. C. Williamson. *Description of the Tumulus opened at Gristhorpe, near
       Scarborough*. S. W. Theakston, Scarborough, 1872.

14 C. Fox (1959), 62–70; ibid., *Archaeologia* 89, 1943, 89–126.

15 J. C. Atkinson. *Forty Years in a Moorland Parish.* Macmillan, London, 1891. 147–9; F. Elgee. *Early Man in North-East Yorkshire.* J. Bellows, Gloucester, 1930. 90–1.

16 L. V. Grinsell. *Dorset Barrows.* Dorset Natural History & Archaeological Society, Dorchester, 1959. 98. For Collingbourne Ducis, Wiltshire, see: R. C. Hoare. *The Ancient History of South Wiltshire.* London, 1812. 183.

17 P. Gelling and H. E. Davidson. *The Chariot of the Sun.* Dent, London, 1969.

18 J. G. Scott. *South-West Scotland.* London, 1966. 35–41.

19 D. D. A. Simpson & J. E. Thawley. 'Single Grave Art in Britain'. *Scottish Archaeological Forum* 4, 1972, 81–104; R. W. B. Morris. *The Prehistoric Rock Art of Argyll.* Dolphin Press, Poole, 1977; ibid. *The Prehistoric Rock Art of Galloway and the Isle of Man.* Blandford Press, Poole, 1979; E. Hadingham. *Ancient Carvings in Britain: A Mystery.* Garnstone Press, London, 1974.

20 D. D. A. Simpson & J. E. Thawley (note 21), 95–9; P. Gelling & H. E. Davidson (note 17), 39–42, 152–3.

21 J. L. Forde-Johnston. 'Megalithic Art in the north-west of Britain: the Calderstones, Liverpool'. *Proc. Prehistoric Soc.* 23, 1957, 20–39.

22 R. Robertson & G. F. Black. 'Notice of the Discovery of a Stone Cist and Urns at the Cuninghar, Tillicoultry ...' *Proc. Soc. Ants. Scotland* 29, 1894–5, 190–7; F. R. Coles. '... a cist at the Cunninghar, Tillicoultry ...' *Proc. Soc. Ants. Scotland* 33, 1898–9, 358–65.

Chapter 8

1 G. & M. Ponting. 'Callanish. The Documentary Record'. Callanish, 1977.

2 C. Innes. 'Notice of the Stone Circle of Callernish ...'. *Proc. Soc. Ants. Scotland* 3, 1857–60, 110–12.

3 C. Houlder. 'Stone Axes and Henge Monuments'. in: *Welsh Antiquity: Essays mainly on prehistoric topics ...* Cardiff, 1976. 55–62.

4 J. Ritchie. 'The Stone Circle at Broomend of Crichie, Aberdeenshire.' *Proc. Soc. Ants. Scotland* 54, 1919–20, 154–72. 168.

5 C. E. Dalrymple. 'Notes of the Excavation of the Stone Circle at Crichie, Aberdeenshire'. *Proc. Soc. Ants. Scotland* 18, 1883–4, 319–24; J. Stuart. *The Sculptured Stones of Scotland* I. Spalding Club, Aberdeen, 1856. xx.

6 W. Stukeley. *Itinerarium Curiosum* II. Privately printed, London, 1776. 42; for Shap, see also: W. C. Lukis *Proc. Soc. Ants. London* 10, 1883–5, 313–20; T. Clare. *Trans. Cumberland & Westmorland Ant. & Arch. Soc.* 78, 1978, 5–15; W. Camden. *Britannia.* A. Swalle, London, 1695. 808. For stone avenues generally, see: A. Burl (1976), 153, 262–3.

7   J. H. Chalmers, C. B. Davidson. *Proc. Soc. Ants. Scotland* 7, 1866–8, 110–18.

8   E. M. Fahy. 'A Recumbent Stone Circle at Reanascreena South, Co. Cork'. *Journal Cork Hist. Arch. Soc.* 67, 1962, 59–69.

9   A. Burl (1976), 124–5, 205–8.

10 R. A. S. Macalister, E. C. C. Armstrong & R. L. Praeger. 'On a Bronze Age Interment with associated standing stone and earth ring, near Naas, Co. Kildare'. *Proc. Roy. Irish Acad.* 30, 1913, 351–60.

11 R. A. S. Macalister. *Ireland in Pre-Celtic Times*. Maunsel Roberts Ltd, Dublin & London, 1921. 339–41.

12 T. Bateman. *Ten Years' Digging …* London, 1861. 22–4, 34–5.

13 T. C. M. Brewster. 'Garton Slack'. *Current Archaeology* 51, 1976, 104–16. 108.

14 S. Piggott. 'The Excavations at Cairnpapple Hill, West Lothian'. *Proc. Soc. Ants. Scotland* 82, 1948, 68–123.

15 A. Burl (1976), 332; L. V. Grinsell. *Folklore of Prehistoric Sites in Britain*. David & Charles, Newton Abbot, 1976.

16 A. Thom. *Megalithic Sites in Britain*. Oxford University Press, Oxford, 1967. 97–101.

17 W. G. Collingwood. 'An Exploration of the Circle on Banniside Moor, Coniston'. *Trans. Cumberland & Westmorland Ant. & Arch. Soc.* 10, 1910, 342–53.

18 C. Fox. 'Two Bronze Age Cairns in South Wales: Simondston and Pond Cairns, Coity Higher Parish, Bridgend (Glamorgan)'. *Archaeologia* 87, 1938, 129–80.

19 E. W. Holden. 'A Bronze Age Cemetery-Barrow on Itford Hill, Beddingham, Sussex'. *Sussex Archaeological Collections* 110, 1972, 70–117.

20 'Kimpton'. *Current Archaeology* 11, 1968, 284–6.

21 P. Ashbee. 'The Wilsford Shaft'. *Antiquity* 37, 1963, 116–20; ibid, *Antiquity* 40, 1966, 227–8.

22 J. N. A. Wallace. 'The Golden Bog of Cullen'. *North Munster Antiquarian Journal* 1, 1938, 89–101.

23 S. P. O'Riordain. 'Excavation of some Earthworks in the Curragh, Co. Kildare'. *Proc. Royal Irish Academy* 53, 1950. (Site 4, pp. 254–8.)

Chapter 9

1   T. C. M. Brewster. 'Garton Slack'. *Current Archaeology* 51, 1976, 115.

2   A. Ross (1974), 25, 29.

3   P. V. Glob. *The Bog People*. London, 1969. 116–17.

4   R. A. Bullen. *Harlyn Bay, and the Discoveries of its Prehistoric Remains*. Swan Sonnenschein & Co. Ltd, London, 1902.

5   Lucan. *Pharsalia*. (Trans. R. Graves). Penguin, Harmondsworth, 1956. 78.

6   A. Ross. 'Shafts, Pits, Wells—Sanctuaries of the Belgic Britons?' in: *Studies in Ancient Europe*. Leicester University Press, Leicester, 1969. 255–85.
7   R. L. Praeger. *The Way That I Went*. Dublin, 1939. 66.
8   R. A. S. Macalister. *Tara*. Scribner, New York, 1931; S. P. O'Riordain. *Tara*. Dundalgan Press, Dundalk, 1964.
9   J. G. Frazer. *The Dying God*. Macmillan, London, 1911. 99–103.

Index

Page-numbers in italics refer to illustrations